A PEBBLE IN THE TORRENT

A tale of love, survival, civic courage, the spy game, integrity, and life after cancer

JAN VÍTEK

Published by New Generation Publishing in 2013

Copyright © Jan Vítek 2013

First published in Czech under the title OBLAZEK V
PEREJICH by Akropolis, Prague 2011

www.newgeneration-publishing.com

New Generation **Publishing**

Translated into English by the author

Editor Peter Hulm

Cover photo by Nikki Meith

FOR MY FAMILY

The record shows
I took the blows
And did it my way…

CONTENTS

I. GREAT EXPECTATIONS THAT FAILED

That evening in late May Father came home in an exuberant mood. His ascetic face radiated joy and pride.

"I have bought a house at Kremze," he said. "I put down thirty thousand crowns, and the rest we shall pay in installments."

"My God, thirty thousand," said Mother in shock. "This is all the money we have, everything we have salted away."

"So what?" said Father. "It is better to put money into stone than in a bank. Now we shall have our own roof over our heads."

"How much is the rest?"

"Forty thousand."

"Have you lost your mind? We can never scrabble together such a sum."

"The crisis is over, business is picking up, and we shall be rolling in dough pretty soon."

"You always see the rosy side."

"And you the dark one. This is why we complement each other so well," said Father in an attempt to mollify his wife.

"You could have asked my opinion. That is the least you could have done," said Mother. "We live so well here. And what will become of Mary and Zdenka when we move?"

By 'here' Mother meant Pasicka, a hamlet of several homesteads at the foot of a hill, Chlumecky Vrch, some two kilometers from the small township of Kremze located in the southernmost part of Bohemia near the German boarder. My parents rented a small farm at Pasicka with five hectares of cornfields and pastures.

Mother did all the farm work, aided by her sister Mary whom she engaged more out of family solidarity than a need for help. One of three daughters of a bricklayer named Trapl, who died while serving as a legionnaire in Siberia, Mother was the oldest. Zofie was the middle one, and Mary the youngest. Mary became the black sheep of the family when she gave birth to an illegitimate child, Zdenka. Who was the father? This was the family's most closely guarded secret. The fatherless girl grew up to become a blond beauty that we nicknamed Princess Dandelion.

Above our farmhouse grew mushrooms, raspberries and bilberries in a fir and pine tree forest. We also had an orchard with a small pond where frogs reigned. On summer nights their concerts sent me to sleep. The orchard itself was on a slight slope and was oval shaped. In my boyish imagination it symbolized, goodness knows why, the four seasons. Down on the right hand side, where windflowers grew, was Spring. The top of the oval, behind which was a cornfield, represented Summer. The left side with its apple trees was Autumn, and the bottom, adjoining the pond, was Winter. Even today, this orchard sticks in my mind as a picture, a painting even, whose colors do not fade or turn yellow with the passage of time. It is an inseparable part of a paradise lost named Pasicka.

Father, also called Jan or, familiarly, Honza, was thirty-four years old at the time. He grew up in a small cottage in the tiny village of Krasetin at the foothills of Klet, the highest mountain in South Bohemia. The cottage had only two rooms but it was home to ten people: his parents, a grandmother, three brothers (including Father), and four sisters. After finishing school, when he was fourteen, he left home to earn his keep as a stable boy at a farm on the other side of Klet, in a German-speaking part of the country. There he learned to speak a German dialect, Sudetendeutsch.

After four years as a farm hand he decided to switch to an apprenticeship with a butcher and pub owner named Stanko at Kremze. The pub stood below the local school in a bend of the road leading to the next village, Chlum. Soon he noticed a lovely fourteen-year old girl with black curly hair who walked every day after school along the road taking her home to Chlum. He began to wait for her in front of the pub, pretending that he was splitting firewood. To tease her, he threw wood chips on her hair as she passed by.

"You stupid blockhead!" the girl shouted.

"Calm down," Jan told her. "Say you'll marry me and I'll wait for you."

"You can wait until the cows come home," the girl replied.

By chance her teacher, Mr Heral, was passing by and heard it all. The next day at school he asked his favorite pupil to come to the blackboard.

"Traplova, what did you shout at the young man yesterday when you were going home?" he asked.

"Nothing."

"I heard you very well. Go to the corner and kneel down for a quarter of an hour to meditate about that nothing."

Katerina Traplova grew up in an adobe cottage near a brook at Chlum. It had just one room and a shed with two milk goats. Kate, as everybody called her, had an unhappy childhood. She had to put up with poverty, hardship, belittlement and drudgery. When she was born, a female relative looked at her in the crib and uttered a fatal remark: the baby, she exclaimed, did not look at all like Franta Trapl, her father. It started him thinking. After that he would not even look at Kate.

13

When he got drunk, which he did regularly, he always accused his wife of having borne him a bastard. However, later on, as Kate grew up, the likeness with him was so evident that he began to love her. As a soldier on the Russian front he wrote letters in which he vowed must return home if only to compensate for all the wrong he had done to Kate. He did not return and his wife soured against the world. Embittered, she turned on her first-born daughter. She loved her other daughters, and cuddled them in her arms, but Kate she pushed away: "Scram. Go and do something useful," she would say. For every little failing, real or imaginary, she beat Kate with a leather whip. Even as a young child Kate had to work on odd jobs in the fields and cut grass with a sickle for the goats whose milk helped nourish the family. When she was nine Kate became a nursemaid for a landowner. She had to wake at four in the morning along with the grown-up maids to light the fire in the big kitchen stove and prepare fodder for the cattle. Then she had to wake up the landowner's two children, and dress and feed them before they went to school. Because of all these chores she often missed the beginning of the first lesson and had to stay on after school as punishment. When she returned home late her mother welcomed her with the whip. Despite all this Kate always came first in her class. When she had finished primary school with distinction, the chairman of the Organization of Legionaries wanted to pay for her higher education. The mother refused the help. But what she told him was: "I will do everything for her future, even if I have to sell the house. I love her so much."

Back home, she was her old self.

"Forget about the school," she said. "What would people say if such a beggar went off to study?"

She sent Kate to a neighboring landowner to be a

cowgirl.

Jan and Kate met again four years later by chance at a country ball. Kate had grown up into a beautiful young woman, but she would not engage in any serious courtship because she was just a poor cow maid. Jan Vitek was also penniless but he nurtured an ambition to become rich one day. The two social outcasts started to walk out together. Kate became Jan's girl.

"I am going to be a cattle dealer," he said to her later. "I need a housewife. Will you marry me?"

"Why not? I have already had to kneel down because of you as a punishment," she said, "so what worse could I expect? And if we marry, I'll be rid of the drudgery in the cow barn."

When my parents married they had nothing but their bare hands to support them. A farmer, Mr Sahan, rented them a room with two beds, two chairs, a table and a washbasin. In the dark a dim light from a naked bulb mercifully hid their poverty. After a year a crib was added. When I was born, my father took me out in swaddling clothes and with his free left hand he made a circular gesture.

"From here up to Zelnava and Zvonkova, all this will be your beat."

He entertained high hopes that I would be his successor and heir to the stock-dealing empire he dreamed of building.

To achieve his dream, Father started with a buggy owned jointly with a buddy who also wanted to make a fortune buying and selling stock. Father's main problem was money. To buy a cow or a pig he needed a couple of hundred crowns. He borrowed the money, at first, from his partner, and paid him back immediately he sold the animal to a butcher. But when the partnership broke up, he did not know where to find such money any more. Soon the family's meager savings were exhausted, and Mother and Father were desperate.

One day Mother ran out of the house, sat on a stone at the roadside and wept. A rich miller, Mr Hrubes, passed by on his way to the pub.

"Why are you crying, Kate?" he asked.

When Mother told him about their financial woes, he asked how much they would need.

"Five hundred crowns. Honza, my husband, wants to buy two calves and a pig," she said.

"I'll lend him the money at no interest," said Mr Hrubes, "but for Christ's sake stop sobbing."

This was how my father's business took off.

He bought the house at Kremze from a tailor who went bankrupt. It had a workshop and a show window where the previous owner exposed his wares. The rest of the house consisted of one narrow alcove as sleeping rooms and a somewhat bigger room as a kitchen and living quarters. By then we were already quite well off, because cattle trading was booming. The Great Depression had ended in 1934 mainly because of rearmament by Germany under Hitler that, in turn, spurred similar activity in Europe and created spinoffs in other branches of the economy. Father made enough money to buy a delivery truck, a second-hand Walter, in which he transported pigs, cows and calves he bought to the cattle market in the district town of Budejovice.

Father sub-let the workshop to Mr Cizek, the husband of Mother's younger sister Zofie, who was an upholsterer and furniture painter. I spent quite some time in his workshop, not because I admired my uncle's skill, but because there was a poster on the wall with portraits of Voskovec and Werich, two famous actors at the time. I looked at them longingly and with profound admiration, intoxicating myself with the fantasy that sometime I, too, would appear on the stage and be applauded by enchanted crowds.

With this vision in mind, at nine years old, I dramatized a popular fairy tale about 'Honzik and Marenka'. The scenario was short, only a couple of handwritten pages. Of course, I cast myself in the lead role while a girl from my class graciously agreed to portray Marenka. We had no poster to advertise the play, so I personally invited all children I knew to come and see the first and last performance one night at a dancing hall at the Hruby Pub, named after its owner. I promised them sweets as a reward. About twenty children could not resist the temptation and filled the first two rows of chairs. Since I bribed each of them with a lollipop they applauded dutifully when the curtain went down.

In the same hall an itinerant theatrical company run by Frantisek Solc appeared on tour regularly at the beginning of May and performed one month every night to a full house. During the war, apart from the cinema (once a week), there was no other public entertainment. The ensemble's repertory varied from musicals to Shakespearean dramas. The principal, Mr Solc, played most of the leading roles because he knew how to act, sing and dance. I admired him, but my real idol was Mr Vasta, who excelled in the role of tragic heroes. He was natural, sober and never overacted. His voice was so captivating that the audience was mesmerized. He moved on the stage with assurance and immense grace. At home I tried to imitate him, reciting poems in front of a mirror.

Mr Solc had a daughter my age whom I sometimes spotted in the hall and a couple of times on the stage in a minor child's role. It was not difficult to find out that her name was Hanicka, but to make acquaintance with her seemed a superhuman problem. I decided I would watch for her in the vicinity of a villa where her father rented an apartment. I rehearsed time and again what I would say to her in a nonchalant manner. But when, by chance, I ran into her in the street one day I stood thunderstruck and unable to utter a sound. Hanicka was on her way home from shopping and carried a bag full of food. As I did not have any better idea I grabbed hold of the bag to help her. She was not alarmed.

"How about telling me your name, or are you deaf?" she teased me.

"Honza Vitek," I managed to blurt out.

"I have noticed you," she said. "You stand usually back in the hall at the pillar. I wonder how it is possible that your parents let you out every night."

"My father has other worries and my mother is kind to me," I said. "Let me carry the bag, please."

"Are you so gallant to all the girls?"

I blushed and shook my head. We walked in silence for a while.

"Tell me one thing," she said. "You always buy a standing room ticket, but still…where do you get the money?"

"Savings from my lunch allowance," I said. "You see I study at the lyceum (high school) in Budejovice. I take a train at six in the morning and come home at four in the afternoon. Father gives me six crowns to buy lunch. I put one or two crowns that I save almost every day in a box hidden in my room. That is my war chest."

"In which grade are you now?"

"Second…but you see school is just a waiting room for me. I don't care about it. What I want to be is an actor when I grow up."

18

"It's a tough life being an actor. You can believe me."

"All the better, I don't want an easy life. I shall follow my ambition, no matter what may happen to me. And now you know everything about me."

"You are wrong, I want to know much more."

From that moment on we met every day. In her presence I lost all timidity, I did not need to pretend anything, I was my true self. Together we read the love poems of Frana Sramek and dreamt about the future when we would appear on the stage together. We were in love, a love that was chaste and puppyish and unrepeatable. Our romance started in May 1941 and continued each May over three subsequent years.

When we met for the last time in 1944, Hanicka introduced me to my actor hero Mr Vasta. I confided to him that I wanted to abandon my studies to become an actor and asked his advice how to go about it. He looked at me with his wise brown eyes and said:

"Don't hurry. Finish school first and come to me after graduation, then we shall talk about your artistic future."

Our gang of boys and girls growing up together at Kremze met regularly on the corner of the Post Office building in the village square. All were children of local notables, barring one: me. Zdenek Simecek and his brother Jiri were sons of the Mayor of Kremze. The father of Josef Brejcha was a postmaster. Mirek Jakl's father was a police officer. Milan Benes was the son of a bank treasurer. Josef Bukovsky was heir to a large landed estate. Silva Simecek and her sister Helena were daughters of a professor. Lida Cermak's father was a dentist. Hanka Klimova was a daughter of the owner of a big sawmill. I was the exception, a son of a cattle dealer. My base origin weighed on me like a hereditary sin. I felt a misfit in their company.

My buddies were always dressed to kill. They did not have to harvest hay, or muck out cow barns and feed cattle as I did. It was small wonder that I suffered from an inferiority complex. Whenever I went to our meeting place I always had a stomach ache and anxiety gripped my breast. I suspected my pals of accepting me out of pity and mocking me behind my back. Thus began my lifetime problem of exaggerated timidity and social phobia. I tried to overcome it by a desperate attempt to excel in everything we did together: to be a better skier, ice hockey, tennis and volleyball player than they were. As a result, I developed an almost morbid ambition.

When I realized that my buddies were mostly egotistical I would ask them questions that would enable them to talk about themselves. As a result, I was considered a good companion, while in fact I was just a practiced listener. But at home during my sleepless nights I invented witty remarks and urbane comments that I would have said if I were more resourceful and quick witted.

It was during my difficult adolescence that I discovered alcohol. During the war Mother concocted a moonshine drink with chocolate aroma that she offered to friends when they came to visit. She kept the brew in small soda water bottles with a patent cap. Once I stole a bottle and brought it to our dancing lesson in an abandoned laundry. Well, everybody danced, except for me, because I was clumsy and my feet refused to follow the rhythm. I changed the records and wound up the gramophone. I offered mother's 'bracer' around. Boys accepted it, but the girls refused. As the bottle stood next to the gramophone, I took a sip each time I changed a disc. After a while I experienced complete relaxation, I felt light and brave, made cheeky remarks about the dancers, and finally I even dared invite Sylva Simecek to dance with me. I stepped on her toes repeatedly but I joked about it. I was not at all afraid that I would be embarrassing and ludicrous, and I was no longer shy. I was the Honza I always dreamed of being, charming, irresistible, intelligent. I was on the top of the world. I felt just great. This illusion gave me trouble for a great part of my life.

There was nothing much for teenagers like us to do during the war apart from sport. In winter we played ice hockey or skied downhill and cross-country. In summer we played tennis, volleyball and football and swam in a pond. With the exception of boxing we engaged in almost all sports.

In addition, I had the theatre, my greatest passion. I was a member of an amateur ensemble led by Vaclav Benes, a tinsmith by profession but an amateur actor in his heart and soul. He allowed me to borrow theatrical plays and various books about acting and directing. As a thirteen year old I devoured a pre-war edition of the famous classic by Stanislavsky *An Actor Prepares* that became my bible.

Our ensemble prepared one performance in spring and another in winter. Given my age, I played minor roles, but I was an accomplished master of ceremonies, introducing the play, actors and the stage manager at every performance. The plays we put on had just two or three subsequent shows. My father never set foot in the large hall, a former gymnasium, where we performed. However, my mother never missed a show, although at home she complained that her son was a ham actor.

So far, war for me had boiled down to putting up with German propaganda via the radio, newspapers and cinema. Towards the end of the war my grandfather was arrested because somebody denounced him to the

Gestapo, saying he listened to the Czech service of the BBC. He spent a month in prison in Budejovice and was subjected to harsh interrogation but he somehow convinced the Gestapo that he was deaf as a doornail and was released.

My turn to participate in the forced war effort came only in February 1945 when I was assigned to Olomouc, in Northern Moravia, to dig trenches against the advancing Red Army. We were billeted at a school and every morning we marched to the outskirts of the town equipped with shovels and pick axes. The very first day I decided that I hated the work. I broke the handle of the shovel and went to see the SA sergeant, our guard and supervisor, complaining about the shoddiness of the work instruments.

"You speak German very well," said the sergeant. "I want you to be my interpreter."

The following day I accompanied him, hands in my pockets, and translated his orders. This I liked even less than shoveling. Two days later I reported sick, complaining of unsupportable heart pain. I was sent to a hospital for tests.

A nursing nun attached the wires of a cardiograph to my breast. The cardiogram showed my heart was as sound as a bell.

"I am a malingerer," I confessed. "I don't want to dig trenches, and I shall not do it. Please help me."

"I must help the machine, for starters," said the nun.

She affixed the wires again and switched the cardiograph on. Then she took the needle registering the heartbeat between her thumb and index finger. Briskly she pushed it up and down. The curving track the needle left on the roll of paper was alarming. It predicted an acute heart attack.

The doctor sent me home to die.

THE PRISONERS WHO NEVER WERE

Of the Czech flag on our house only a blue triangle and a red stripe remained. Its white part was ripped away by German soldiers to be used as a sign of surrender when they encountered the American army. Mother had kept the flag hidden somewhere during the whole war until the day before, when she handed it to Father, who put it up on a pole fixed to a window frame.

It was just as well that the soldiers tore it apart. On that May morning all flags in the village disappeared as if by magic. The main street and the village square were completely deserted. All would-be patriots were in hiding. Kremze was paralyzed by fear. A punitive German commando sent by the SS Headquarters at Krumlov had arrived following a denunciation that villagers tortured German soldiers whom we had taken prisoner. The commando was a truck full of soldiers armed to the teeth and led by a first lieutenant with SS insignia. The soldiers invaded the school where the citizen's revolutionary committee was in session, arrested the ten men present, and dragged them out hands tied behind their back. They lined the men up against the school wall and pointed a machine gun at them. The first lieutenant announced that they would be shot if the German prisoners were not released within an hour.

The problem was that we had not captured a single German soldier! But who would explain that? Whom will the first lieutenant believe?

If there was someone whom he might listen to, it could be only his countryman and fellow officer SA Major Hassenblas who lived in our house at the end of the war as a billeted guest. When I entered his room he was just packing a rucksack. He was dressed in a worn-out checkered jacket and gray trousers belonging to my father because he thought that it would be better if he surrendered as a civilian.

I begged him for help: "*Herr Oberst, Sie müssen uns helfen.*" Hassenblas was a mining engineer from Düsseldorf who supervised the preparatory work to open a nickel mine. The deposit was located some ten kilometers from Kremze. The nickel did not amount to much but during the war every gram of this precious metal was welcome. Experimental boring and the construction of a narrow-gauge railway employed some two hundred forcibly recruited intellectuals, predominantly lawyers, teachers and professors from Budejovice. For them it was incomparably better to be here than somewhere in the Reich. Hassenblas realized that Hitler was kaput and he treated the Czechs accordingly.

"*Nur Sie können unsere Leute retten,*" I insisted: "Only you can save our people." "*Mein Vater war auch verhaftet*" "My father has also been arrested." Father had disappeared somewhere in the morning. I was not sure that he was arrested, but I knew that this possibility would make Hassenblas think. He and Father were about the same age and they talked together for hours almost every night. The two men began to address each other as Du Ernest, Du Jan, and they established a relationship that under normal circumstances would surely have developed into a lasting friendship.

Mother came in and with tears in her eyes begged Hassenblas to save the hostages.

"*Bitte, bitte, bitte,*" she repeated in an incantation of the only German word she knew.

Hassenblas sat down at the table, holding his head in his hands, thinking. He stayed silent a long time. Finally, he got up, took off the civilian clothes, and slowly, hesitatingly, began to put on his uniform.

Without a word he left the room and started walking slowly towards the school. I followed him from a distance. I saw how he raised his right hand in the Nazi way in front of the first lieutenant, who returned the salute. They both lit cigarettes and talked for a while. I could not hear what they said. Then they threw away the cigarette butts and shook hands instead of the Nazi salute.

The commandos folded away the machine gun, jumped onto the truck and departed. Hasenblas came back, changed into the civilian suit, put the rucksack on his shoulder and left to give himself up to the Americans. Mother burned his canary yellow uniform, ignoring my pleas to let me have at least the cap as a souvenir.

Czech flags appeared in windows and on houses again. The hostages became heroes of the revolution. Father was not among them.

Thus ended the Second World War at Kremze.

But in Prague the fighting was far from finished.

THE YOUNG LIONS

We were a small group in a column of three, all young boys with rifles over our right shoulders and ammunition boxes on a belt containing four clips of five cartridges. I inherited my gun from a German private when he passed through Kremze on his way to surrender to American army units who were not far away at Chvalsiny, some fifteen kilometers from us. The Americans were so busy disarming German soldiers that they had to stop their advance.

The private gifted me his gun with relief bordering on joy. He could have been a few years older than I but he looked like a man in his fifties. He showed me how to put in the cartridge slip, take aim and slowly push the trigger. His voice was colorless, and there was a glitter of pity in his deep-seated eyes.

You are a cretin, who does not know what he is doing, his look said. Then he offered me a handshake: *"Alles gute, mein junger Freund"*: "All the best, my young friend."

We were standing in front of the school where I had spent five years in elementary education. Our class was on the ground floor. The first deity after God was a red-haired and freckled teacher named Ms Foltova. She liked me and I liked her. I worked hard to please her. On one of the walls hung a simple picture depicting a policeman directing traffic. It had a caption that said: 'Road junction in Prague.' Whenever I looked at it, which I did a million times, an intriguing question crossed my mind: whether, if ever, I should see our capital. Prague—the word sounded like a siren's song. I desperately yearned to go to Prague.

Now Prague was calling for help. However, I did not want to go. I had a perfectly valid reason: I did not want to die at seventeen. Such stupidity, I told myself. With twenty cartridges we can make no difference, we shall be just risking our skins. I don't even know how to aim properly. I have never fired a shot, so what use could I be as a fighter?

I feverishly sought a way out of this mess without appearing to be a coward. I could simulate something, but what? A twinge? A paroxysm? I was a stupid asshole who had allowed myself to be bamboozled. The grown-ups wearing the red sleeve bands of the Revolutionary Guard stayed away in safety while they sent us, young nitwits, to get slaughtered. Some of these 'revolutionaries' were also compromised because they had enriched themselves on the black market. I recognized among them an informer whom Tony Tesar had identified to me. Tony was of my age but he did not belong to our gang because he was half-German. Before the war his father had served in the Sudeten, a German-speaking part of the country, and had married a German wife. I first met Tony and his younger brother Hans at Pasicka where the Tesar family were our neighbors. They moved to Kremze almost at the same time as we did. After the German occupation of Czechoslovakia Tony and Hans had to leave our school and attend a German one. They did not want to go, they cried, begged and pleaded, but to no avail. They were born to a German mother and thus, according to the law, they were German citizens. I was the only one who remained on speaking terms with them afterwards. Tony and I were close. We built an 'eagle's nest' in a wood that became our secret hangout. We constructed airplane models. One time we made a kayak out of wooden planks. It took water despite our sealing it with asphalt. During our sessions in the eagle's nest Tony confided to me that his mother, who was forced to join the Nazi Party, received anonymous letters in which Czechs denounced other Czechs for listening to the BBC, or said they had slaughtered a pig illegally, or fled from forced labor camps in Germany and were hiding in abandoned barns. Certain denunciations, slipped into Tesar's mailbox at night, Tony's mother burned after reading. But there were squealers who came to see her in person and she had to pass their indictment on to German authorities because they might have gone to the secret police themselves and denounced her as well. But she always sent Tony to warn the endangered people to expect a police raid and tell them why. When Tony recounted these stories to me I realized for the first time in my life that the world is not black and white, that even in the most odious regimes there are honest people, and that good and evil coexist in some kind of perverse symbiosis.

All of sudden a gunshot broke the morning calm. It sounded like the crack of a whip, followed a few moments later by a long staccato of a machine gun.

"It comes from Klet," somebody said.

A man named Mican joined us, running from behind the school where he had observed the mountain with field glasses. He breathlessly reported that he had seen two armored carriers on the connecting road between Krasetin and Chlum.

"They are looking for a short cut to the Americans," said our self-appointed leader, who used to be a sergeant in the army.

"Chlum will get it," said another volunteer. I knew him only by sight. In fact, I knew practically nobody among this handful of volunteer combatants. I had spent five years at the lyceum in Budejovice, and this time away had broken all childhood ties and fogged up all memories. There was no one from our student group; I was the only fool present. The men wearing red bands also disappeared when the shooting started. We stood alone in front of the school like a forgotten platoon.

"We'll give Chlum the deep six," said our leader, who carried a black holster with an automatic pistol on his beer paunch.

"You must be kidding," somebody cried. "I am from Chlum and so is Karel. We must do something to help."

"Our mission is Prague," decided the leader. "Prague is calling."

One after the other we climbed onto a captured German truck. I was last because I was trying to think of a way to slip, fall and pretend that I had broken my ankle.

The leader pushed me from behind.

"Get moving!" he shouted.

I had the gun in my right hand while clutching the

sidewall of the truck with my left. I thought about the uncountable number of human beings this army vehicle had transported to killing fields. Now it was my turn.

With immense sadness I looked at the mountain Klet that would still be there when I was dead and gone. There, on a wooden beam of the lookout tower, I carved a heart with a knife and inside it I put the initials B+J, for Blazenka and Jan. This, I thought, will also outlive me.

Then my eyes turned to the parsonage next to the church…In my memory as at that time, I see and hear quite clearly Father Hrubes examining my knowledge of German. When I was in the fourth grade of the lyceum at the end of the first semester, I received an F in the German language and a warning that I should be excluded from further studies if I didn't improve. Under the Nazi occupation good grades in German were all-important. My mother implored Father Hrubes to help me. He did so. He proceeded like this: "How do you say father?" "*Das Vater*," I answered. Immediately he smacked me. "*Der Vater…DER!* Repeat it ten times!" It was not a sophisticated method of teaching but it worked. In three months he smacked me up to an A+. Strangely, though, he awoke in me a desire to learn foreign languages and showed me the way.

The lime trees surrounding the church were not in blossom, but it seemed to me that I could smell their sweet, intoxicating perfume, and feel on my lips a butterfly touch of the first kiss Hanicka gave me there, unforgettable and irreplaceable. I was overwhelmed by self-pity, regrets for wasted hopes and unfulfilled loves, and my desolation was such that I was on the verge of crying.

The driver turned the key of the starter. The engine coughed and died. I felt a shivery flicker of hope that the truck was kaput. But on the second try, black smoke

29

puffed out from the exhaust pipe and the engine started. Now my only chance was to simulate some sort of a fit. If I had a piece of soap I could pretend an epileptic seizure. Why else was I an actor? But I had no soap; therefore I had to come up with something else. I had three hours to invent it, before we arrived to Prague. I'd be damned if I cannot manage it.

A man with a red band came running out of the school.

"Russians have liberated Prague!" he shouted at the top of his voice. "The uprising has succeeded!"

All my worries and sadness disappeared immediately. My heartbeat doubled. It was as if I had grown wings. I floated in pure bliss and happiness.

I jumped down from the truck first.

"Hurrah!" I cried not as a salute to victory but to life, wonderful and unique, which was waiting to receive me with open arms.

THE AMERICANS ARE COMING!

May 1945: the mother of all Mays. I promenaded in a US Army uniform, tasted American chocolate, ate American K rations, smoked American Camel cigarettes, drank American grapefruit juice, listened to Glen Miller, Ella Fitzgerald, Frank Sinatra, Bing Crosby and Dean Martin. I experienced America with all my senses, I soaked up America though every pore, I craved for America and I dreamed of America—a land of freedom and unlimited possibilities.

Towards the end of the war I had begun to study English secretly from a handbook for self-learning loaned to me by Father Hrubes. When Americans appeared I already knew several hundred words and basic phrases: "How do you do? Good day. Give me a cigarette. I love USA." The pronunciation in the handbook was transcribed phonetically and I tried to imitate it as best as I could. The American soldiers I talked to understood my "How do you do?" but when I spoke the other words they shook their heads and asked: "What did you say? I don't understand you." My pronunciation was misleading at best, if not outright wrong. But in the end I somehow got across the meaning of what I wanted to say. Then the soldiers said it correctly with an American accent and I repeated it several times after them. Which is why I have never learned to speak British English. Moreover, I used to listen regularly to the American Forces Network in Munich, which only reinforced my American accent. There was a positive side to this, because when I worked in the Neutral Nations Supervisory Commission in Korea I had no problem understanding American liaison officers no matter where they came from, whether Texas or Brooklyn.

As it was very hot in July, we spent a great deal of our summer vacations—the first in a free country—at the pond. We talked about the future and our plans, what each of us would like to do, for we were young and we lived in times when everything seemed not only possible, but also easily attainable. Ludek Burianek wanted to be a painter, Zdenek Simecek an architect, his brother Jiri a professor, Lida Cermakova a lawyer, Milan Benes a bank director, Hana Klimova a doctor, Josef Bukovsky an agronomist. I knew for sure what I wanted to be: actor, stage director, dramatist, film producer, all of it! Unlimited creative possibilities lay wide open for me, and it sufficed, it seemed, just to go for them.

"I will be an actor," I said modestly when my turn came to speak of my future. "Or rather a theatre director," I added.

The first play I will stage is Edmond Rostand's *Cyrano de Bergerac*, I told myself. It goes without saying that I shall play the lead role. I knew the play by heart. So I leaned against a pine tree on the shore of the pond and began to recite the closing monologue.

Surrender, I? Parley? No, never! You too, Folly,— you? I know that you will lay me low at last; Let be! Yet I fall fighting, fighting still! You strip from me the laurel and the rose! Take all! Despite you there is yet one thing left...

One thing is left that is void of stain or smutch, I bear away despite you: my coat of arms.

I didn't expect applause, but not general and profound indifference either.

Zdenek said: "What a scorcher. I am going to take dip."

He jumped from the board into the pond. The others followed one by one: Jirka, Lida, Pepik, Ludek, Hanka, Milan. I watched as each plop made centrifugal circles on the water, big at first, then gradually weaker and weaker still, until all that was left was the listless surface, above which beat down the hot summer air.

I remained standing on the shore. I was sad and gloomy as one is when one must leave and say goodbye forever. Absurdly on that splendid summer day, I was overpowered by deep melancholy. It occurred to me that, perhaps, our life is also no more than a pebble that ripples briefly the placid surface of eternal time.

It was the last time that we were all together. We did not know that we would never meet again. Nor did we know that our youthful hopes and dreams were doomed. In our blissful ignorance we were carefree, playful and happy.

Come Christmas, I parted with the local amateur theater

by playing the lead role in a romantic comedy, *Mistresses* by Jarka Bily. The first night was on the 25th of December 1946 at half past seven in the Sokol hall at Kremze. I portrayed a character called Mirek, a pampered, godless womanizer, who is transformed and finds the right way to live when he meets a *'femme fatale,'* the love of his life.

Good God, what a cliché, I thought.

But how little a man knows about himself and about what will happen to him in life when he is seventeen.

PORTRAIT OF THE ARTIST AS A YOUNG PLAGIARIST

We were on board a train returning home from school in Budejovice to Kremze. My buddies played a card game while Lida and I were sitting at the window looking with drowsy eyes at the countryside moving backwards at the unhurried tempo of a short-winded regional train. It was early September, the beginning of the seventh year of my five days a week trips to and from the lyceum.

"I want to change schools," Lida said casually. "I will continue my studies in Krumlov."

It was as if a bomb had exploded next to me. I was shell-shocked.

"Christ, when?"

"Starting on the first of October. I have already informed the director."

"But why, for goodness' sake?"

"It's closer to home, and there are lots of accommodation possibilities in Krumlov. I want to rent a room so that I need not commute every day."

The train's wheels clattered monotonously while I hunted high and low for a rationale to her decision. In fact, she might have had a great idea, I realized. In fact, the more I thought about the more I liked it. It might be a solution for my troubles, too. I finished the previous year with a D-minus in mathematics, and this year had already started disastrously. On top of it, my French professor was picking on me. I was fed up.

My problems with mathematics began in the first grade of the lyceum. We had a professor, Josef Soler, whose method of teaching was dull and ineffective. He wrote formulae and quadratic equations on the blackboard, mumbling explanations that no one heard, let alone remembered. I stopped paying attention to him after the second lesson. Soler used only written exams to check our knowledge. I copied from my neighbor, Salamoun, who was a mathematical ace. This was how I covered up the black hole in my knowledge of arithmetic. I successfully hid it from Soler. However, a new professor appeared at the start of the second semester last year and tested us at the blackboard. He did take pity on me and let me off with a D-minus, for which I was most grateful. But during the first fortnight of the current semester he treated me mercilessly and had already given me two Fs. It was a sign that the worst was yet to come. Maybe I shall be lucky in Krumlov to have another merciful teacher, I thought. As things stand, I have nothing to lose. And if I can find a flat or a room in Krumlov to escape from my parents' control, I would be on the top of the world.

"What's the second language there, French or English?" I asked.

"English."

That clinched it. I entered the lyceum in Krumlov in October 1946.

On my first day in the class my new classmates sat for a written exam in Latin. As a newcomer, I was excused. Opposite me, in the second row, was a blond girl who began sending SOS signals to me. I had a crib of Ovid's works, found the corresponding text, and laid it on the girl's lap when Professor Vondracek could not see me. The girl stiffened, then her legs started to tremble. The crib fell on the floor with a thump. It was a well-used paperback with many loose sheets, some of which flew towards Vondracek's feet. He showed admirable tolerance. He smiled, turned his back towards us, and looked out of the window. The whole class watched me with amusement as I gathered up the sheets and the rest of the crib. As an opening scene to my new life it was not bad. It gave me a certain reputation that I nourished through my subsequent exploits.

Krumlov itself was almost depopulated by the deportation of German inhabitants, now drawing to its close. I saw people walking in long columns towards the railway station. They were allowed to take with them only what they could carry. One old man had a bundle in each hand and three hats on his head. I felt sorry for him. A well-known local politician, Mr Sedlak, spoke of a reckoning and historical justice. "Baloney," said my father, who knew almost all German peasants in the region since he did business with them before the war. Most of them were poor people who were guilty only of ignorance when they proclaimed their allegiance to Hitler. Because of the hardships of her youth my mother was particularly sensitive to injustice and suffering inflicted on people, so she took a train every week to Budejovice where the Germans waited in a concentration camp for deportation and took them bread, salami and other food.

First to invade Krumlov were the so-called gold-diggers arriving from different parts of the country. Here they established their base from which they launched looting expeditions to deserted German villages. Real settlers came in the second wave. They occupied empty houses or flats to start a new life. The castle dominating the town was in a lamentable state. Its round tower was flaking away and its walls were covered with large dark brown patches of dripping plaster.

I shared a flat with a friend, Jarda Pesek, who was three years older than I and had a job as accountant in a flourmill. We lived in two large rooms on the first floor of a bourgeois house at Soukenicka Street that must have belonged to a rich German, and had been looted before we came. Consequently, our flat was equipped, austerely, with furniture that Jarda had commandeered from some deserted houses nearby. In each room there was a single bed, a wardrobe, a table and two chairs. The toilet was in the corridor. We had to fetch water for washing in jugs from downstairs where the only thing left was a faucet. We lived like gypsies, but we wanted for nothing, for it seemed to us that we had all we needed.

The lyceum was not far away, about a kilometer and a half. It was located near the bridge over the Vltava River that carried a lot of chemical wastes from a paper-mill. It smelled really bad. In our class, Professor Cihlar, the Director, taught math. He was a short, lean man with a well-cultivated goatee. He was very kind to me, tolerant of my math ignorance; he did not require much from me, and I humbly accepted a D at the end of the first semester. Moreover, he forgave me unexcused absences and other trespasses, most probably because I was the mastermind of the lyceum's theatrical and recital ensemble, which offered cultural enrichment to the forlorn life of a half-empty little town. We performed gala performances of poetry, staged a play for children, and put on a comedy for adults, all with great success.

I played lead roles, directed, recited, and led a bohemian life. Krumlov for me was a movable feast, a banquet of life-giving gratification and heavenly bliss, which lasted almost six hundred days and nights. I looked forward to each day like a little boy to Christmas, and to each night like a drunkard to a shot of alcohol after a long dry spell. Krumlov days and nights were full of inspiration, my consuming passion, and offered giant expectations to an unconscious, vain youth.

THE GYM TEACHER

I endured yet another of Cihlar's lessons and i was grateful to him that he did not ask me to come to the blackboard to solve an equation. He had given up on me, I guessed. Or at least I hoped so.

I left the classroom. The large corridor was full of kids from lower classes. Then along came a woman walking with the stride of a trained sportswoman. Her prominent blue eyes focused on me briefly, then turned away. Professor Vera Sokolova. As she was passing by she raised her right hand to glance at the watch, let the hand fall and continued walking. I gave a nod. Even if somebody observed us very carefully, they would not have the slightest suspicion that we had just confirmed a date.

She had attracted my attention since the first days in the lyceum. She was the only graceful person on the professorial staff. I would have had to be blind to overlook her although I was not her student. She taught gym and geography to the younger children. I admired her figure, slim at the waist and broad at the hips and bust.

37

The staffroom was on the same floor as our class. During every break I placed myself strategically at a window not far from the staffroom and I waited for her. I never changed the position. When she walked by I made a slight bow. In the beginning I did not want to flirt with her. Seeing her and miming a greeting was for me just a break in my boredom.

After a week or so she began to notice me, too. Since that time, whenever our eyes met, she smiled lightly and nodded her head. We did not exchange a word. Then I accentuated my bow a little like an actor on stage, and her smile became more radiant betraying undisguised pleasure.

What will happen if I disappear for some time? I asked myself. It occurred to me that I should put her to a test.

For three consecutive days I spent all my classroom breaks sitting on my bench. The fourth day I appeared again at my strategic place at the window. To my surprise she stopped in front of me.

"Good day, Professor," I greeted her politely.

"Good day. Were you sick or did you play truant?" she asked and marched off without waiting for a reply.

I was jubilant. She missed me! This was an infallible sign that she took a real interest in me, though I did not know why and what for. However, this was not important. What mattered was that she was hooked. What should I do now? My poor head swarmed with ideas, most of them foolish, of how to approach her. I rejected them all. I decided not to hurry but wait patiently for a chance, an unexpected occasion, and then grab it.

Then one afternoon the whole lyceum marched to the local cinema to see a French picture, *Children of Paradise*. She took a seat in the last row and I swiftly sidled up to her.

"May I sit next to you, Professor?"

"If you wish, student," she said with maliciously tainted civility. But she smiled, which could mean that my presence was not unwelcome.

"Do you know that in the lead role is the famous French mime Jean-Louis Barrault?" I said in an attempt to engage a conversation.

"And do you know that I also read posters?" she replied curtly.

That was not a good omen. Luckily, I was saved by the lights going off in the theatre as the operator started to project the film.

I did not follow the picture much; in fact, I hardly noticed it. In the beginning I hesitated: should I attempt and approach or should I not? In the final analysis I had nothing to lose. So I must not be a coward. It is now or never. I prepared a plan in a flash. I waited patiently while the love story developed on screen. When Barrault began to shed glycerin tears I pressed my knee to hers and held my breath in a tense expectation. My heart stopped beating for a while. Nothing. She did nothing, said nothing. After several minutes, an eternity, I nestled my thigh to hers. Again, nothing happened. Would it be possible she did not notice my advances? That was out of the question. Or was it possible that the physical touch aroused her, too? In order to find out, I laid my hand in her lap. Now she must react one way or the other. Either she flings my hand away, or she slaps me, but something is sure to happen. After a while she put her hand in mine and pressed it gently. I vibrated with joy and bliss. I wished the film would never end.

When the names of actors started to roll on the screen she finally dropped my hand and pushed it away subtly.

"Quite a good picture," she said. "Pity we cannot

see the second part right away."

"I enjoyed it very, very much," I said ambiguously.

"Goodbye, student," she said in a professorial tone.

I was as proud as a two-tailed dog. I found the courage to act. I had not failed. And I was not rejected. That was the main thing. My mood inflated like a balloon… then I slowly but surely deflated. An ice-cold cascade of misgivings quenched my elation. What had happened? Not much, almost nothing. She pressed your hand, palmed it once or twice. It was like soothing a pet rather than an amorous caress. Don't be a bloody fool!

The following day I was waiting in the corridor. As she came nearer to me, I tried to find a clue in her face and eyes, a clue to her feelings of what happened between us. She smiled non-committally as usual, nodded and disappeared into the staffroom. I was not any wiser.

What to do? How could I meet her alone? Where and when? It was not easy, since I was afraid to betray that I was flirting with a professor. I found out where she lived and considered the possibility that I would simply parachute in on her. However, I did not have the guts to do it. What about writing her a letter? Why not, it might be the optimal solution. When I started composing a draft in my mind I came to grief on how to address her. Vera? Verunka? Dear Vera? I realized my total inexperience in such matters since I had not, as yet, written a single love letter. Moreover, I was not in love. I lusted after her as a mature woman. The fact that she was a professor made her even more desirable.

No, a letter was out of the question. Anyway, how would I sign it? Your loving Jan? Eternally yours, Jan? What if it fell into wrong hands? No, I must not leave any trace.

I tore a sheet from my Latin glossary and wrote on it in capital letters the following anonymous message:

TONIGHT AT TEN IN THE CASTLE GARDEN

I folded the sheet into a small square and put it in my pocket.

Lessons finished, I lingered on in the class to make sure that I was the last one to leave. On the bridge over the river I came to a standstill. I leaned my back on side rail and waited. I whistled silently. I spotted her leaving the school building several minutes later. Luckily, she was alone. I set out walking towards her. When I was about to pass her by I stopped and extended my hand. She was so surprised that she took it and I slipped the folded message into her palm.

"Have a fine day, Professor," I said, and ran away like an urchin who had thrown a stone into a neighbor's window.

The die was cast. Now it just remained to while away the time until the fatal hour. When I came home, I took a piece of bread and salami out of the wardrobe. I cooked a cup of tea on a table hotplate. This was my standard fare, though sometimes I bought sausages or tinned pork meat for a change and breakfasted on Mother's marble cake and instant coffee.

Having eaten my lunch, I cleaned the table and lay out my school texts and notebooks. I decided that, for once, I would study and do my homework in English and math. Our English teacher, Dagmar Polivkova, one of three female members of the professorial staff, was a frail, old-maidish spinster in middle age who was convinced that she spoke Oxford English. In fact she had a typical middle-European accent. Small wonder that she disliked my guttural diction that I learned from American GIs. She asked us to write an essay on a trivial subject matter, 'One day of my summer vacation.' Nonetheless, I attacked it with gusto. I recounted a hazy, lazy, sunny afternoon on the waterside of a pond. I spiced my narration with a flashback on my first girl friend, Blazenka, whose body was so soft and inviting. Here I paused a while to recall again—I don't know how many times already—an unbelievably happy, miraculous, blissful early evening in my attic room at home. I resisted the temptation to include it in another flashback describing Blazenka's bosom, which was like a pot of honey. That would be too much for a narrow-minded schoolmistress. Let alone that your first lovemaking is a unique, incommunicable utterly personal experience that you keep in your innermost sanctuary as a sacred mystery until the end of time.

The three equations that Cihlar gave us to solve were beyond me. After half-an-hour of fruitless effort I gave up.

What to do with the rest of the afternoon? There was a full-size mirror on the left side of the wardrobe door. I took a pose in front of it to rehearse Aragon's poems that I had chosen for a literary evening next week. I knew them by heart already, so I concentrated on diction, intonation, gestures and mimicry. After an hour or so of repetition I stretched out on the bed to relax. I was staring at the ceiling trying hard not to think about tonight. No dice. It haunted me, kept coming back. She will not come. Why should she come? Even though she feels lonely and forlorn. I passed in review, mentally, all her colleagues, one after the other, but could not see anyone worthwhile. Most of them were married anyway. What about outside the school? Gold-diggers, adventurists, scum. She would not touch any of them with a ten-foot pole. With modesty I also eliminated all my classmates as schmucks. Under the circumstance, in dire need, I might do. I was young, handsome, likeable, and getting famous in town as an actor. I certainly had some assets.

With this blissful hope I fell asleep. My roommate, Jarda, woke me up two hours later when he came home from work.

"I am loaded," he announced, "let's get out and celebrate."

Every time on his payday Jarda invited me to dinner at the city hotel called Mestak. It was located on the town square a stone's throw from our flat. As we were walking there, Jarda told me that Blazenka had called his office from Budejovice to say that she would be coming to Kremze on Saturday afternoon. The prospect of spending a weekend with her lifted my spirits sky high. It also helped to chase away for a while my worries about tonight's date. And misgivings about what would happen in the castle garden...or would not.

The barroom was full. With luck we found the two last places at a table in the adjoining restaurant where food and drinks were more expensive. I was glad that Jarda took me out. In the noisy, boisterous company of gold-diggers and members of the Revolutionary Guard, in fact looters, the wait to be served, which otherwise would have dragged interminably, passed very quickly. There seemed to be no air in the oblong room, just pure tobacco smoke. The voices of several dozen drunkards melted together in an ear-deafening roar. We had to shout to hear each other. The topic we were trying to discuss was sport. At Kremze we played together football, volleyball, tennis and ice hockey. Jarda was the goalkeeper of our hockey team. Since now he was working in Krumlov he decided that in the coming season he would join the local ice hockey club. He coaxed me to do the same that whole evening, but for me it was a non-starter. The last four years I was the right-winger for my old team, with Zdenek Simecek at the center in the first line and Pepik Matuska on the left wing. I could not let them down, for it would be treason. To make Jarda happy, however, I promised that I would think about it.

When I left the hotel, it was already nine o'clock. On the way a dreadful possibility made me tremble like a leaf: what if Vera showed my invitation to the Director? What will happen if Cihlar reads it? He surely will kick me out of school; I should be out in a flash. But so what? I don't care if I graduate or not. If I am expelled I shall take it as a sign by destiny to follow my dream...Even if I should end up as a ham actor. Or, maybe, Mr Solc will engage me out of pity and I shall be on the stage with Hanicka. This tempting vision calmed me down. Stop agonizing, I told myself, cross the bridge when you come to it.

It started to drizzle. This was the last thing I needed. I ran to our flat, opened the wardrobe, and fished out an American army raincoat and a garrison cap. Having put on the coat, I stepped in front of the mirror to make sure I wore the cap in the flashy way of GIs. Satisfied, I saluted myself. At home at Kremze I preciously hoarded a complete US officer's uniform, a gift from Captain Jeremy Hawks, whom I befriended. He had urged me to go to America. Before the war he was Professor at Chicago University, and he said he would get me admitted there as a student. But I did not want to leave my parents and give up a glamorous career in the theatre of which I was certain.

I set out for my date at double speed. There were only twenty minutes left to reach the castle. I ran over the wooden bridge under the castle and then started to climb a hillside that provided a shortcut to the garden. I stopped a couple of meters behind its entrance under a big broadleaved tree. I touched the ground. The grass was still dry there. I leaned my back against the trunk and looked at the luminous watch face. It was ten o'clock sharp.

The night was pitch dark. Gradually my eyes became accustomed to the gloom and I could see the access road quite distinctly. My calm surprised me. No hectic heartbeat, no pinching in the stomach. Cool. If she comes, fine. If not, also fine. It was like waiting for the outcome of a bet of no consequence. Out of superstition I bet against it. She will not come. Why should she have an affair with an immature student? Why risk it? If it were divulged, I might be expelled but her career would be jeopardized, if not ruined completely. It will be better for her not to come.

I shall wait a quarter of an hour and then I leave.

I took off my garrison cap and put it in my pocket. I did not want to look ridiculously martial if she came, nonetheless.

After some twenty minutes I spotted her in the entrance. She wore a long, brown overcoat with a protective hood. She looked like a Franciscan monk.

"I did not believe that you would come," I said when she stood before me.

"Why?" she asked, taking off the hood and revealing blond, shortcut hair I liked on her. "Why did you think that I would not come?"

I shrugged my shoulders.

"I did not believe, but I was fervently hoping…"

"I know that you like me, and I like you, too," she said. "I also know that you want me as much as I want you. In a couple of months we shall part forever…This is all the better because we do not need to lie to each other, or to pretend something."

I put my arms around her and kissed her. She pressed her body to mine, but our coats dampened our craving and lust. They were like asbestos plates. We pulled them away from our bodies and kneeled on them in a long, clumsy caress.

"Wait a little," she whispered. Freeing herself from my embrace she spread my army raincoat on the ground and placed her brown coat on it. Then she stripped off her knit sweater and rolled it in a coil for a pillow. She did all this thoughtfully with female care. When she finished she lay down on the bedding and took me in her arms.

"Don't rush," she said between two kisses.

I did not hear, and even if I had heard I would not have paid any notice, for my hands were hungrily discovering her body. I tore off a button on her blouse opening it to find two white, soft little knobs that fitted into my palms as if they were made for them. Her skirt rolled up and I saw that she had no panties. This was the last thing that I registered before taking off, rapidly and unexpectedly, for a world of unbearable lightness somewhere in outer space.

The dazing feeling did not last, the flight ended with a brutal fall.

The blissful dizziness was disappointingly brief.

A bit later she was sitting at my side, her head resting on her knees. I did not know what to say. I put my hand around her shoulders that were trembling. I petted soothingly her bowed head.

The tree that protected us against rain started to leak. Drops were pattering down.

At long last she raised her head.

"I shall go first...wait a little here...let's leave one after the other," she said.

She got up, arranged her blouse, put on the sweater and the coat. She left without a word.

For several interminable minutes I gazed listlessly into the night. Then I picked up the raincoat, shook drops of water out of it, slipped it on, and leaned back against the trunk of the tree as if seeking support against shame, disgrace and humiliation.

How long did I stay there like this? Half-an-hour? Eternity? Or a few seconds? I lost trace of time. All I know is that I had a guilty feeling that I had damaged something precious and irreplaceable. As if I held the glass globe with snowflakes dancing inside, like the one that Orson Welles grasped in the film *Citizen Kane* and that, like him, I dropped to the ground. It broke into zillions of microscopic bits; mere stardust remained.

I heard rapidly approaching footsteps. Is she returning? Why?

Vera came to me breathless, head all wet, but smiling.

"We have forgotten to make another date," she said. "Come to my place on Thursday. I live in Nadrazni Street number twenty-six. But don't come sooner than ten o'clock at night because of the neighbors. OK by you?"

"That is in two days from now. What if you have some hitch?"

"I can't see any, but to be sure you know what we could do..." She hesitated a little thinking it through. "On Thursday, observe me as I go to the staffroom during the break. If there is no hitch, I will look at my watch when I pass you by. If I don't look at the watch, it means that the date is postponed to Friday."

I was one of many secret signs that we developed over the time to protect our love affair from snoopers and to meet clandestinely in security.

Although she was six years older than me, she was as little familiar with the breviary of lovemaking as I was. But we learned diligently and passionately. We made big and rapid progress together.

One night after the parting kiss Vera whispered:

"When you speak about us some time…and you will…please, be gentle."

THE ACTOR PREPARES

I was late. the rehearsal of Cyrano had already started. But I arrived just before my scene. Running, I took down my overcoat made of white felt that Father had bought during the war when real wool cloth was rare and very expensive. At my request, the tailor was generous with padding to make my shoulders seem extra large. I was very proud of my overcoat, for I thought it gave me an irresistible, manly look.

There was a bespectacled girl in the first row of the hall. I threw this precious piece of my wardrobe into her lap.

"Hold it for me," I told her.

I ran up the board to become Cyrano on the stage. We rehearsed the scene in which a messenger brings a letter from Roxana. I think it is for me, but bit-by-bit I realize that it is for the stupid but charming Christian. During this scene I have to say "yes" seven times; first with eager expectation, then with gradual disappointment, and with resigned frustration at the end. The stage manager, Karel Zahorik, kept interrupting me, making me repeat my little word again and again. "It lacks gradation," he said. He gave me confused directions because the intonation of my voice ought not to rise but, on the contrary, gradually go down. He had a point, however, in complaining that I could not find the right vocal shade to convey Cyrano's change in feelings from hope to disillusionment. After half-an-hour we all were fed up. Zahorik announced a break.

As I jumped down from the stage to have a word

with Zahorik sitting in the third row I was stopped on my way.

"Your cloak, Master," said the bespectacled girl with undisguised irony.

"Oh, yes...thanks." I took my overcoat, giving her a probing sideway glance. I have, as yet, been impassible towards girls who wear glasses. But there was something intriguing, even special, about this one

"It's not my day," I said to Zahorik.

"You got better towards the end," he said, picking up papers that lay on a small lectern in front of him. *Cyrano* was supposed to be our first attempt at producing a classic piece. So far, we had staged a children's play, a comedy, and most recently a literary gala of Aragon's poetry.

"Come, I will introduce you to a new recruit," said Zahorik, leading me to the bespectacled girl. "This is Honza Vitek...meet Miss Blanka Cechova."

"I've had the pleasure already," I said.

"Yes, you mistook me for a coat hanger," said the girl with specs.

I did not know what to say, so I kept silent.

"Blanka is an excellent alto and plays the piano," said Zahorik.

"I go at it," she said with a ringing, joyful grin. She wore a close-fitting dress of green velvet that accentuated her well-turned figure and gutsy curving breasts. A silver breastpin adorned the dress, and a string of pearls encircled her slim neck. She was dressed for a social occasion rather than for a rehearsal in a cold, empty theatre. She had slightly protruding Slavic cheekbones and peach colored cheeks. Her nose was long in the classical Greek style. At its base hovered two lenses in an ivory frame. Her pitch-black hair was combed into a pony tail, stapled by a brooch at the top, and descending like a waterfall. For a fragment of a second I imagined it spread out on a white pillow. But I blotted out the seductive picture immediately. Perish futile temptation!

"Where do you study?" I asked, to say something.

"Where are the snows of yesteryears," she recited borrowing a verse of Apollinaire. "I graduated from a lyceum in Budejovice a year ago. Now I slave in the city administration like Karel."

Zahorik nodded in assent. He worked in the cultural department. Which is why he became our stage manager, since the responsibility for our ensemble was in his job description.

"Blanka has not missed any of our performances," he said. "I could not convince her to join us, however."

"Well, you did succeed, since I am here," Blanka said and blushed for some reason.

"All, right let's go on," decided Zahorik, clapping his hands. "On stage!"

I did not act in the rehearsed scene, so I sidled up to Blanka, who resumed her seat in the first row.

"If I ask you a little inquisitive question, will you answer?"

"Try me, we shall see."

"What exactly do you do in the city hall?"

"I work in the secretariat of deputy Mirko Sedlak."

"Oh, that one…He has the reputation of a wolf."

"What do you mean?"

"Just what people say…that he likes young pretty girls."

"Gossip. Don't believe it. Mirko is very timid."

"Timid! A politician? That would be the eighth wonder of the world."

"Yet, it is true."

"Well, if you say so," I said and changed the subject. "When my turn comes, watch my profile carefully and pay special attention to my nose so that you know why I portray Cyrano...because I don't need a false one."

She laughed. It encouraged me to ask a question that was the hidden reason why I was talking to her.

"If you stay here until the end, may I accompany you home?"

"It is a big if, but yes, why not? I live at Parkan. Do you know where it is?"

"I have never set my foot there yet but I like discovering new places...and people."

We were interrupted by Zahorik's angry shout:

"Honza, where the hell are you?"

We started to rehearse the scene of a duel between Cyrano and the simpleminded nobleman de Valvert. The cause of the duel is Cyrano's big nose. During the fight Cyrano composes a ballad, each strophe ending in a threat: I shall run you through.

It was a Calvary. We did not have swords so we used our right hand to fake the fencing. It was pathetic. No, utterly ridiculous. I should take a couple of lessons in épée fencing, it flashed through my mind, but where and with whom?

I thundered again and again for a dozen times:

"A move a pace-lo, such and such!

Cut over-feint!

What ho! You real?

At the envoi's end I touch!"

I pretended to attack de Valvert, who was played by a local teacher, Krivanek. I took three quick, short steps forward and then two steps back as in an attack and retreat. Since my throat was sore and dry I just let out a shriek instead of the roar that should run right through Krivanek's beer paunch.

"Stop. That's enough," said Zahorik disgusted. "Let's call it a day. The next rehearsal will be on

Monday at eight. Do me a favor and be punctual. That goes for you, too, Honza."

After this last dig I was sure that most, if not all, of what I endured from Zahorik during the rehearsal was intended to denigrate me before the bespectacled girl. Was he jealous? Nonsense, there was no reason.

Blanka sat in her place wrapped in a fleecy green coat. I asked myself where she got it. The only explanation was she must have come wearing it, but had taken it off to showcase her fancy evening dress. That thought should have started alarm bells ringing, but it did not. I was in heaven because she had waited for me. Wow!

"I am freezing to death," she complained. "Shall we go?"

I waved goodbye to Zahorik and other members of our ensemble who were gathered around him. Blanka got up and we left together.

In the beginning of December 1946 Krumlov, which had been depopulated by the deportation of its German nationals, slowly but surely revived. The original Czech inhabitants, who had been expelled from the town in 1938 after annexation of Sudetenland by the Reich, returned to claim their confiscated property. Among them was the family of my classmate Kuba. Then came new settlers who seized the best villas and flats in town. A lot of houses, robbed of all valuables and furniture by looters, still remained empty. Now, at eleven at night, streets were deserted, with no living soul around.

"You lead," I said to Blanka, lending her my arm.

"To the left and then upward," she said. She locked my arm as a matter of course as if we had known each other always.

She had high-heeled shoes that made her to walk in short steps. I had to adjust my stride by changing step a couple of times.

"I am sorry to disappoint you, but I must tell that your nose is not Cyrano's size, at least as I imagine it," she said with a ringing smile that was her hallmark. "You will have to make it much bigger."

"If we continue like tonight it won't be necessary, because we will never make it to a dress rehearsal, let alone the first night," I said. As I did not want to talk about my lousy performance, I changed the topic abruptly. "Tell me, rather, what are you reading?"

"*Colas Breugnon* by Romain Rolland."

"I don't know it. I read Rolland's *Jean-Christophe*, all three volumes, but nothing else."

"In the Czech translation the book was published under the title A *Good Man Still Lives*. But I read it in the French original. A friend of mine brought me a copy from Paris…It's a sort of apotheosis of the simple, meaningful life…The Czech title is quite sententious."

I took note that she wanted to impress me with her knowledge of French, so I played along and asked:

"Did you graduate in French?"

"And in mathematics and physics…"

"A very rare combination…languages and science…With such a background I could see you in the Charles University in Prague rather than in an office in this godforsaken town."

"I did not like the idea of spending the next four or five years in a lecture-room…Frankly, there was no specific field that interested me, and I wanted to be independent, to earn my keep. I shall give it a go, a year or two, then I might change my mind, who knows…Now, in return, you tell me what book you are reading."

"Not reading, Miss Blanka, but stu-dy-ing," I replied, emphasizing each syllable. "I am studying

Karel Capek's dramatic works and his message to the world. Have you seen any of his plays?"

"Just one, *Bandit*. I liked it very much."

"It is a charming comedy but rather superficial, nothing comparable with *White Disease* and *R.U.R.* I am fascinated by the latter, Capek's play about robots. You know, when they started to produce robots their inventors and the director of the first factory did not do it for profit. They all had a noble goal: to do away with drudgery, free people from work, give them time to live their lives, do things they like, lead a full satisfying life. But it backfired. Because work is not only a means to make a livelihood and a curse, but a basic, essential need for human beings. Having been liberated from work, strain and even pain, people lost energy, gave up all activity and lost the ability to live...Moreover, the production of robots gets out of hand, and here is yet another of Capek's messages for our society obsessed with technology. Robots gradually become indispensable and stopping their production seems impossible. The sales manager says: 'How could you ever have thought the managing director was in charge of production? Production is governed by supply and demand. Everywhere in the world they wanted to have their robots, and all we did was respond to the flood of orders.'

"Capek puts the responsibility not only on those who made robots but also on all those who contributed to its worldwide spread, and especially on those who, in their thirst for power, used them as soldiers to kill people. The whole world is responsible for this gigantic catastrophe, although the measure of responsibility is different from one person to another. I suggested to Zahorik that we stage *R.U.R* instead of *Cyrano*...Maybe I shall do it myself some day and if I do, you will get a free ticket."

"If you forget, I'll hire a claque to hiss you," smiled the bespectacled girl. "Besides Capek, who else is your favorite author?"

"Let's be more specific…Let's leave dramatic authors out, because you would have to suffer a rather rambling lecture about the difference between the Ibsen and Chekhov's schools, one rational, the other emotional…Let's agree to discuss fiction."

An almost full moon stared out from the clouds in the sky. At this hour of the night we had the streets to ourselves. Blanka walked close to me on rough paving stones, staggering from time to time on her high heels. She slid her hand into my pocket. Our fingers interlocked. It was pleasant and exciting. We talked about our favorite books: Stendhal's *Red and Black*, Maupassant's short story *Dumpling* (*Boule de Suife*), Hemingway's *For Whom The Bell Tolls*, Huxley's *Brave New World*. We considered Virginia Woolf and Faulkner overrated. We admired Tolstoy, Turgenev, Dostoyevsky, Mann, Zola, and Feuchtwanger. Her hand pressed mine in assent each time when we agreed. In fact, it was extraordinary that we had the same literary tastes and were on the same wavelength. I did most of the talking. Blanka contented herself with short remarks but posed a lot of good questions—that I answered with eloquence and pleasure. At one moment I had a sneaking suspicion that I was being artfully manipulated, that some kind of invisible but strong female web was being woven around me, but in my egotism I rejected the thought and forgot it. I considered Blanka an elegant, gracious, educated and very intelligent young woman who fully understood and shared my opinions and feelings.

"In Tolstoy's correspondence I discovered an interesting thought…" I paused in the middle of the sentence and pointed to a tumbledown gate of a surely uninhabited little house. "This is the second time I am seeing this wreck!" I cried. "Miss Blanka, aren't we are walking in a circle?"

"A little…"

"On purpose?"

"A little…I wanted us to have more time to talk…because I wanted to know the way you are when not acting…who you are in reality."

"Jesus Christ!" I said in shock.

"But now we are back on the right track…Please, finish what you were saying about Tolstoy."

"Well, it's about an answer to the eternal question: what is the sense of life? Tolstoy wrote that the sense of life is to live."

"And that's all?"

"Isn't that enough? It's a whole program."

"Live to live it up…or the other way round? That does not sound like Tolstoy. He was a true believer and, so far as I know, he wanted us to follow the example of Jesus."

"But not always, Miss Blanka, not always. When he was young, and even in his prime, he considered bliss the utmost good. He deprecated all other values. He was a nihilist and hedonist. He was over fifty when he changed. Only then did he begin to preach that the sense of life is an effort to achieve the highest possible level of morals, love and faith. But I agree with the young Tolstoy. Yes, the sense of life is to live…and at full blast, I add."

I fell silent for a while waiting for her objections. As she said nothing I tackled the subject from a different angle.

"Do you know what Goethe said?"

"No. But I am sure you will tell me."

"In connection with our journey through this valley of tears, Goethe said that man should study until thirty, from thirty to forty make a career, and from forty to fifty make money. I have thought about it and one thing I know for sure: I don't care about career and money."

"So what will you do after graduation?"

"You've uttered the magic word: graduation. The problem is that I must somehow be admitted to the final exams. That depends on Mr Cihlar, the Director, who teaches math. I do everything I can to please him, which is why I put together an ensemble at school and organized cultural performances where he can make festive speeches…I grovel to him whichever way I can because math and I are sworn enemies. If Cihlar does not have mercy on me and give me at least a D, then goodbye graduation."

"I heard you want to study acting."

"Wrong. If I do graduate and go to the Arts Academy in Prague, I want to study stage directing and dramaturgy. I don't want to be pushed around by nobodies like Zahorik all my life."

I was about amuse Blanka with a story how, at the tender age of nine, I dramatized a popular fairy tale, when she stopped in front of a villa on a slope.

"We have arrived," she said pointing upwards. "I live in the attic and I have wonderful views of the castle. Especially in early morning when the first rays of the rising sun fall on it."

"Who is the lucky man who commandeered this villa?"

"Attorney and city council member Oberhanzel. Lucky man? Hardly. He is a grumpy, acrimonious little man and has a hellcat for a wife," smiled Blanka. She offered me a hand to shake: "Thank you for accompanying me."

"Hold on," I replied. "A real gentleman always sees the lady to the door."

We entered a small garden. On the left was a

wooden toolshed and next to it a greenhouse. Several stone steps led up to the porch of the villa. Blanka unlocked the door and standing on the threshold offered me a handshake again.

I knew well that it would be appropriate now to shake hands, thank her for an unforgettable evening, express the hope to meet again soon, turn around and leave.

Instead I stepped nearer to Blanka and on the spur of the moment took off her spectacles.

"I cannot leave without knowing the color of your eyes…"

What I saw was the most beautiful pair of golden-brown eyes in the whole universe. They were looking at me affectionately, impatiently and hungrily. They were pulling me down into an abyss of passion from which there was no escape. I did not try to resist, or to defend myself. I was unbearably happy. I felt great and high.

"Kiss her, stupid," an inner voice commanded. I obeyed gratefully, repeatedly.

"Take off your shoes," she said, catching her breath between two long kisses.

"Why?"

"We must not wake up the landlord when we go upstairs…"

A pale roundish moon shone into the room through a window without curtains. Blanka lay on the bed. She loosened her long, pitch-dark hair. It extended to the nipples of her breasts. She seemed sinful temptation personified. And the only manly thing to do was to succumb.

PUNISHMENT MATH

When the Latin lesson ended, Professor Vondracek beckoned to me to come to him and told me that I should go immediately to the headmaster's room because Director Cihlar wanted to speak with me. On my way I debated with myself but I could not see any reason to be in trouble. Probably he wants to talk about the next performance by the school ensemble.

I knocked at the door, entered and greeted him with the clear conscience of a choirboy.

Cihlar got up from behind his paper-littered desk. He wasted no time on preliminaries and launched a frontal attack right away.

"You are a depraved and shameless youngster, a disgrace, a slur on the good reputation of our lyceum. My patience with you is overstretched."

Cihlar's penetrating eyes spluttered with rage. I was struck by lightning. He must have found out about Vera and me! Jesus Christ! We are both damned! To hell with me, I don't matter at all, but Vera is absolutely vulnerable. She must have been sent away from school already, since I did not see her during the first break this morning. The only thing I can do for her is to take all the blame. It is true. I started it. I am a man of no scruples, Mr Director, a rogue, a rascal or whatever you want to call me. Vera is a poor victim of my lust. I am disgusted with myself. I must tell him something like this. But first I will hear what exactly he knows.

"Don't try to appear innocent. You know what I am talking about!" shouted Cihlar.

"No…I have not the slightest idea…"

"I am talking about your visits to Miss Cechova. You spend two or three nights a week with her. When the house is locked, you climb to her room on a ladder from the toolshed. Last night you damaged the greenhouse belonging to the landlord, Mr Oberhanzel. He has filed a complaint with me and demands that I punish you in an exemplary way."

Oberhanzel the city council member was Chairman of the Committee on Education. That added extra weight to his complaint. He was a bastard who forbade Blanka from receiving male visits. She had to smuggle me in. Lately, he had installed a thumb-latch inside so that I could not use a copy of the door key Blanka gave me. Which is why I had to climb a ladder.

All this swept through my mind together with a feeling of relief that Vera was not involved. Blanka was a different case. It means that I am in a jam but not right in the shit. Blanka and I are adults and have the right to enjoy a love affair. The old coot! I saw red when I thought of Oberhanzel. I will wring his neck, just wait, the time of reckoning is coming. I will burn down your villa, even if I end up in a slammer for the rest of my days.

"I am going to compensate Mr Oberhanzel for the greenhouse," I said.

"This is the least that is awaiting you. I have not finished with you yet. You will be flabbergasted by how I shall deal with you. I could expel you right away for immoral behavior. But that would attract undesired attention to our school. So I have decided to handle things differently without much fuss but no less efficiently. Today is Monday. In a week from now I shall reexamine you on all mathematical subjects that we have covered this year. Take it as a pre-graduation test warranted by your lousy academic achievement. You will come to the blackboard and the exam will be held in front of your classmates. They will be witnesses to your failure and it will constitute a valid reason for barring you from graduation. At the end of the semester you will receive a *concilium abeundi* (advice to leave, a form of expulsion). We'll part forever. Good riddance. Don't bother to thank me; consider it as my present for your birthday tomorrow. And now, out!"

I did not return to my class. I left the school building like a moonwalker. I let my feet carry me wherever they wanted. It started to rain. A strong wind blew into my red-hot face cooling it, mercifully, with splashes of raindrops.

I stayed home and did not go to school any more. What for? There was no point. Also, I wanted to avoid answering maliciously sympathetic questions because the news about my forthcoming execution had surely spread like wildfire.

I cancelled all rehearsals. I called up Blanka and told her Oberhanzel is a treacherous sod and we must be more careful. I wrote Blazenka telling her not to come to Kremze next weekend. No need to warn Vera, she must have known by now that this was the end of our affair. We expected it would come. Still it pained me the way it happened, and so prematurely. I cancelled my reservation of a small stateroom at the city hotel where I wanted to celebrate my birthday. I felt like making my last will.

For the first time study became my priority: a whole week, seven days and seven nights. Is it possible to catch up on all the math lessons? And was it only one year? In my desperation I pored over the textbook and scanty notes I had taken during Cihlar's lessons. The more I peered into the mysterious realm of equations and theorems, the more painfully I realized hopelessness of my endeavor. Nonetheless, I sat through the days and stayed awake throughout the night with the resignation of a convicted life-timer, contemplating the math enigmas, while mountains of crumpled papers containing false solutions grew up around me. On Saturday my head was torpid and blank.

I slept the whole Sunday. On Monday morning I set forth to my place of execution.

The math lesson started at nine o'clock. Cihlar invited me to the blackboard immediately and asked me to solve three equations. Each of them was like a hammer blow to my head. My classmates, eight boys and two girls, were full of compassion. They shared the drama of my superhuman effort. Kartak, a top mathematician, tried with pursed-up lips to prompt me with a formula. Jana Xandrova was staring at me as if she wanted to hypnotize me. Her lips too were moving silently. Even mischievous Pepik Knop put his thumb up in a sign of support.

I don't know now, as I did not know at that time, how long I took to finish my labors. Equally, I have never grasped how I succeeded in solving the three mysteries. A miracle must have happened. Or maybe Cihlar inadvertently chose his puzzles from the miniscule islands of knowledge surviving in the vast ocean of my mathematical ignorance. Or maybe I used the ability that later became the tool that enabled me to earn my keep as a journalist: the capacity to master a complex issue in a short time, interpret it intelligibly, and forget most of it, if not all, soon afterwards. Or most likely of all, the Holy Ghost inspired me, having finally heard my mother's daily prayers for her wayward son.

I sat for the graduation exams at the end of May. I was calm. I had no stage fright. I faced the board self-confidently. I spoke slowly, carefully. I paid attention to my diction as if I were on the stage. This is your one-man show, I told myself; watch your behavior and presentation. I felt the adrenalin rising to my head. It cleared and stimulated my brain. I looked straight in the eyes of the chairman and tried to guess his reaction to what I was saying. I was encouraged by his occasional nodding and by his slight smile that was amused rather than ironic.

During my studies, surviving barely from one class to another, I learned how to handle difficult test questions by deflecting my answers from the unknown parts to those bits with which I was familiar. In chemistry, for instance, I always ended up at fractional distillation, which I knew perfectly. In my graduation exams I made a masterly use of this art. I excelled in all oral exams, which made the chairman look into my past report cards. It must have intrigued him when he compared my poor grades with my performance before the examination board.

When we all passed, he made a brief speech in which he congratulated us and wished us much success at the University. He paused for a while as if he clarified for himself a particular thought and weighed the words in which to express it. Then he said:

"In life it does not matter what you know, but how well you manage to sell it."

"My remark was meant for you," he told me shaking my hand. "I am sure you will find your way in the maze of life."

VICTIMS OF COMMUNISM

Father arrested. Come immediately. When I received Mother's telegram I put textbooks and papers in my briefcase so that I could do some work in the train during the journey home.

I lived in a boarding house at Husova Street, not far away from the Central Railway Station. Over the past eight months I had changed my domicile three times. The previous September, Father brought me to Prague in his Walter delivery truck to a sub-let room that Uncle Sklar had found for me in the apartment of a young widow in a small house at Zlichov, on the outskirts of Prague. The widow was small, plump and enterprising. The very first night she slipped into my bed and showered me with passionate kisses, attacking me without any preliminaries. I was dumbfounded and, yes, so scared that the following day I packed up my two suitcases and left.

I was lucky. The first advertisement I found in a newspaper turned out as good as a winning lottery ticket. It took me to a large room in an apartment near the Powder Tower in the center of Prague. The rent was moderate and the landlady looked very pleasant and amiable. She told me that she had one condition: no female visitors. I asked her if my sister, who would occasionally come to Prague, could sleep over in the room. The landlady agreed, provided that my sister's visit was short. When in the beginning of October my girlfriend Blazenka came to see me we were not cautious enough and, more particularly, we did not notice that there was no solid wall behind the wardrobe but a connecting wooden door to the kitchen where the landlady could hear all what we said and did. Thus on a Sunday morning we were both put out on the street. Blazenka took a train home, while I found a provisional refuge in the studio of my classmate in a boarding house on Husova Street in the popular borough of Zizkov. After a short wait, when another tenant left, I was able to rent a tiny, narrow room like a monk's cell in the house.

A local train from Budejovice dropped me at the railway station at Mric shortly before midnight. From there I had to walk some two kilometers to Kremze. I took a shortcut over the meadows. I could do it blindfolded because for six years during which I studied in Budejovice I walked there, and most often ran, twice a day. The sky was clear, the stars bright and big, as high in the mountains.

I climbed over the yard gate that Mother had closed and secured by a bar. There was a light in the kitchen. Mother was waiting for me. I knocked gently on the window.

"You took a lot of time to come," Mother said when she opened the door.

"I had to take a slow train from Prague to Budejovice, there is no fast train in the evening," I explained. "Please say what's going on."

"They came for him yesterday at five o'clock in the morning," she said. "One policeman and two detectives. They almost broke down the door and then searched the whole house. They confiscated all bills and business papers, all the money, our bank books and his beloved car, the Walter."

It was not a lamentation but a factual account.

"What will become of us?" asked Mother crying. "He may be in prison for a long time. They have said on the radio that the time for exploiters is over and that they will be annihilated as a class."

"Father was no exploiter. He has never hired anybody. He only enslaved himself and you."

"But that changes nothing since he has achieved such a big turnover. How many times have I told him to slow down, but no, he never listened, he kept saying let the wheels keep turning. And this is where he has ended up, in prison."

What had happened was that when the Second World War ended, there was a period in which Germans from the Sudeten were forced to leave their farms and these were taken over by state-appointed trustees, mostly gold diggers, who plundered the rural homesteads. Father bought beef cattle from them. This was how he made an enormous turnover, but with little profit.

"That was his megalomania—keep the wheels turning. Now they have stopped. He saw too big. He boasted that last year he bought and sold cattle worth a million crowns. Now the Communists want people like him to pay a millionaire's tax. But how? And with what? We have so little cash. I don't know what he did but we have always been short of money, and now we have lost everything."

She was beyond consolation. I had to listen again to the litany of woes: she made a mistake marrying Honza Vitek, all she experienced with him was drudgery from morning till night, lot of worries and pain, never a bit of joy. Tears were running down her face. It was still lovely and delicately modeled, hemmed with thick, curly hair, but which had started to turn silver at the temples, I noticed for the first time. And there were wrinkles under her eyes. Katerina Traplova was a beauty when she married at twenty. However, living with her was not easy, because she was stubborn, unbalanced and moody. Her soul was pure, her heart noble and charitable, as so often with people who have experienced in life more than an appropriate portion of suffering, humility and poverty. Father never contradicted her. He listened to her and nodded in mute assent. When he thought she was right, he obeyed; otherwise, he simply did what he wanted. He loved her immensely, implicitly and truly.

Mother rested her elbows on the kitchen table with hands clasped together as if she were praying. Her fingers were short, strong and brownish as a result of hard work; they knew nothing else, and were never adorned by a ring, not even a wedding one, because Father was too poor to buy one at the time. I was suffused with a hot flush of tenderness for her. I wanted to embrace her, kiss her hands and say: Dear Mom, I love you so much. But I did none of these things; I just sat there in sullen silence. I shall never forget that, nor shall I forgive myself.

"What will become of us?" Mother said once more. "How shall we pay for your studies?"

Her words struck my heart like hot iron. What studies? Last Friday I was expelled from all universities in the republic...You don't know, Mom, but I have become an outlaw, for they have branded me as a reactionary element of bourgeois origin, and on top of it indicted as the enemy of the people because I had participated in a demonstration against the new regime. You should have seen the young Communist in a blue shirt chairing the university purge committee. How he smirked haughtily when he told me to go to the Ostrava coalmines and work there to remold my character. As if I were a piece of scrap iron!

"Are you hungry?" she asked. "I have completely forgotten to give you something to eat." She brought a half of rye bread and a piece of salami that Father made himself, and a bottle of beer. Bread, salami and beer were Father's favorite meal. I think I have never seen him eat anything else.

"They have said on the radio that all kulaks will be evicted from their homesteads, their fields will be joined together and belong to collective farms. I am afraid that they will chase us out as well."

"Mom, they are just frightening people," I said to calm her. But I did not believe it. I recalled in my mind the long columns of Red Guards with rifles on their shoulders that I had seen marching in Prague streets on that cold February night of the Communist putsch. I also re-lived the horror I felt when workers' militia hammered us with rubber truncheons as they were chasing us down the stairs from the Prague Castle to the Little Town Square. Our new masters were capable of everything and were merciless.

"Can you stay with me, or must you return to university?"

"I have no exams and Easter holidays will start next week," I said, evading a clearer answer because this was not a propitious time to tell her the truth. "We can go to Budejovice tomorrow to try to find out what are the accusations against Father. Maybe we shall be able to see him."

On this hopeful note we said goodnight to each other.

Once again, I lay in the green-colored bed of my adolescence. Its straw mattress rested on wooden planks, making the bed hard and austere. I could not fall asleep. I thought incessantly of Father, imagining him pacing in his cell—four steps one way, four steps back—and what must be going through his head. He was a self-possessed, wise, hardworking man. Pity I was not more like him. I called up his lean, ascetic face, his prominent nose (yes, this I inherited), and his protruding ears like Clark Gable's. When he clenched his fists they resembled two big stones. I frustrated the hopes he had pinned on me when I refused to be a cattle merchant and became a student instead and, worse still, an aspiring actor. I don't remember that he ever tried to talk me out of it, or forbid me from going my way. Rather, he seemed to have written me off. This attitude pained me more than if he had thrashed me. Perhaps now, I thought, when he realizes that commerce has no future, he will accept the fact that I want to be different.

But different how? What can I do? What are my possibilities?

As always when I was cornered I started with the

question: what could be the worst possible outcome? In this case that Father would remain in jail, which meant that I must return home and find some work as a digger or a farm laborer to help Mother. It would not be pleasant, but I would do it. Once I sort of accepted the worst-case scenario, I examined the other options. At best, I could return to the Institute of Modern Languages to continue my English studies, and I could start learning additional languages. It is a private school where the expulsion from state universities does not apply. This presupposed financial support by my parents, which could not be taken for granted. Or I could find the itinerant theatrical company of Mr Solc and join it. It would be great if I could share the stage with Hanicka and thus fulfill our dreams. Or I could flee the country to Germany and from there to America. All things considered, this might be the best solution. Picturing myself as an emigrant on ship from which I would see the Statue of Liberty, I finally dropped into a deep sleep.

Father was released after a fortnight in jail. He was accused of fiscal fraud and of cheating on payments to the state trustees from whom he bought cattle. His honesty and square-dealing saved him because his bookkeeping tallied to the last crown and proved that the charges against him were groundless. But most of all he was lucky that he was arrested and interrogated shortly after the communist takeover when prosecutors and police inspectors were still those of the old Czechoslovak Republic and its laws were still valid. If he were arrested a year later when the police and judiciary apparatus had been purged, laws changed and class justice established, he would surely have been condemned.

But we did not get back our delivery truck, money

or bankbooks because Father's business was nationalized and all property and capital confiscated by the State. By some miracle, we did not lose our house.

Father was forty-eight when his life's work collapsed under him. He took it as a man. He did not grumble or wail over his misfortune. Without hesitation he accepted a manual laborer's job at the Forest Administration, and a month after his release he was already felling trees.

On the eve of my departure to Prague I finally revealed to my parents what had happened to me and what my options were.

"I can be a miner, because that's what they told me to do, and I am sure they will not let me work elsewhere. Or flee the country, so long as it is still possible. Or bury myself in the Institute of Modern Languages and study French and Russian along with English for at least two years."

"Go to that school," advised Mother. "Knowledge of languages will help you in life."

"But it would cost a lot," I said, "at least a thousand crowns a month for tuition, and another thousand for board and lodging."

There was silence in the kitchen for a while. It was interrupted only by the loud ticking of the old alarm clock standing on the cupboard.

"We'll scrape it together," Mother said. "I'll go out and get a paying job, no matter where or what, in agriculture or in forestry. We'll get the money somehow. Right?" She turned towards Father.

He nodded in his habitual way.

"We shall survive," he said. "This fucking regime is all bullshit and thievery, and it will tumble down some day like a rotten shithouse."

These were the only foul words I have ever heard

from him. But he had to wait forty years before his prediction was fulfilled. Mother, who hated the communist regime even more than he, passed away two months before its downfall.

II. HOW I BECAME A GIANT INSECT

"Honziku," called somebody behind me. Turning round, I saw in the feeble light of a street lamp a girlish figure muffled in a beige overcoat. It was half past ten at night and Wenceslas Square in Prague was almost empty. I hesitated a moment, not being sure that I had heard right and that the call was addressed to me. I could not see the girl's face clearly, as she wore a scarf that partly covered her face and cheeks.

"Honziku," repeated the girl. Her voice seemed to float to me from far, far away on a rushing tide of time, unbelievable, unreal. It could not be possible!

I took two steps toward the girl, who pulled the scarf down with a light movement of her hand. Now I saw her face framed by brown, curling hair falling to her shoulder.

"Hanicka," I sighed, utterly amazed. I held back my questions, because I did not want to debase this miraculous encounter by some banality. Instead, I came close to her, took her in my arms and kissed her gently.

"Hanicka Solcova," I said as tenderly as I possibly could.

"When I went by you, I was not sure, but then in a flash I realized it was you."

Her teeth glistened in the dark like small pearls. Way back, I used to tease her that she must have forty-eight of them in her mouth. A hurricane of memories took hold of me. I tried to orientate myself in them and to find a hold. When did we see each other the last time? Yes, in May 1944…and now it was the end of September 1949.

Hanicka, too, must have counted the time that had passed by since she asked:

"How many years went by since we were together

72

the last time?"

"Four years and four months, "I said, "almost exactly."

I drew her to me and kissed her tenderly and shyly as I did under the lime trees at Kremze, those trees that were in full blossom, whose sweet smell filled the air with an intoxicating aroma I have not tasted again since.

We were standing there motionless in each other arms. Then Hanicka pulled her head back.

"Do you have time?" she asked.

"You mean now?"

"Do you have to hurry home?"

"No, I have no reason to hurry…"

"Will you accompany me? It is not far away, I live in Rimska Street, a few hundred meters from the Museum."

When I nodded, we linked our arms and set out towards the statue of St Wenceslas. There we turned right, following a path in the small park that adjoined the Museum.

"Where were you wandering tonight?" asked Hanicka as we walked in the park.

"I did not wander…I was in the cinema Blanik to see the picture *The Postman Always Rings Twice*. And you?"

"I was on my way home from the Rokoko Theater. I am in a play by Goldoni, *The Servant of Two Masters*." Then she added hurriedly, as if she wanted to change the subject, that she had seen *The Postman* at the Barrandov Film Studios. "They project foreign films there, particularly American ones, before they go into distribution," she explained. "I have a special pass. You could go with me, if you want. The showing is on every second Friday of the month at four o'clock in the afternoon. I do hope to see you, I don't want to lose you again, now after I have found you," she said in a tone which surprised me by its unusual urgency that I grasped only too late. To cover it up she laughed hilariously.

"You have not changed a bit, you still don't know to count."

"How come?"

"You count fast but wrong. It's five years since we were together the last time at Kremze."

I secretly used my fingers recounting the years.

"You are right, it's already five years…Me and numbers, we're sworn enemies."

"That's why you very wisely wanted to be an actor," she smiled. "I often thought of you when reading theater reviews in the newspapers, hoping that one day I come across your name. Tell me, do you study, or do you have a job?"

"Take a deep breath…I am an English editor in the Czechoslovak News Agency. But I have been there only a couple of weeks."

"Editor? You write for newspapers?"

"Well, not exactly…I write short texts in English to go with photo reports and captions under pictures. They are mimeographed and sent out to foreign illustrated magazines. I have no idea which ones they are, or where. I have had no time to find out. Today, for example, I wrote about a country mailman who delivers letters, telegrams and parcels on foot or riding a bicycle in some godforsaken part of Southern Bohemia."

"Where did you learn English?"

"Partly from American soldiers who liberated Kremze. I took English at the lyceum and then I studied it for two years here in Prague."

"So, you gave up theater?"

"It's a long story, Hanicka."

"Never mind, I want to hear it, you must tell me

everything when we come to my place."

Her studio was located in Rimska Street on the first floor of an old tenement house. Hanicka opened the door and switched on the light. We entered a narrow corridor that led into a large living room that was at least three times the size of my den in Nusle (almost on the outskirts of Prague) that I inherited from Zdenek Simecek. When his great love, Lida, had departed to America without saying goodbye, he left the university, took a job in a small town and settled down there. Pepik Bukovsky, too, chose exile. Milan served in a forced labor army battalion. The Communist putsch in February 1948 disrupted the plans and dreams of everybody in our bunch at Kremze. I did not try to contact my buddies who stayed in the country because I had no desire to explain what I was doing and why. But to Hanicka I would tell all. For to whom else could I confess if not my first love?

When Hanicka took off her overcoat, I saw a buxom young lady, who reminded me, somewhat remotely, of the frail, slim little girl of my memories. Her face was roundish, and her smile resplendent. There were remnants of theater make-up under her eyes, those eyes that resembled to two oval emeralds.

"Make yourself at home," she said kicking off her shoes one after the other into the corridor. Instantly, she seemed to be a couple of inches shorter. She shook her curly brown hair.

"My god, what a day!" she said. "I have nothing to drink, but I can make you coffee or tea."

"Coffee."

"Milk, sugar?"

"No, thanks, just coffee."

When Hanicka disappeared into the kitchenette, separated from the living room by a curtain, I started to look around. There was a double bed alongside one wall, a square coffee table with two armchairs in the middle of the room, and a couch in the corner. The floor was covered by an imitation Persian carpet. But my attention was attracted to two framed theater posters on the front wall. I knew both of them well from Kremze during the war. They appeared regularly every May on the local tobacconist's in the village square and at the entrance to Stanko's pub. One featured a scene from a popular music show *On the Green Meadow*, the other a scene from *A Midsummer Night's Dream*. They both carried a block-lettered announcement: SOLC THEATER COMPANY PRESENTS. Underneath was white space for information about the night's performance, time and ticket prices. This information was handwritten on a rectangle of paper and pasted into the white space as necessary. Sometimes it was Hanicka who did it with my help.

Hanicka brought my coffee, and tea for herself.

"Don't stand there like that, why don't you sit down," she pointed to the couch. "Give me a minute, I have to change."

When I sat down I found myself facing a low cupboard under a large three-piece window. On a plaid cloth on the cupboard stood a small empty vase, and next to it lay, upside down, a photograph in a silver frame. I picked it up and turned it over. I saw an amateur snapshot of a young and very attractive man who resembled the then popular heartthrob actor Raul Schranil. The photo showed this good looker posing in a sports car with his right hand on the wheel and a cigar in his left hand, with the air of a philanderer. I immediately found him repulsive. I decided that under no circumstances would I try to find out who he was, and should Hanicka volunteer even a passing mention of him, I would pretend an utter lack of interest. At this very moment she emerged out of the bathroom wearing a light blue dressing gown made of Chinese silk.

"Take off your jacket, your necktie, too, and make yourself comfortable," she commanded.

Then she sat down next to me and raised a teacup as if in a toast.

"To our reunion," she said. "Champagne would be more appropriate, but I have not a drop of any alcohol. I never drink. My father was a binge drinker and that gave me a disgust of alcohol for life."

"But he was an actor of genius," I said. "I can still see him in the role of a vagabond feigning steps on the stage and singing 'a white road in front of me, the sun shining down on me, and I am free as a bird...' He knew how to act, sing, dance. He was an accomplished performer."

"But to live with him was hell."

"And what about your mother? It now occurs to me that you have never told me anything about her."

"Mom left us when I was eight. It doesn't pain me any more." Hanicka took my hand and pressed it gently. "Let's talk about you for a change. You wanted to be an actor. And you would be a good one...So what happened? Why didn't you follow your dream?

I heard reproach in her words. It made me to try to vindicate myself.

"That would require a long monolog," I warned her.

"I promise to be an attentive listener. I want to know everything in full."

"Well, OK...You may be surprised but I succeeded in graduating from the lyceum, or rather I squeezed through somehow. Then after summer vacations..."

I stopped, wondering where to begin. How Father brought me in his delivery car to Prague where Uncle Sklar had found me lodgings in the flat owned by a merry, enterprising widow…how I packed up and left the following day…No details, I decided, just the bare essentials.

"I came to Prague to enroll in the Arts Academy that had just opened and where I wanted to study stage management. There were two of us who applied: me, and a certain Mr Palous. Naturally, it made no sense to open a section for two students. We were told to come back next year. So what now? The first idea I had was to find your group, or any other road company that would engage me as an actor. However, I was somehow loath to leave Prague, so signed myself up for the Law Faculty of Charles University. At the same time I attended English courses at the Institute of Modern Languages. I thought it would be helpful to know English in case I went to Hollywood someday…I had a lot of pipedreams at the time…Then there was the putsch last February. We students assembled at Charles Square and from there we marched to Prague Castle to demand that President Benes not yield to Communist demands and pressure. The so-called People's Militia units were waiting for us on the steps leading to the Castle. They attacked us and beat us with truncheons. As the stairs are very narrow a crush and panic ensued. A girl next to me fell. I helped her to her feet and we ran together down to the Charles Bridge. Her name was Volfova. Her father was a Czech diplomat in Washington before the war, so she spoke English perfectly. As we remained friends, I had English conversation lessons with her for nothing."

Meanwhile Hanicka was trying to find the most comfortable position and she finally ended up with her head in my lap and with her legs hanging over the armrest of the couch.

"After the communist takeover, political purges took place at the university. Every student had to fill a questionnaire full of catch questions. One was: 'What is your attitude towards violence?' The right answer was that violence committed in the interest of the working class is just. But I purposefully wrote that I condemn violence as such, no matter by whom and for whatever reason. I was fully aware that I was signing myself into a sentence. I would have been expelled anyway, because of my bourgeois origin, since my father was a wholesale dealer. The chairman of the inquisition committee read aloud what I had written and said: 'There is nothing to discuss, the case is clear.' My whole future was decided within minutes: there would be none for me. The expulsion ended all my hopes of enrolling in the Arts Academy since it fell under the administration of the university."

"So you gave up," said Hanicka.

"No. Definitely not right away. First, I tried to find your theatrical company. I wanted to be an actor, damn the Academy. But I learned that road companies were disbanded. Is it true?"

"Yes. For my Pop it was a fatal blow. He began to drink daily and heavily."

"An artist like he must have found another engagement easily…"

"He was not looking for it in the beginning because he was so desperate…Finally, after a several months of bingeing, he was hired as a comedian at the theater in Pilsen."

"My father ended up even worse. They confiscated all his money, quite a lot, his car, and he was imprisoned for a while, having been charged with fiscal fraud. The accusation was hollow, groundless, so he was released. Now he works as a lumberjack."

"And you…what happened to you?"

"I was looking around for gigs in small theaters in Prague. The director of the Alhambra cabaret, Mr

Snizek, took pity on me and hired me as his sidekick. I copied dialog on the typewriter and fetched beer most of the time. Then I got a break. I was to bring on stage a cup of coffee on a tray and say 'Your coffee, sir.' But before the first night show Mr Snizek disappeared. We learned confidentially that he was in Paris. To leave the country seemed to be the best solution. I discussed it with Dana, in whom I had full confidence. Her father had been dismissed from the Ministry of Foreign Affairs and his future was as bleak as mine. Then sometime in early December last year Dana told me that her father was organizing a joint escape with several of his friends and she invited me to join them. Our meeting place was in a hotel at Cheb, a small town right on the border. There were nine of us: the Wolf family, an elderly couple, three young ministerial officials and me. The plan was to cross the frontier in two groups: the Wolfs and the couple would go first during the night from Tuesday to Wednesday, and the rest of us the following night. But on Wednesday afternoon a man appeared in the hotel room where we were waiting and hurriedly told us that the first group had been spotted by a border patrol, there was an exchange of fire between the soldiers and the guide, who was wounded. The man added that we should leave the hotel forthwith, one after the other, and take different trains or buses from Cheb."

"When did all this happen?"

"Last Christmas. We thought that during the holidays crossing would be easier because the border would be less guarded. However, it was snowing on Tuesday and the patrol might have seen fresh footprints. That's a guess. We never learned what really happened."

"Do you still want to run away?"

"Not much...the frontier is almost hermetically

closed. A friend of mine, Gusta Kriz, was caught by border guards and sentenced to ten years of hard labor in uranium mines in Jachymov. I really would hate to end up there."

Meanwhile, Hanicka had changed her position again. Her head rested on my shoulder, her left hand held gently my right hand, and her feet rested on the coffee table. Her legs were well formed, without hairs. She must have shaved them. Her gown slid down and revealed two alabaster thighs.

"At the end of May I was to take a state exam in English which would have entitled me to teach in secondary schools. Oh, I did not want to be an English teacher, but one never knows, a certificate of competence might be useful one day. There was a hitch, however: I had to sit for the exam at the Charles University from which I had been expelled. They threw me out of the Law Faculty but not from the Philological Faculty, where I was inscribed as a candidate, but that did not make much difference. There certainly was a blacklist of expelled students against which all applicants were vetted in order to prevent undesirable elements slipping back into the university. Desperation breeds crazy ideas: mine was that I should change my name. I decided that I would apply not as Vitek, but as Vítek, changing an i for a í, to mislead the university ferrets. To disguise the scent even further I also changed my place of birth from Chlum to Kremze, as well as my date of birth from 17 March to 4 July. Now, comrades, try to find me in your black list. If they tried, they failed. I passed the state exam with flying colors.

"With my certificate in hand I went to see the Director of Basic English, a private school in Spalena Street. I knew that summer courses would begin there shortly, so I gave it try. The Director and owner of the school, Mr Vicha, hired me on the spot, all the more readily since I accepted his offer of a meager 600 crowns a month in salary, and did not bargain about it. I taught just two days. When I arrived on the third day the students were unusually quiet. In the last row I saw two strange gentlemen. They were plain-clothes policemen. They took all of us to the infamous police station at Bartolomejska Street for interrogation. We were kept waiting…Are you sleeping?"

"When I fall asleep I will tell you," smiled Hanicka. "Go on, I am all ears."

"During the long wait my shirt became covered with sweat. I feared that police would search my studio and find the book *I Chose Freedom* by Victor Kravchenko. I got it more than a year and half before from an American diplomat I met by chance on a tram. After that we saw each other a couple of times to chat about films, theater shows and, above all, about politics. The last time I saw him was shortly after the failed students' demonstration…Kravchenko was a Russian diplomat, who in 1944 sought asylum in the USA. In his book he described forced collectivization and famine in the Ukraine. In my holy innocence I started to translate it into Czech! Should they discover the manuscript, I would not need to worry about board and lodging for many years. Luckily, the police only took down our names and addresses, and told us that the school was closed because the owner had no legal authorization since all private schools had been outlawed. Then we were released.

"I began to look around for another job. But there was a catch. Everywhere, before they even asked my name, they wanted to see a testimonial of my political reliability. What I needed was to camouflage my bourgeois origin…"

"Meaning that you are not a son of a merchant?"

"Right. Searching for the way to do it I recalled that

Mr Benes, a tinsmith by profession but an amateur actor in his heart and soul, with whom I had played in a number of performances, was also Chairman of the Communist Party at Kremze. 'You must make me a proletarian, fully devoted to the people's democratic regime,' I told him. Benes fidgeted and equivocated. He said he was no longer Chairman but a simple committee member, and was afraid that there was too much risk involved. I succeeded in talking him into a vague promise that he would think it over. It is to his honor that in the end he brought me a clean sheet of paper with the rubberstamp of the local Communist Party. 'Write it yourself if you dare,' he said, 'but as for me, I have not seen you since the end of the war...'

"There were two institutions that in my opinion could use a man with perfect English and German and partial knowledge of French and Russian: Prague radio and the Czechoslovak News Agency. Radio Prague offered me a job as translator and two thousand crowns per month. The Agency offered five hundred crowns more and the title of Editor. I started there two months ago. Tomorrow, I am going to make my first reportage trip, to write a story about how sugar-beet turns into white gold."

"If I understood you correctly you live under a false name, "observed Hanicka.

"Not false, just slightly changed."

"And with a fake background."

"They made me an outlaw. I am just defending myself."

"Don't you feel strange?"

"Why? I take it as a role. Every morning when I wake up I tell myself: "Honza, get on the stage, the show begins'...On reflection, maybe you are right...I sometimes feel strange, like Gregor in Kafka's story *Metamorphosis*. Have you read it?"

"No, I don't read Kafka, I don't like him, he is too morbid for my taste."

"Gregor wakes up one morning feeling that something strange has happened to him, and then he finds out that he is changing into a giant insect. People, including his family, loathe and despise him. His tragedy and suffering lies in the fact that in his inner self he remains a human being…I will bring you the book, you must read it."

"You surprise me, Honziku. I remember you as a romantic, a dreamer. And now I see in you a…," she hesitated, "a down-to-earth realist."

"And what's wrong with that?"

"Nothing. I am just surprised by you."

"If you want to know, I am still a dreamer," I defended myself. "But I dream about different things…"

"Like what?"

"Well…like…that one day we shall live in a better society, more transparent and just…But to live to see it we must survive the regime that we have now. My father says that it is criminal and that it will collapse soon. However, I think it is more complicated, and that he is wrong. We shall have to live under this regime for some time…maybe quite a lot of long years. The thing is not to get steamrollered by this regime, to wait out this lousy era and preserve yourself for the better time to come. I don't want to become a martyr, our family has suffered enough. And maybe I have an excessive self-preservation instinct…My favorite writer, Hasek, in his book *Good Soldier Svejk* created a philosophy for our time: how a vulnerable, powerless individual can outlive a senseless and dangerous society, keep his mind sound and still stand up straight. Svejk knows that he must look after himself with the only tools he has at his disposal: cunning, mimicry and wit. I don't want to become a hero either. And if I cannot survive otherwise in these times of darkness and gloom, I will be Svejk."

"Do you believe you can do it?"

"I don't know. But I have no better idea as yet."

"And what if they find out?"

"Find out what?"

"That you are not the man you pretend to be."

"That I am a class enemy who tries to dupe the Party and the regime? That would require some effort from the bureaucrats; they would have to send somebody to Kremze to verify my background. It cannot be ruled out. But what could happen to me then? They would sack me, and, at worst, send me to dig uranium ore."

We were silent for a while. My arm embraced her shoulder. Her hand caressed my palm.

"Hanicka, my sunshine," I said as in those days of our puppy love, gently and tenderly, "I am a reprehensible egoist, I babble about myself too much. But tell me how are you and what do you do?"

"Some other time…"

"Tell me at least which role you perform in the Rokoko Theater?"

"Perform? I am a mere stand-in. You know, I did not inherit much from my father. I shall never be a great actress."

"How can you say such a thing, I don't believe it."

"I am sure. I would gladly do something different if I could. I am completely burned out inside. Let's leave it for another day. Do you believe in destiny?"

"No."

"I do. Therefore I think that our encounter was not an accident, but destiny. We were destined to get together again. I am terribly happy that I met you."

"Hanicka, my sunshine, I have never felt more over the moon than when I held you in my arms again."

I looked at my watch. It was half past three in the morning. I rose slowly from the couch.

"I shall have to go," I said.

"Where and why? There are no trams anyway at this hour."

Hanicka also rose. We were standing close together looking into each other's eyes.

"Honziku, we are in debt to each other. I owe you and you owe me."

She hugged and kissed me, long and hungrily, almost desperately.

"Do you have somebody?" she whispered.

I understood what she wanted to hear.

"No, there is nobody in my life," I lied, denying Blanka as shabbily as Peter denied Christ.

We embraced and kissed passionately. Hanicka unbuttoned my shirt and pulled it down. Her breasts slid out of the gown and touched my chest. My whole being was shaking with burning, lustful pain. I knew I would not leave.

"Stay with me," I heard her voice, wooing and pleading, coming to me from far away as an echo. "Don't leave, please, stay with here and help me through the night."

It was a night full of tenderness and dizziness. Hanicka was more experienced than I, so I let her to guide me on the mystic pathways of caresses to the pinnacle of consummation and ultimate bliss. This was the mother of all lovemaking of my youth.

Before dawn I fell into a brief, semiconscious sleep. When I woke, I saw in the shaded light of a bedside lamp that Hanicka was smiling at me, her face radiating love and devotion.

"You were snoring, Honziku."

"I must have slept on my back…Sorry."

"Think nothing of it. At least I knew I was not alone."

There was an undertone of suffering and sadness in her voice, but I did not take proper note of it, because I was preoccupied with immediate anxieties about getting quickly to my den in Nusle, changing clothes and preparing for the reportage trip. Instead of asking why she was sad and melancholic, I jumped out of the bed as if I was in the army.

"Hanicka, my sunshine, I must run!"

She did not try to hold me back. I gathered up my trousers, socks, shirt and shoes thrown in disarray on the floor and quickly dressed. I needed to don a clean shirt at home, put a notepad and pen in my briefcase, and be at nine o'clock in front of the Czechoslovak News Agency. I must not keep the cameraman and the driver waiting. I went to the bathroom, splashed cold water on my face and combed my hair. Hanicka also got up. She wore her Chinese nightgown.

"I'll make you a coffee."

"Thanks, but some other time, now I really must hurry up."

For a while, we were standing in the little corridor, embracing and kissing.

"Come tonight, Honziku. I'll be waiting for you."

"I don't know when I'll be back, maybe late at night."

"It does not matter. Come anyway, I'll be up waiting."

"If I do not make it, I'll come to the theater tomorrow."

"No, not the theater, come here, please."

This time I had an impression that the undertone in her voice was one of beseeching urgency and suppressed anguish. But I was too preoccupied with myself to take time to think about her, let alone to try to understand her feelings. She was standing in the door when I left, looking vulnerable and lonely.

I did not go to see her that evening, nor for the three following days. I needed time for reflection. Blanka or Hanicka? The risk that I should bitterly deplore my decision was about the same as the hope that I should be happy because of it. Blanka was a proven haven. We had gone together for almost three years and had got used to each other. She left Krumlov to join me in Prague where she found a good job at the Koospol export company. She had a sub-let and wanted me to move in with her once we got married, a desire she urged me to agree to. Hanicka was an unknown equation. But she was my first love. I felt an undying feeling for her that flickered forever under the ashes of time. After the night we had spent together, it flared up again at full blast. Blanka was a year older than I, she had an elegant presence, a wide Slavic face, and wore spectacles behind which there was a pair of the most captivating eyes I ever saw. Hanicka was a year younger, and whenever I thought of her, an American saying sprang to my mind: 'She is a looker.' Of course, it occurred to me that I could maintain my love affair with both of them. An affair, yes. However, I was unable to be in love with both of them at the same time because, as Bing Crosby crooned, 'I am a one girl guy.' I was telling myself: Don't be hasty, give it time, to hell with reason, follow your heart, one morning you will wake up and you will know for sure what you want, you will be utterly convinced that one of them, and she alone, is the right and only lifelong love for you.

That Friday in early autumn was an exemplary Indian summer's day. The sun dried up the puddles from yesterday's drizzle and its rays lightened the remnants of overripe tree leaves with dazzling colors of deep yellow and crimson red. It was unseasonably hot. Girls unbuttoned their overcoats like roses opening on bright mornings and all of them seemed to me more graceful and charming than ever. They smiled at me passing by. I grinned at the whole world and the whole world grinned at me. It was a day made for love, and on its wings I flew through the park at the Museum towards Rimska Street, where Hanicka lived. I should be bringing her a bunch of flowers for the occasion, but when I pictured myself running along the street with a bouquet in my hand I immediately rejected the idea. I will just embrace her and whisper the three little words, of which I was fully and totally certain.

I took the stairs to the first floor three at a time. I pressed the doorbell shortly and twice. Maybe Hanicka is still asleep, so once I tell her the three little words I'll apologize for waking her up and invite her to lunch. I waited a while. Nothing. Silence. I rang again and longer. Then I knocked at the door. Nothing. Silence. Joyful expectation turned to sheer desperation. I rang and knocked several times. Where can she be? Shopping? After some twenty minutes I left, crestfallen and frustrated.

The head office of the Czechoslovak News Agency was in Opletalova Street, not far from Hanicka's home. I ran this short distance twice that afternoon, but in vain. Maybe she went to an early lunch before a rehearsal at the theater. This seemed to me as the most probable explanation. I decided that I would go to see her at the Rokoko Theater. She did not wish me to go there but I had a valid and pressing reason: I must tell her the three words today. Any postponement was out of the question.

Between two trips to Rimska Street, my boss, Frank Lion, chief of the Foreign Photo Service Section, called me into his office. He was suntanned all the year round, wore sunglasses at all times, and when he smiled he showed protruding upper teeth that used to be white.

"I like your head 'Sugar-Beet Blues,'" he said. "However, as regards your maiden effort I had to cut it and jazz it up a little. When my secretary types it over, look at the changes I made, and should you have a problem I'll be delighted to enlighten you."

I was about to leave when he stopped me

"I have another matter to discuss with you," he said searching for something in a heap of papers on his desk. "That you mangle rhymes during office hours is bad enough but what's worse is that their content and intent is objectionable, if not outright treasonous, according to your colleague Goldschmied who showed me your doggerel. If I were of the same opinion, I would have to fire you on the spot. However, I think that they simply display your political immaturity that, at your age, is comprehensible. So I'll let you go but heed my advice: keep your masterpieces locked away at home, and not in a drawer in the office. And this," he threw two sheets to me, "burn it right away."

I made two resolutions. One, from now on I would respect Frank Lion not only as a professional but also appreciate him as a human being. Two, I would put off a shootout with comrade Goldschmied. For now I had to focus on a matter of vital importance for me.

I stayed at my desk pretending to be busy until six o'clock. Then I walked leisurely down the Wenceslas Square towards Rokoko. I had plenty of time. The evening performance did not start until seven. I arrived in the theater with twenty minutes to spare. I approached a female usher, showed her my press card and told her I want to interview Ms Solcova. The seasoned Cerberus was not impressed. She looked at the program and said that there was no such name in the cast. I insisted that she must be mistaken and demanded access to the dressing room. We argued and raised our voices, attracting the attention of a dresser who wanted to know what our problem was.

"Miss Solcova is an extra," the dresser told me, "but she has not shown up for two days in a row. Since no one noticed, she was not replaced."

I returned again to Rimska Street and rang the bell again and again without answer. Then I ran back to the theater, and bought a ticket for a gallery seat to kill time. I remained seated during the intermission puzzling my head for an explanation of what might have happened. At the same time I mulled over and over her hidden reproach that I was a dreamer turned realist. A down-to-earth realist, she said. Why down-to-earth? Maybe she did not want to hurt my feelings by calling me a shameless or obscene realist...Nonetheless, she hit me where it hurt. I remembered protesting that I had not changed so much: I still had a dream...a dream of something different...a dream of a better and humane society. I was just shooting off my mouth when I said it. Now, however, when I thought it through, it dawned upon me that I had expressed a dormant idea that had always been close to my heart. Therefore, nothing would ever stifle it. It would haunt my days and prevent me sleeping at night. It would become the guiding star of my whole life. Life must have a purpose! At the same time I realized that Svejk's philosophy would, therefore, not be enough. I should have to actively pursue this ideal and stay committed forever. One day, at an opportune moment, I would discuss all this with Hanicka. But first of all I must tell her those three little words..

Around midnight I returned to the house. It was not locked and I slipped inside. The stairs were poorly lit, the corridor was dark, but by now I could find my way

91

to her studio with my eyes closed. In the quiet of the night I heard the ringing of the doorbell inside the studio. The response was the same deadly silence.

Back home, I lay in my bed with my eyes wide open. In my mind I saw the man in the photograph on Hanicka's cupboard. He radiated arrogant self-confidence. I was jealous of him, and I hated that. So I tried to think of something enjoyable, evoking the moment I met Hanicka for the first time at Kremze. She was twelve. I was a year older. I recalled how I would look out for her at the village square until I finally caught up with her when she was returning home from shopping. "How about telling me your name? Or are you deaf?" she asked while I was facing her, speechless. When I managed to utter my name she said: "I shall call you Honziku." We saw each other every day during that memorable month of May in 1941, as well as every May over the following three years. I recalled the last of our sacred months together, and our first timid kiss under a lime tree in full blossom…At long last I fell asleep.

On Saturday at eleven o'clock I stood again at her door. I rang, I knocked, rang, knocked. I did not know what else I could do, so I lingered, confused and lost.

The door opposite opened and out came a woman with a shopping bag. She glanced at me and asked:

"Are you looking for somebody?"

"Yes, Miss Solcova. She does not answer. I guess she is not at home."

The woman looked at me for a long while with undisguised compassion. Then she said:

"Miss Solcova has committed suicide."

There was a mute, unspeakable question in my wild-open eyes but the woman guessed it.

"Gas," she said.

I staggered. I leaned against the wall so as not to collapse. I realized that Hanicka's embraces and kisses were calls for help but I, an idiot, did not perceive them because I was such a bloody egocentric dimwit.

"When…did it…happen?"

"They took her body away the day before yesterday."

Why did not I come after the reportage trip? She wanted me to come, she needed me, she relied on me I might have been her only hope, a new chance, and I failed miserably. Oh, Jesus Christ, how can I go on living with such a burden of unpardonable guilt on my conscience? It will haunt me until my dying day!

"You are pale as ashes. I bring you a glass of water."

"No, thank you…that…it will pass."

I shall never know what pain and suffering drove Hanicka to her death. She will never hear my three little words "I love you."

When somebody dear to you passes away this is what you regret most: words unspoken and deeds undone, because there is no second chance.

In hindsight I came to realize that our first and last night of love was Hanicka's goodbye present.

III. INFILTRATING THE PARTY

The transformation of a human being into cannon fodder begins when you sit on a chair and an army barber, just for fun, runs a dry shaver from the front of your head to your neck and from the left ear to the right ear, making a white cross on your head. He admires his creation for a while before finishing. Then he offers you a mirror to take a look. Your first reaction is horror mixed with shame and humiliation. But seeing all the other guys' naked skulls you can't help getting a kick out of it.

Every morning at six o'clock we would run out of the barrack gate of the 35th Regiment in Plzen. Our boots were hobnailed and we trampled the street cobblestones like a herd of wild mustangs. Shirtless and hairless we must have been a sight worth watching. All the girls from an apprentices' boarding house across the street would get up before their wake-up call so as not to miss the spectacle. In return every night they would perform a striptease for us, taking their bras off and parading behind windows with no curtains. It was an amateurish show but exciting enough to fill our nights with longing and lust.

Father had a regular footlocker made for me that looked like a wooden baby coffin with a rounded lid and a metal handle on the top. Inside there was a removable shelf for toilet articles. Provocatively, I put in two books: Stalin's *Problems of Leninism* in English and *Good Soldier Svejk* in Czech. At the first inspection our political officer ordered me to get rid of Svejk, the personification of an antimilitarist who through feigned idiocy and incompetence repeatedly manages to frustrate military authority and its stupidity. I hid the book under the mattress. Every night after taps I read this bible of rank and file soldiers under the blanket with the help of a torch. Without it army baboonery would have driven me crazy.

The Commander-In-Chief of the Army was General Alexej Cepicka, whose qualification for this post was that he had married the daughter of the then President, Gottwald. Cepicka had a brilliant idea. He issued a special order instituting an obligatory siesta after lunch. We had to undress, put on a checkered sleeping gown and lie in bed for an hour. He marked me for life: no matter where I am, an after-lunch siesta is for me sacrosanct and inviolable.

Following six weeks of Prussian-style military drill designed to break your will and make you obey blindly any stupid order, I was assigned to undergo special training for non-commissioned officers at Stribro. There was one pub and one cinema showing old films on weekends only. Two thirds of the inhabitants were soldiers who on Saturday night took over the town en masse. It meant a free for all and survival of the fittest. Only some three dozen of the strongest men with sharp elbows and iron fists got into the pub, where they stood on each other's feet. Nonetheless, all of us wanted a weekend furlough because it gave you a feeling of being free and having the possibility of leaving the barracks if you liked. In the end most of us stayed behind the garrison's walls and drank light beer bought at the Army shop, pepping it up with Alpa, a massage lotion for enfeebled muscles that contained a slight dose of industrial spirit.

Something must happen, I thought. I was not born to ruin my body on the parade ground, to shoot a gun and kowtow to higher ranks. And something did happen. Second Lieutenant Kriegl and I founded an artistic ensemble called STRIBRO 50. The number fifty stood for the year 1950. Kriegl was an excellent guitar player; I still can picture him playing and singing American hits such as *Summertime* or *My Blue Heaven*. He found six other musicians to form a band. I did not play any instrument, nor did I know how to sing, but I could recite and act. I became Master of Ceremonies, introducing the band and amusing the spectators with jokes. Soon we started to export our cultural program to nearby villages that did not even have a cinema and where we were welcomed with open arms. I also took care of the box office, which consisted of two soup plates on a small table at the entrance. When the upper plate was filled with money I swept the bills and coins onto the plate underneath. The incoming spectators thought we had gathered nothing, which made them feel ashamed of their village and led them to reach deeper in their pockets. We split our pickings equally.

In the spring of 1951 our NCO school began intensive preparation for the traditional marching parade on 9th May in Prague to mark V-Day. One can hardly imagine a stupider clownery than a parade march where you have to kick your foot up as high as the bottom of the soldier in front of you, hold a gun close to your chest and turn your head right to the tribune as a salute to Party bosses all at the same time. You have to do this hour after hour, day after day, for three long months.

The army daily *Obrana Lidu* launched a competition for the best reader contribution about the preparation for the parade. When we were traveling by train to Prague from Stribro, my buddies mostly slept, or for part of the time played cards. Out of sheer boredom I pulled out some letter paper and began to describe our state of mind during the training and on the train. I wrote about my closest friends, their life and army regulations. I rhapsodized about our enthusiasm for the parade and about our resolution to be the best unit on the parade ground. I put the couple of scribbled pages into an envelope and posted it when we arrived to Prague.

Copies of *Obrana Lidu* were distributed to the army for free. Three days or so after I had sent in my contribution, I opened the paper to see my production in black in white under the headline 'On the way,' signed Private First Class Jan Vítek (I already had one pip). The text was printed in italic. My pals rolled over in laughter when they read my narration because it was a cocktail of fact and fiction. The very same day a ginger-haired First Lieutenant came to our billet and wanted to speak with me. He introduced himself as Alois Mestek, editor of *Obrana Lidu*. He told me that my piece was the best contribution the paper had received so far and gave me a book as a present. When he learned that I had worked in the Czechoslovak news agency he nodded his head approvingly and said that he had sensed the hand of a professional in the style. I was quite amused, since I had worked in the agency only few months and wrote in English. Mestek pressed me to become a regular contributor to *Obrana Lidu*. He tempted me with promises of perks such as a week of training for embedded correspondents in Prague. That clinched it. I promised to write as regularly as inspiration struck me, and we shook hands on it.

In our ensemble, we needed to enrich and diversify our repertoire. To fill this gap I wrote a theatrical play set in our unit. I made the main characters antagonistic. Josef was an exemplary soldier and a member of the Communist Youth Association who took his military service seriously and was always among the first to volunteer for difficult duties. Honza was his very opposite, a typical free rider simulating zeal and effort while taking it easy. He made fun of Josef, stultifying him on every occasion. After basic training, the unit is sent to guard the frontier, hence the title of the piece, *On The Border*. In carrying out their duty the two antagonists clash a number of times. In the final scene Honza tries to desert and flee the country. Josef stops him at the point of a gun. Honza derisively calls him a coward and dares him to pull the trigger. He turns his back on Josef, puts up his hands and says: "Don't let me go too far, you could miss me." He crosses the border. It is an early, foggy morning. There is a resounding shot and the curtain falls.

When I conceived the play I thought about people who fled the country as well as about the unlucky ones who did not succeed and were caught or killed. What had happened in Cheb was still haunting me, and I could not put it behind me. Writing the play was a way of exorcising painful memories and getting them out of my system. I was skating on thin ice because I developed it on two levels. At the level of subtext it could easily be understood as a parody of military stupidity and political brainwashing. But we took care to stage and interpret it at the simplistic obvious level, which is why it went off without a problem.

Kriegl portrayed Josef and I, of course, had the role of Honza. We rehearsed the play at a military summer training camp in the deserted border region, whose original dwellers had been expelled to Germany after the war. The rehearsals gave us a credible and welcome pretext to skip political lectures and other clowneries that poisoned our life. Following the premiere at the camp we toured backwoods villages near our camp to bring a bit of culture to their inhabitants on weekends. Kriegl shot me dead at least a dozen times. The last time it was in a real dump of a place where we performed on an improvised open-air stage. There was a beautiful pony-tailed girl sitting in the first row. Kriegl spotted her, too, but I beat him to approaching her. She invited me to her place for coffee, which, for some reason, we took a long time to drink. Meanwhile, Kriegl gave an order for everyone to leave the dump, which was some twenty kilometers away from our camp, quite a distance to walk as I found out. When I arrived at the entrance gate in the early morning the guards, alerted by Kriegl, told me I was under arrest for having been away without authorization. This meant a couple of days in the jug. However, as there was no prison at the camp the judgment was postponed until our return to the garrison.

Shortly after this incident, a black sleek Tatraplan, an official car for the top brass, stopped in front of the Commander's tent. We passed it as we were marching into camp from a shooting exercise. No sooner had I dropped my gun and gear than a duty officer appeared and ordered me to pack up all my belongings and put the gear and gun back on. Flabbergasted, I did as I was told. Then he escorted me to the Tatraplan.

"There he is," he said to the driver, a sergeant, as if handing over a package.

"Put your stuff on the back seat and get in," the sergeant told me.

"Where are we going?"

"Division HQ."

"Why?"

"I don't know and I don't care. My order is to transport you to the HQ. Period."

The Division Headquarters in Plzen was some one hundred and twenty kilometers from our summer camp, or about two hours' drive. But each minute of those two hours was among the longest in my life. It's just a bad dream, I told myself. They cannot drag me before a military court because of a short unauthorized absence from camp. It is just a minor offence that normally is handled by the commanding officer. So why, my god, am I being taken to a prosecuting attorney?

Never fear, never steal, Father used to say. The latter was out of the question, so I made the firm resolution that I would not fear. Lock me up they can, release me they must, I consoled myself with a popular adage. I also decided that I would not ask any questions of the driver, and that I would passively await whatever the future might have in store for me.

At the HQ we stopped in front of the guardroom. The sergeant told me to leave my gear there and surrender my gun. Then he handed me over, again like a package, to a non-commissioned officer who took me to the first floor. In front of a brown office door he stopped, waited, tightened his belt and arranged his cap.

"Comrade Major, I am bringing Private First Class Jan Vítek," he said when we entered the office.

"All right, dismiss," said the major without taking his eyes from a document he was reading.

I stood at attention cautiously examining the major. Despite that he was sitting behind a desk it was clear that he was very solidly built, he had large shoulders, a thick neck and an imposing head. Receding, already thinning, hair emphasized a bulging forehead. His hands were big and strong like that of a manual worker. Finally, he pushed the document away and smiled. Wow, a smiling prosecuting attorney, that's an eighth wonder of the world!

"Sit down, please, comrade," said the major, pointing to an easy chair in front of his desk. "Do you smoke?" he added invitingly.

When I nodded he offered me a box of Partyzanky, the cheapest brand. I took a cigarette, thanked him, and lit up. If this is an interrogation, then the major goes about it in a soft way, I thought. But I am not going to fall for it; I'll be on my guard.

"You were an editor in the Czechoslovak News Agency," said the major in an analytical tone. Without waiting for my answer he added: "As a journalist you understand newspapers and you have a certain knowledge about their production. We have decided to start a division newsletter and we are looking for a competent editor." The fear with which I entered the office disappeared as in the wave of a magic wand. I had to try hard to hide my relief and to suppress my perplexity and surprise when the major added: "Do you think that you can handle this job?"

I frantically reviewed what I knew about newspapers…that you read them and throw them away. That was about all. Should I admit my ignorance? No way. The proposal looked like a wonderful occasion to shirk military service, an offer that you simply cannot refuse. Moreover, if I leave the camp and join the division staff, my commander will surely not take the trouble to write a report about my offence since he will be glad that he got rid of me.

"Of course, Comrade Major, I know all about newspaper writing, editing and production," I said. "I will do my utmost to give you full satisfaction and not to let you down for your confidence," I added, anxious to please. If he wanted me to run an observatory I would declare myself an astronomer.

We lit up another cheap cigarette and with the first puff the major expressed the thought that as an editor I should have a higher rank.

"You will be promoted to sergeant," he decided. "I'll let you go now. The duty officer will show you your new quarters. Think about how the newsletter should look, its format, number of pages, layout and so on. Prepare your proposals in writing. We shall discuss them tomorrow afternoon."

Some encounters are of fateful importance. For me one of them was meeting Major Vaclav Prchlik. He was older than I, maybe five or six years. As a Party cadre he had been sent to the Military Academy and became a political officer. Because of his extraordinary intelligence he rose quickly in his career. When I met him he already headed the Political Department of the Army Division in Pilsen. From the very first moment Prchlík made a great impression on me, one of a personality with charisma. And little did I know how profoundly he would change the course of my life.

I was given an assistant, Mirek Taborsky; a typesetter, Josef Srp; and a printer, Vaclav David. Luckily, Mirek Taborsky had more newspaper experience than I because before joining up he had worked for two years for a major Prague daily, *Mlada Fronta*. He handled all the necessary chores such as preparation of manuscripts for layout, proofreading and printing.

The newsletter was a fortnightly, printed on eight pages in A4 format. For me, who had to supply most of the copy, it was a voracious glutton that gulped down manuscripts like strawberries. The Editor-in-Chief was, in fact, Prchlik, who suggested themes, reportage topics and news I should cover. To help me gather the material he took me along on his trips to different regiments and barracks under his political command. We would sit together on the back seat of his Tatraplan, but more often on the hard and narrow seat of an army jeep bumping along on unkempt back roads in field training camps. Prchlik would be tired from exhausting meetings and his big head would wag left and right for a while, always ending up on my shoulder. Thus we traveled thousands of kilometers, smoked uncounted numbers of cigarettes, had long discussions about the army, politics and life in general. Sometimes we would sit quiet, lost in thought and ruminating. We became very close friends. In private we were on a first name basis, Vasek and Honza.

I had a feather bedded life. I slept in my office, no waking up at the crack of dawn, no limbering up in the morning, no lights out, no army bullying. I had a permanent pass so that I could go out into town and return whenever I wanted. I spent practically every weekend in Prague with Blanka, whom I had married shortly before entering the forces.

Prchlik often woke me up when he came to my den, usually around seven in the morning. He always directed his steps first to the radio set and pulled out a knob to turn it on. Out came an American voice or jazz hit broadcast by the American Forces Network in Germany.

"Honza, if you listen to the Amis, do me a favor and switch it to another station afterwards," he would admonish me.

"I need to refresh my English lest I should forget it," I would reply.

There was a reason why he tolerated my listening to the AFN. It was the Cold War and Prchlik wanted to learn how the opposing side viewed political and economic developments in the world. Usually, I briefed him on the main news while we traveled in the car to some outpost garrison and were sure that the driver could not hear us because engine noise covered our voices.

Came October, I had only a couple of days left to serve.

"What will you do when you leave the army?" asked Prchlik as we bumped along in the army jeep on the way back to Pilsen from visiting a frontier garrison.

I did not answer because I knew what he was getting

at with this question. It was not the first time that he had raised it with me.

"I told you, Honza, that you must join the Communist Party, otherwise you have no chance in life...I'll put it another way...it is like ice hockey. You have two possibilities. Either you can be in the anonymous crowd in the hall and the only thing you can do is to applaud and whistle...Or, you can be on the ice, have a stick and puck, you can play, defend and attack. In other words you have a chance to do something, to show what you are capable of doing. Kibbitz or score? Make your choice."

I felt it was my last opportunity to square things with him once for all. I took that chance. I told him about my father, who he was, about my expulsion from the university, and about the falsified cadre testimonial to cover up my social origin.

"With my bourgeois background I can apply for work in the Jachymov uranium mines at best, not for Party membership."

"Class origin is not your fault, it is not a hereditary sin."

"Maybe. But if the vetting commission starts digging into my past it will discover all the other things that I faked."

"It will not, just forget it."

"How can you be so sure?"

"Because I shall chair the Commission. I know you. I will vouch for you. I know you better than you know yourself."

"But it is still a non-starter. I would have to leave the Church. Our priest at Kremze would be informed, he might tell it to my mother, and she would die of shame."

"So the question of leaving the Church will not come up. I'll see to it."

He deprived me of the last argument I had prepared for not joining the Party. I did not know what to add, so I just looked out of the window at the passing countryside and kept silent.

"What's the matter?" asked Prchlik. "Have you got yet another confession?"

"No. But I am perplexed. You are the first man who wants to do something for me."

"I am not doing it disinterestedly and gratis as you may think. I am opening a long-term credit line with you."

"What do you mean…what credit?"

"Credit of political commitment…I think that in the near future there will be a profound, tectonic change in the Party and our whole society. It must happen, because the present state of affairs is hopeless and unsustainable. Party democracy is purposely stifled. The Party itself has become an instrument for maintaining absolute power. And as power tends to abuse, in our totalitarian system abuse of power is full scale and omnipresent. This must change," declared Prchlik. "And there is more. Party bureaucracy is like a thick sieve that prevents new, cleansing and progressive thinking from penetrating to the people. The result is passivity and stagnation in the political, economic and cultural spheres of our society. It may still take some time but a catharsis must come, and I hope it will begin with the departure of Stalin and Gottwald. They both are old and ill; they will not be around forever. We have to prepare the ground for the coming change. That means, in the first place, to awaken the consciousness of our people so that they will not only accept the changes but also welcome them as a political and economic renewal. This is the most important challenge and mission for a select politically conscious Party avant-garde. We have to get together, join our forces..."

"Sorry to interrupt, but when you say, select avant-garde...It sounds like some sort of a conspiracy, and that's playing with fire. It can be interpreted as a disruption of Party unity, or worse."

"Sure, we shall be taking a risk. So we must proceed very carefully, vetting everyone thoroughly, and, above all, beware of stoolies. I am convinced that with further erosion of the leading role of the Party and economic decline, our ranks will swell. If you call it conspiracy, then it will be a conspiracy of progressive forces against dogmatists, responsible Party members against irresponsible ones, the unselfish against the opportunistic, the honest against the corrupt. You, as a journalist, should be part and parcel of it. Therefore you must join the Party so that you can write in newspapers and prove that you are one of us and that I have not misjudged you. Do you understand?"

I realized that Vasek was doing me a great honor in opening to me the inner sanctum of his heart. I felt that his trust and his faith in me forged an unbreakable bond between us, no matter where we were and what might happen.

"OK, I will do what you want, you can count on me...but what changes are you talking about...do you want to change the system?"

"No! The socialist system is the only one possible, just and right. However, it should not be a Bolshevik socialism that we have now, but a genuine socialism that, for lack of a better definition, I call democratic socialism...this is what I dream about."

"I did not know you were a dreamer."

"To dream is human," said Vasek with a broad smile.

Then, his large shoulders sagged down; his bulky body slumped into the seat.

"Maybe, it is not the best idea," he said in a dim voice from which all passion and enthusiasm was gone. "Yet, someone has to do something with our party and society. And who else could it be if not us?"

Vaclav Prchlik became the Head of the Governing Political Administration of the Czechoslovak Army. At the end of 1967 he pre-empted an attempt by the then President and First Secretary of the Communist Party Antonin Novotny to call on army tank units to support his collapsing reign. Prchlik sent reliable general staff officers to the units to convince their commanders to stay in the garrison and disobey the President. In a press conference in early1968 he critized the Warsaw Pact military alliance and stopped short of calling for its dissolution. Prchlik, was at the top of the Soviet list of enemies. After the invasion of Czechoslovakia in the night of 20th August 1968 he was degraded from the rank of Major General to a Private, and spent several years in prison.

MY SHINING TOMORROW

Two weeks after my return to civilian life, I received a notice to appear before a Special Screening Commission that would review my eligibility to become a member of the Czechoslovak Communist Party. Vasek told me that the commission would sit in Prague but did not specify the date. I was surprised that the vetting was so swift in coming. The wording of the notice was in a typically military style: You are, herewith, summoned to be present at 15.30 hours on 12th November 1952 in the Conference Room of the Hotel Krivan, Zitna Street, number 34.

I saw in it a joke of destiny. Hotel Krivan was the place where shortly before the call-up I had celebrated my marriage with Blanka. Then it was a hot summer day, today a nasty cold wind was blowing, it rained, and there were dirty puddles on the pavement. I took off my drenched Montgomery coat in the hotel entrance hall and put it on a coat hanger near a mirror. I wore dark-blue clothes, a white shirt and a red tie. I combed my wet hair and looked at myself in the mirror with some satisfaction: if nothing else, I should make a good impression.

The conference room was easy to find, thanks to arrow signs the organizers had providently placed to ensure that candidates would not get lost. There were several chairs in the corridor near the conference room door. A young man of my age sat upright on one of them. His shortcut gave it away that he was recently demobilized.

"Are you here for a communion?" I asked, sitting down on the chair next to him.

"For an admission interview," he said stiffly and turned his head away from me to signal that he did not want to deign to talk to me.

Inwardly, I uttered a four-letter word and wrote him off. At the same time the door of the conference room half opened and a head and a shoulder with uniform sporting the rank-badge of a captain appeared.

"Comrade Pavelka?" said the officer in a tone that was more an order than a question.

"Present!" the young man cried, jumping to attention as on a parade ground.

"Come in," said the officer.

Pavelka adjusted his jacket and in an unconscious gesture slid his hand around his waist as if to arrange a non-existent military belt. Then with a military step he walked into the room.

I got up, went to the window and lit a cigarette. While I was smoking, tipping the ashes behind a central heating unit, another candidate turned up whose looks also betrayed a recent civilian. He dressed like a politically conscious builder of shining tomorrows: blue trousers, blue shirt with the emblem of the Czechoslovak Youth Association. The incongruous complement was a brown leather jacket.

"How's it going?" he asked.

"Dragging on," I said. "As I see it, they are half an hour behind schedule."

"Shit," said the newcomer

This exhausted all conversation. What followed was like waiting in a dentist's waiting room with painful anticipation.

After a long time Pavelka re-appeared, he was red-faced and wilted.

"If you are Comrade Vítek, you should go in," he mumbled and left without saying goodbye.

Between the two front windows of the conference room I was confronted with a glaring slogan: WITH THE CZECHOSLOVAK COMMUNIST PARTY FOR PEACE AND SOCIALISM. Below it were framed portraits of the President Klement Gottwald, and Minister of National Defense, Army General Alexej Cepicka. At the head of a large table covered with white cloth sat five officers: three majors and two captains. The Chairman, Major Vasek Prchlik, was enthroned in the middle. On his right sat a chubby major with a self-contented look. Next to him I recognized Captain Hnilicka, a political officer of the 35th Regiment in Pilsen, where I began my military career. The third major had a longish face, decorated by a fair, Lenin style beard. The captain on the far left sat stonily with his elbows resting on the table. His eyes were black-circled as if after a drinking bout. I noticed that the members of the commission no longer looked like fresh daisies; they rather seemed tired and annoyed. Most probably, they were suffering from the fatigue of a marathon session. The Party needed new and strong blood. Therefore, Gottwald had entrusted Cepicka with enrollment in the Army. The servile son-in-law carried out this task with feverish enthusiasm. This is why screening commissions in the army were so overworked.

"Sit down, comrade," said Vasek, pointing to a single chair in front of the table. I looked furtively at my watch: it was quarter to five.

"Comrade Jan Vítek has been recommended as a new member by the division Party organization in Plzen, where he served as sergeant and editor of the division magazine," Vasek said to open the hearing. He took a piece of paper from a heap of documents he had before him on the table and began to read from it the justification of the proposal. It sounded like a litany for someone who had just died: politically conscious, loyal to the cause of the people, hard-working, well educated, talented, popular, appreciated… "He created a magazine that became the best in the Czechoslovak army and for this achievement he received an exceptional reward from the Minister of National Defense. The Divisional Party Organization expresses its unanimous conviction that Comrade Jan Vítek will become a valuable asset to our Party, which is why it recommends that he be admitted as a new member," said Vasek concluding his introductory speech. He put the paper down and asked if there were any questions.

Captain Hnilicka cleared his throat, smiled at me encouragingly and put the first question.

"Comrade Vítek, what was the reward you received from the Comrade Minister?"

"It was two…" shelf warmers I almost said but stopped in time before doing it. "Two volumes of Sholokhov's *And Quiet Flows the Don*, illustrated and hard covered."

Then the major with Lenin beard asked:

"I would like to know, do you study the classics of Marx–Leninism?"

"As yet, I have not had an opportunity to attend an evening university or course," I admitted, "but I try to deepen and improve my education by consistent self-study."

"What exactly are you studying at present?"

"Stalin's *Problems of Leninism*. I study it in English."

"In English?" wondered the major. "How interesting, this I hear for the first time. Why exactly in English?

"I have already studied it in Czech," I lied, "I am reading this classic work again in English…mainly because of special political and economic expressions that I don't know well or at all. I look them up in a dictionary and write them down in order to memorize them perfectly, which could come in very handy if I were to be again an English editor in the Czechoslovak News Agency, where I had worked before my call-up."

My laborious explanation must have satisfied the major, since he stopped his cross-examination at this point. I felt a great relief.

"Are there other questions?" said Vasek.

"Comrade, do you have siblings?" asked the captain with the hangover look, coming to life for a second.

"No," I assured him.

The captain nodded and instantly sank back into his own world.

"Any other questions?" said Vasek again, to encourage his tired team.

"Tell us some more about your father," said the chubby major. "What did he do for a living and what is his present occupation?"

I anticipated this question, so I had prepared a tactical plan to obfuscate the attention of the Commission by a recital of unobjectionable and dull details in order to sweep this rather delicate matter under the carpet.

"My father was born on the seventeenth of June in the year one thousand nine hundred as the second son of bricklayer Jan Vítek, who had seven children, of whom four were boys and three girls." I began to tell the story like a well-prepared student at the blackboard. "The family lived in an old wooden cottage at Holubov in Southern Bohemia. A meadow went with the cottage that provided fodder for a cow, representing all the fortune of the family. His father, my grandfather, would go to Bavaria every spring to work as bricklayer, and would return home at the end of autumn. The money he earned in Germany was spent on a complete reconstruction of the cottage. It had to be enlarged so that the whole family, including grandmother, would not have to live, work and sleep in just one room. In winter all the Víteks were busy making various wooden implements, such as handles, broomsticks, shovels and baskets to eke out a living. Every summer, the children went to the nearby forest to collect oven-wood, lopped branches, pinecones, and gather raspberries. My father told me that by selling raspberries he would earn money to buy clothes, shoes, as well as school copybooks and pencils. He attended a grammar school at Holubov and a secondary school at Kremze. When he left it he was fourteen years old and after that he was on his own. This is why he went to earn his keep in the Sudeten where he served as a stable boy and farm hand for four years. He had several employers, all of them

German farmers whose sons were fighting in the First World War. He learned how to run a farm and to speak a German dialect. After the war he went into apprenticeship with a certain Soukup at Kremze who was a butcher and innkeeper. At the end of his apprenticeship, he met his future wife, Katerina Traplova, daughter of a bricklayer from Chlum, near Kremze, who was killed in the war as a Czech legionary in Siberia. As a married couple they lived, at first, in a sub-let room in the house of a farmer at Chlum, where I was born. Later on, they rented a small farm at a hamlet, Pasicka, with about five hectares of cornfields and a meadow. During the Great Depression, however, the owner of the farm had to sell it, and my parents moved to Kremze. There they rented a small house that they bought a few years later. My father worked as a laborer at a lumber mill at Mric near Kremze. My mother, who used to be a cow maid before her marriage, gave seasonal help to local farmers…"

"Sorry to interrupt you, comrade," said Vasek. "What we want to hear is not a family history but what your father does for a living today?"

It was clear to me that he was trying to stop me getting entangled in my own web.

"He is a forest worker," I said with great relief that I could leave out a part of my father's life that was a liability from a political point of view. "He is employed at the State Forest Company. For some time he was a logger but now he drives a truck delivering lumber to a paper mill at Loucovice near Krumlov."

"Please explain to me, comrade," said the chubby faultfinder, "how is it possible that your parents could buy a house when they evidently were very poor?"

He tricked me. I bitterly regretted a slip of the tongue when I mentioned the purchase of the house. How to get out of it?

"Frankly, I don't know," I said. "They managed to save some money when they had the farm at Pasicka...And I recall...hazily...that during the war they repaid a loan to a rich miller named Hrubes...He knew my mother when she was a child and liked her...I also know that my mother washed and ironed shirts for the miller's two sons...I guess it was Hrubes who loaned money to my parents to buy the house."

"Is your father politically engaged, does he belong to a party?" asked the major with the Lenin beard.

"No, he has never been politically involved."

"Why?"

I hesitated a moment. Then I decided I had nothing to lose.

"Father says that politics is filth."

They all were struck dumb with amazement. The sleepy, hung-over captain opened his bloodshot eyes. The chubby faultfinder almost jumped up in his chair. Vasek shook his big head and opened his mouth to intervene, but the bearded major was faster.

"And what do you think about politics, comrade?" he said raising his voice and putting special emphasis on the last two words.

"Politics is the art of governing, and as such it is neutral," I said. "The crucial thing, on which all depends, is who is in control of politics and whom it benefits. I am for politics of the people, executed by the people, and carried out for the benefit of the people."

"In this respect we are all in agreement because the ultimate goal of the government entrusted to our Party is the wellbeing of all working people in our country," said Vasek hastily, to head off the possibility that somebody in the Commission got wind of whose words I had just paraphrased. "Now tell us, comrade, how you see your future, what do you want to do in life?"

"I want to be an honest journalist, and write a

couple of good books," I said.

"We need you in the army press. You have some experience already in this field, so think about it seriously," said Vasek. Then, turning to the others, he added: "Let's vote…who is for the proposal that Comrade Jan Vítek should become a member of our Party?"

He raised his hand first. All other members joined him like golems, those beings made completely of inanimate matter in Jewish folklore.

"I congratulate you, comrade, on joining the Party," said Vasek solemnly. He got up and reached out his hand.

I did not know what to say. So I just shook Vasek's hand, made a little bow to the others, and marched out.

It was ten minutes past five. In half an hour I had become a different being.

As it was raining hard outside I decided to stay in the hotel and wait in the restaurant for the worst to pass. A waiter came, I ordered a coffee and rum, lit a cigarette and began to recapitulate events and sort my thoughts out.

I did not join the Party—I had pupated in it.

I shall have to be very prudent not to give myself away.

I must not accept any Party post or function, even the least of the least.

Above all, and foremost—my mother must never learn about it, for she would die of shame and sorrow. This was my uppermost concern.

I had no qualms about my comportment and performance in front of the commission, nor about the half-truths and untruths I had told them. I was living in a totalitarian system that governed by fear and lies. I could not fight openly. I am not Jan Hus, or Don

115

Quixote: thus I justified myself my action. Hypocrisy is the only weapon of the weak and powerless. It is mimicry that will help you to survive. In the cyclone it is better to be a straw of grass than a majestic oak tree.

Although I was twenty-four years old, I was still very naïve. Nonetheless, I understood that up to now my life had been easy because chool, the news agency and military service were not much more than playgrounds. Real life begins now. I did not have any conception of what was awaiting me, or a clear goal. Had I fulfilled my dream of becoming an actor I would know precisely what I want to do and achieve. Now the future was a dark horse.

I had only one idea. In an embryonic stage, this had always been inside me. At that moment it appeared fully formed. It was very simple: I would be as honest and decent a man as possible. It was a credo that would last my whole life.

The waiter brought me a second round of coffee and rum. I sipped them slowly since I did not want to slide into drunkenness. More than by alcohol, however, I was intoxicated by cognizance of the fact that I definitely, at long last, had buried my bourgeois past and my expulsion from the university, and buried all this like a cadaver twenty feet deep.

Ionesco wrote that the world is an egg. Once you get inside its shell, nothing bad can happen to you, you are safe for the rest of your days. I had drilled through the shell and now I felt in absolute security.

How foolish I was!

It never crossed my mind or came to me in my worst nightmares that, thirteen years later, the cadaver would be dug up by military intelligence who would use it to break me down in this very hotel in an inhospitable room on the second floor.

IV. THESE NIGHTS WERE MADE FOR DRINKING

In the daily Obrana Lidu I was welcomed not as a rookie but as an equal among equals because two of the most respected editors, Ota Brozek and Oldrich Mestek, vouched for my professional competence. Moreover, my personal file, sent to the daily by Major Václav Prchlík, contained so much praise that, with this in hand, I could easily put myself forward for a post as minister.

Given my knowledge of four languages, the Editor-in-Chief, Colonel Ada Hradecky, assigned me at first to the foreign news section, which was headed by Jiri Hochman, a tall, thin man who had a well-merited reputation as a womanizer. The couch in his office would have a lot of stories to tell. On the very first day Jiri asked me to write a commentary about the housing crisis in Great Britain. I sweated it out with clenched teeth. The following day I asked for a transfer. I did not want to do political journalism. I could not admit it, of course. So I said to Hradecky that the job in the foreign news section consisted of copying stuff from the Czechoslovak News Agency, dumb drudgery, and I wanted to do some original and creative writing. This is how I landed in the military training department, run by Jarda Homuta, where the star reporter was Ota Brozek.

Soon, Ota and I became an inseparable couple. We signed our articles and reports together, although each was penned by only one of us. As a result, our names appeared in *Obrana Lidu* practically every day. We gained a reputation as prolific scribblers.

But I found no satisfaction in this work. I missed something. I could not put my finger on it for some time. Finally, it dawned on me as we were sitting with

Ota in the Pinkas pub, drinking beer and meditating about writing. I began to lament that I was fed up with machine-line production of stories about model sergeants who, with patience and understanding, transformed slackers into exemplary soldiers.

"It sticks in my throat like an unpalatable dumpling and I simple cannot swallow it," I said.

"You exaggerate," said Ota. "You have been with us only a couple of months. You will get used to it."

"I am not the kind of person who gets used even to the gallows," I said. "What we write are lullabies. I am through with your department. I must find something else."

"Do you have some clear idea or is it just the beer talking?" asked Ota.

I was looking pensively at my beer mug where every sip left a circle on the glass.

"I want to write about what really goes on in the army. For instance, what we told each other on the bunk after taps, what got under our skin, and what drove us mad."

"Such as political indoctrination?" suggested Ota.

"Gosh, you are damn right. If there is something that soldiers hate, it is the crap and blabbering of political officers."

"So put it on paper."

"Ota, you know that political indoctrination is a sacred cow that is untouchable."

"There is no taboo, it just depends on your imagination: how inventively and intelligently you present the issue to get the message across," said Ota. "Put it down even just for yourself so that you get it out of your mind."

The following morning I got up early. At five o'clock I was already pounding away on my typewriter. I wrote about a political officer nicknamed Organ-grinder who grinds out the expected rubbish while most rank and file soldiers slumber or play cards, and Private First Class Vyklouz is overcome by a violent urge to self-abuse that he desperately tries to chase away.

Jarda Homuta crossed out the punch line, of how Organ-grinder drove himself into the nuthouse. The censor killed Private First Class Vyklouz.

After the publication of the piece, we received some outraged letters from the garrisons I visited recently at Plana, Tachov and Stribro, complaining that I made a fool of their political officers and denigrated their meritorious work of deepening the political consciousness of soldiers. I had to visit all these army units again to explain that the feuilleton was a generalization, and definitely did not depict their political officer whose lecture I had heard and who mesmerized his audience with his eloquence, so he could not in any way be a model for the fictitious Organ-grinder.

In addition, to cover my back I stopped at the Division HQ in Pilsen.

"I am really in the shit," I said to Vasek Prchlik.

"I have heard something to that effect," he said. "But I shall be delighted to listen to your version. Spill the beans, don't hide anything, because I shall know it anyway."

After hearing me out, he said that it was a serious mess I was in, and that he would carefully investigate the complaints, which would take some time.

"And be more prudent in the future," he admonished me.

"You know, Vasek, I try hard to be more prudent than the proverbially cautious innkeeper Palivec in the novel *Svejk*...But I am afraid that I shall turn out as badly as he did."

"I will see what I can do about it," said Vasek.

On return to the editorial office I felt an odd man out. My colleagues were cold and distant.

"Had I been in service as the chief editor, your...well to be polite...such rubbish would not be published," said Major Polcar, number two on the newspaper. "I don't get you, Honza, did you lose all judgment? It's as if you wanted to take a whack at the Party."

I felt like I was being put in the pillory. Colleagues looked at me, but no one, except for Ota, spoke to me.

Some ten days later I was summoned to the editor-in-chief.

"Hradecky has called me onto the carpet," I said to Ota, "and I hope you will not desert me. After all, the feuilleton was your idea."

Ada Hradecky was a big, stocky man with a waxy yellow face. With his medals-bedecked breast he considered it his foremost duty to defend the editorial office against adversities and the whims of the army establishment. He invited us to sit down.

"What are you, Ota, doing here?" he asked.

"We are in it together," said Ota.

"Very well. So listen, busters," began Hradecky. "I have just received, courtesy of the Ministry, a letter from the Chief of the Division of Political Administration signed by Major Vaclav Prchlik."

He made a brief pause while measuring us with a fatherly look, and then he continued:

"Prchlik writes that the feuilleton *The Organ-grinder* was very thoroughly discussed at a joint meeting of all political officers of the division. They reached a consensus that the feuilleton was a critique in principle of the general shortcomings of political education as such...and that it expresses a valid view which should lead to an introspection and become a stimulus to rooting out all forms of banality and phrase-mongering in the political education of rank and file soldiers and active-duty non-commissioned officers..."

"In other words, it's constructive criticism," observed Ota.

"Lucky for you, Honza. You escaped by a hair's breadth," said Hradecky.

Vasek is a real friend, I thought with gratitude and respect. Besides Ota, no one knew about my relationship with Prchlik; and I did not consider it necessary to initiate the Editor-in-Chief. But even Ota had not the slightest idea of a special bond, a moral pact in fact, that bound Vasek and myself.

"Feuilleton is a genre we should cultivate because it makes the newspaper more readable," said Hradecky. "When can you deliver another one?"

"Together, Ota and I, we could sweat out two feuilletons a week," I said enthusiastically.

"On one condition," said Ota, "that you free us from scribbling moralizing yarns on drill and training. You know, the problem is not only to find suitable subject matter. We must also screen them carefully. It means crosschecking all tips and information, verifying all facts and figures. We must make sure that that the story is foolproof and cannot rebound on us like a boomerang. It takes a lot of sweat and time."

I perceived the aim of Ota's speech and I hastened to elaborate on it.

"On top of it, we could write special reports about emergency events such as a fire or flood disasters, and we could do some investigative journalism. For instance, we could look into the problem of suicides in the army and car crashes..."

"Hold your horses, Honza," said Hradecky. "No investigative journalism, but the rest sounds all right."

"We could create a department of special reporters," said Ota driving home the point of our plea.

"For you and Honza?"

"If you give us a break," said Ota, "we can guarantee a steady flow of interesting and gripping stories."

Hradecky mulled the suggestion over, and then he said:

"I give you three months to show me that my confidence in you is well placed. Afterwards, we shall see…"

Three months became three years, during which Ota and I wrote feuilletons twice a week under the title 'From Bunks To The Printing Press.' The stories were satires denouncing various abuses in the army, including bullying, harassment and pilfering. Most of the subjects came to us from whistleblowers, both active duty soldiers and career officers. We tackled controversial problems that made us very popular but at the same time got us into trouble. Very often after publishing a feuilleton we had to fend off complaints by enraged commanders and Party committees. Army big shots usually followed the principle that the best defense is attack. To do that, they used a Sophistic approach. We are the representatives of the people, they would argue, thus if you criticize us, you are criticizing the Party because we are carrying out its policy as well as the policy of the people's democratic society. It was not easy to deflect such attacks. Stormy discussions usually ended with a compromise: the big shots admitted that the facts in the feuilleton were correct, and we admitted that the style and language might have been more diplomatic. However, on a number of occasions our livelihoods were at stake.

THE FOX IS CALLED TO THE HENHOUSE

The phone on my desk was ringing. I lifted the receiver to hear the melodic voice of our master's secretary.

"Drop everything and come on the double to see Jirka. He wants to talk to you."

Jiri Kupka was our new Editor-in-Chief. Those who envied him said that he had been named to that post because his father, a great writer, was an honored artist well connected to a number of members of the Central Committee of the Party. The truth is that Jirka was an accomplished journalist and author in his own right. And above all, he was a decent man.

We called his secretary Roly-Poly. She was a buxom young woman with remarkable breasts the size of two halves of a soccer ball. When I passed her going to the boss's office I asked her if she had any idea why I was being carpeted. She puckered her lips and recommended me to search my guilty conscience. Then she turned in a way that allowed me to admire the side view of her overripe breasts.

Jirka was sitting in a leather chair and was smoking a cigar. There was a pile of page-proofs of the next edition of the paper before him. He said Hi, and he would be with me in a jiffy. I sat down on a chair and peered at the cover of the *Newsweek* that lay on the coffee table. It carried a headline saying 'Brzezinski Launches A New Assault on Communism.' He was my favorite author, and whenever I got chance to read *Newsweek*, I looked first for his copy.

"I have two things to talk over," said Jirka. "Good and bad. Which do you want to hear first?"

"Start with the bad one."

"Hawk Eye has just brought me this," said Jirka and fished out a page-proof. Hawk Eye was a nickname of our censor whose job was to ensure that no unorthodox thoughts or politically undesirable news appeared in the paper.

"It was a cold autumn day when I lay on the firing line," Jirka read from my yesterday's fancy. "I aimed my gun carefully and pressed the trigger. I did it six times. Each shot was a bull's eye. I am happy that I fulfilled my pledge…signed Private First Class Jan Fuckingale."

Every year at this time *Obrana Lidu* carried a column entitled 'Resounds,' featuring solemn pledges by soldiers to accomplish outstanding achievements in honor of the Great October Revolution. Some of them were real letters from soldiers and commissioned officers. The others were penned by editors.

"Fuckingale," repeated Jirka as if he abhorred the name.

"So what," I said, "if I used a common-place name such as Jan Novak, we would be flooded by letters from all army units that their Jan Novak never shot six bull's eyes. Thus Fuckingale, because there are not many of them, if any."

"Even if I connive at the fact that you fabricated the news item," said Jirka in a tone full of authority, "the way it is written is unpardonable, because it creates an impression that you despise the whole campaign. Either you rewrite it from scratch, or I take it out of the paper."

"Take it out."

"And I shall also cross you off the list of editors who will receive a bonus."

"Fine by me." I shrugged shoulders. The bonus was one hundred and fifty crowns. Without them, I would survive.

"How well do you speak English?"

"I manage. Why do you want to know?"

"I got a query from the Ministry. They need some

people for the Neutral Nations Supervisory Commission in Korea who know English very well. You used to be an English editor in the Czechoslovak News Agency, so they want me to ask you whether you want to go to Korea…"

Who has thought of me? Who has gone through my personal file? An anxiety crossed my mind. I suppressed it and said:

"I don't know. Certainly not today, we are planning a beer party."

"Don't be a jerk, Honza, this a great opportunity for you to see a foreign country."

"Yeah, but at the other end of the world…"

"That's an added advantage. You'll get a chance to see a part of Asia."

"I like it here, why I should leave? And God knows what kind of beer they serve over there."

"That's enough! Don't crack jokes. This is a serious matter because the Ministry could call you up for special military practice under the law. So be so kind as to behave like a mature man. Such an offer is not refused without giving it a serious consideration."

It occurred to me that I should ask what I would do in Korea. But then I decided against it. There was no point in protracting a senseless discussion. I am not going anywhere. Period.

"OK, I will sleep on it," I said.

We parted on that note. As I was leaving I once again took pleasure in giving a lustful glance at the voluptuous profile of Roly-Poly.

The editorial office of *Obrana Lidu* was located in a four-storied building dating back to the Austro-Hungarian Empire. Our den was at the end of the corridor on the third floor marked with a sign 'Special Correspondents.' Behind the adjective 'special' were two things. One, we could choose for ourselves the subject we wanted to write about. Two, we were not obliged to keep rigid office hours, and we could stay home to write. If by chance all three of us were in the office, Jirka would say: "Why are you hanging around, get out. Because if you are not here, I can entertain a faint hope that you could be doing something useful. Scram!"

Ota Brozek has not turned up yet. Maybe he was taking his 'forty-eight-hours-nap' as his wife would say when he slept away a binge. But Franta Kejik, whom we had adopted as a kindred soul, lounged in a small, squeaky armchair, the only luxurious piece of the otherwise austere furniture. Franta had a checkered, politically incorrect past. He fought as a volunteer in the Spanish civil war against Franco's fascists. Later on he fled from occupied Czechoslovakia to France to join its army to fight Germans, and after the French defeat he went to England to become a navigator in the Royal Air Force Czechoslovak Squadron. He returned home with a rank of Pilot Officer. During the Communist purges he was degraded and discharged from the army. Therefore, he had problems getting a job, and it was to Kubka's credit that he had agreed to take him on. Now, as Franta wallowed in the armchair, his long feet resting on a heap of old newspapers, his good-natured Moravian face lit up with a smile that despite bad, unkempt teeth was captivating.

"Come with me to Pilsen," he said. "I have a car, we can return tomorrow."

"Are you going there on a reportage trip?"

"Not exactly. Between you and me, to see a friend."

"Did you take an advance for traveling?" I wanted to know, and for a good reason, because Franta was always broke. He developed an original approach in tapping you for money. He would sit on your desk and ask if he could use your phone. Then he would dial a number and after a short wait would feign the following conversation: "Hi, this Franta Kejik speaking. I want to know when I can stop by to pick up my honorarium...only tomorrow? I need it now...OK, I'll drop in on you tomorrow afternoon...Have a nice day." Then with a saddened face he would ask if you could lend him five crowns. In those days five crowns bought three beers. He would never ask for more than five crowns because, as he declared, little debts need not to be repaid between friends.

"Don't be afraid," he assured me, "I am loaded, I have got six hundred crowns."

It did not take long for me to make up my mind. I had a carry-on with a toothbrush and pajamas always ready in the office. Pilsen was my second hometown, where I knew all the army garrisons, their commanders and political officers, and, most important, whom to trust and whom to avoid. Moreover, I needed to find a subject for a feuilleton in the Friday edition. So I said in English:

"OK, count me in."

"Great. We'll have a ball."

When we were alone we exchanged a couple of English phrases because it made us feel good. His English was much better since he had a genuine British accent, while mine was typically American, picked up from listening to the American Forces Network broadcast from Munich.

Our driver was a good guy, Karel Simr, but we were, nonetheless, cautious and talked only about football and girls. You never know what the driver hears and to whom he might report it. Franta got out on the main square in front of the District Military Administration, and I descended after a couple of kilometers at the Division HQ. I sent Simr to book accommodation at the Grand Hotel and wait there for us. We wanted to get him out of our way because in the evening we were to meet at the Pilsen brewery beer-hall as a starting point for an all-night drinking bout.

It was raining. The guard at the door hid in the box and was smoking in secret. In the archway I spotted two men in uniform. They were enraged, gesticulated and cursing like mad. I recognized one of them, Vasilij Basiljak, because we both had served as recruits in the 35th Artillery Regiment. Vasilij came from the far-east end of the country in Slovakia where he was born in a little village. He was choleric by nature, which is why he was in trouble every so often and received one punishment after the other. Surprisingly, this did not discourage him from his ambition of becoming a career soldier. Evidently he had succeeded, judging from his Sergeant Major's insignia.

"My god, Honza, what are you doing here?" he exclaimed with joy, shaking my hand so forcefully that he almost cracked my finger bones.

"And what about you, are you in trouble again?"

"Not me, but we have a fucking problem with shitty Armastav," he said and added a long litany of four-letter words.

It transpired that I had in front of me a two-man delegation, Vasilij and a First Lieutenant named Karlik, representing the Association of Tenants of a housing development at Stribro. They came to file a collective complaint with the Division Commander against Armastav, an army construction enterprise that built their tenement houses but had not finished the access roads and pavements. As a result, all the residents drowned in mud and filth in the spring and fall and in slush in winter. This had been going on for three years, despite many protests and petitions.

"Come along," said Vasilij. "We have a jeep here,

come and see that shit with your own eyes. Now in October it is fucking bad."

Stribro was some sixty kilometers away, about an hour's ride on a narrow, curvy road. Vasilij and I reminisced about the time we spent together in the non-commissioned officer school, and how we swapped duties. Anti-tank guns in those days were still pulled by horses. I did not like horses from the day a mare threw me right on the village square at Kremze; in fact, I was afraid of them. Vasilij loved horses. So when I ought to have been in attendance in the stables Vasilij replaced me, while in return I took on his duties of cleaning corridors and WCs.

The army housing development consisted of about a dozen four-storied buildings arranged in a half-moon. In front of them was a large flat area intended to be a playground for children and a park with banks and water jets. None of this ever materialized. Instead I saw an area of foul brown mud that in some places had turned into thickened sludge. The inhabitants had to cross it whenever they left their apartments or returned home.

"How do you manage to wade through this cesspool?" I asked.

"All people here have gumboots," explained First Lieutenant Karlik. "We put them on at home, flounder through, and then we change gumboots for our ordinary shoes. On return we proceed in the same manner. The biggest problem is with small children, because they have to be carried. My wife could tell you all about it. I can show you in my office the copies of complaints to Armastav, some accompanied by veiled threats, as well as copies of petitions addressed to the Minister of Defense and even to the Central Committee of the Party. All without result."

"Besides the thirty unmarried officers sixty-two

families live here with more than eighty children," said Vasilij. He smiled bitterly. "We should grow wings like birds."

Suddenly, I knew I had a story idea for a feuilleton, and that I must write it, if only because of these people in this awful place braving sludge or sleet every day, no matter whether exposing their troubles would help them or not. Maybe they will have a good laugh and be happier for a while, and they will not feel so deserted, defenseless and cast down.

As the jeep jolted its way back to Pilsen, I huddled on the back seat in an almost horizontal position, rolled up my coat to serve as a pillow the way I used to on reportage trips and closed my eyes. I tried to focus on the feuilleton I wanted to write. I should not pillory Armastav alone. That would be an easy and cheap target. I must give the feuilleton a subtext and a social dimension. That meant that I must also aim it at Party hacks in the Central Committee of the Party and brass hats in the Ministry of Defense. But how to write the story so that the censor does not kill it? What if I present it in the form of an allegory? Censorship had taught people how to read between lines. I must think it out properly so as to ensure that the message would not stick out like a sore thumb…I might get it past…

When I appeared at six o'clock that evening in the Pilsen brewery its bar room was as noisy as a beehive. The cigarette smoke hung in a thick fog and it was not easy to spot Franta. I discovered him sitting at a long table under a window. Next to him was a small, corpulent man with a balding head. What he lacked on top was compensated by a puckish beard and mustache. Franta introduced him to me as Peter, his old buddy and comrade-in-arms from the Czechoslovak Squadron in England.

I squeezed in among the beer buddies on a bench on the opposite side of the table. I noticed the strokes on Franta's beer mat, indicating how many drinks he had ordered. There were only three but he would down beer in little sips as if it were wine, so it I concluded they had been sitting here several hours.

It turned out that after the war Peter had also been an English editor in the Czechoslovak News Agency. Following the Communist takeover he was summarily fired, together with other employees who had fought in the West.

"Peter works as mechanic in communal services," said Franta.

"What you learn in your youth comes in very handy when you are in the shit," smiled Peter.

I recalled that when I had come to the Agency looking for work there had been several vacancies for English speakers. Now it dawned on me why, and it crossed my mind that maybe I took Peter's place. The idea haunted me for a long time afterwards. But in front of Peter I kept mum about my position in the Agency. I felt ashamed of it.

I lifted my glass of beer. We toasted. I was launched into orbit on one of the many boisterous and sensational evenings and nights of my bohemian years…

…until your thick eyed and groggy awakening, when your head spins, your mouth reeks like a cesspit, your throat is a Sahara, and your lungs are strangled by an overdose of nicotine.

I half-opened a left eyelid. A laser light burned a hole in my spectacles glass. A pneumatic drill wailed deep in my skull. It was Franta's electric shaver.

"Rise and shine," he said. "It's almost lunch time. I am hungry. I must be back in Prague at five."

I tried to close my eyes again. I could not. I knew I

would not escape into merciful slumber. I was still wearing my shirt, underwear and socks. Evidently, I had only succeeded in taking off my tie, trousers and shoes last night. I searched for a box of cigarettes. It was empty. I began to put on my trousers and inadvertently touched the back pocket where I usually carried my wallet. It was not there. Hastily, I checked all the pockets of my jacket.

"Jesus Christ, I lost my wallet!" I cried. "Or it was stolen."

"Stay cool," said Franta. "Try to remember when you held it in your hand for the last time."

"I wish I could. I don't remember."

"You still had it when we were stopped and checked late night."

"By whom?"

"By the police."

"No, complete blank, zero, I have a total black-out."

"You sang the *Marseillaise*, and the policemen did not like it. Luckily you managed to convince them the *Marseillaise* is a revolutionary song of the French working class, which softened them up."

"Did we get a fine?"

"No. They sent us away to sleep it off."

"It means that we went to the hotel?"

"We were on our way but then we saw that the Kakadu night club was still open. It was there where we lost Peter. When the club closed at four o'clock, I put you in a taxi. Did you have money in the wallet?"

"I don't know, three hundred crowns, maybe…Jesus Christ, I had a service card there enabling me to enter all military installations! I must have lost the wallet in that bloody club. What happened there? My brain has been lobotomized."

"Nothing extraordinary. Except that you danced with a gypsy girl, or rather shuffled on the dance floor."

"You could not have kicked me and pulled me out of the joint?"

"You should know yourself by now. When you are in orbit you stay on it till the bitter end."

"It must have been the gipsy girl who stole it!"

I sobered up quickly, faster than under an ice-cold shower. The loss of the service card completely overwhelmed me. At that time, there reigned an artificially created paranoia about capitalist plots and omnipresent Western spying activity. In such an atmosphere it was very likely that I would be accused of selling the card to foreign intelligence.

"They will arrest me," I wailed. "They will lock me up."

"And throw away the key!" Franta gave a loud laugh.

I was on the verge of weeping with rage against myself. The drinking bout in Pilsen will never be forgotten, because I shall have to pay a high price for it. What was bound to happen one day was about to come to pass. My guardian angels had had enough. They were fed up with me. They had watched over me when I was in orbit and guided my landings for a long, long time. This time they have deserted me! Shall I lose my job? Will they lock me up? Of course, sure as hell!

On the way back to Prague I got an idea that sometime I should record my life in orbit and that it should be entitled '*These Nights were Made for Drinking*'.

V. WATCHDOG IN THE LAND OF MORNING CALM

A week later, after the heroic spree in Pilsen, Roly-Poly stormed our office. When she saw our threesome sitting at the desk, she gasped.

"What's the matter, boys? Why are you all here? Did your wives throw you out?"

"You should know better," said Ota hypocritically. "We keep office hours."

"If you have come to fetch my feuilleton," said Franta, "I am just about to finish it."

It was not true. We had to lock up Franta in the office and threaten to keep him there until he delivered the promised copy. When he was done the floor was full of crumpled papers, all with a new beginning because Franta could not write a story until he had produced an opening sentence with which he was happy.

"Honza, you are in a pretty pickle," announced Roly-Poly merrily. "Major Zapletal called from the Ministry: you are to report to him at half past two in the afternoon."

"Who is this Major Zapletal? Does Jirka know him? Is he from counterintelligence?" I asked with apprehension.

"No, but Jirka thinks that it is because of the service card you lost." Roly-Poly confirmed my misgivings. "When you return Jirka wants you to see you, and you should tell him how it went and what the consequences will be."

"I expected it, but not that soon," I said when we were alone.

"No panic, stay cool," said Ota.

"We must think it over carefully," said Franta.

We agreed that the best thing to do would be to go to the Pinkas pub where we were used to contemplating our creative problems and hard luck situations. We arrived there at lunchtime. The bar downstairs was full but we found a small table free in the restaurant on the first floor. The waiter, who knew us well, automatically brought us three dewy glasses of beer.

"Cheers." Thus Ota opened the deliberations. We took a long sip, and he continued. "Let's start with tactics. What will you say when Zapletal asks you to explain the loss of the service card? It must be a plausible story."

We agreed on a fabrication that I should present. No pubs, and above all no night club. I was on a reportage trip to Stribro, slept quietly in a hotel in Pilsen, went to a self-service in the morning, where I paid for my piece of salami and a croissant. And that was the last time I had my wallet with all my documents in my hand.

"Deny, deny and deny again," stressed Franta.

"Let's expect that at best Zapletal will buy it. But on the other hand let's be prepared for the worst: that you will have to go before a tribunal. And if so, what might be the penalty."

"If the worst comes to the worst, they will impeach you for selling the service card to the CIA," said Franta. "Luckily, you are a civil employee and as such you cannot be judged by a military tribunal."

"That's really a stroke of luck because a military tribunal is like fighting a bull," said Ota. "I know an excellent lawyer, however. We went to school together. He specializes in criminal law, and I am sure he could get you a lenient sentence."

"I will testify before the jury that you are obedient to the law and a politically reliable citizen," said Franta. "I will not leave you in the lurch."

"At worst, you will get a suspended sentence," said

Ota.

"Do you have a clean rap sheet?" Franta asked.

"You bet he does," said Ota. "As your superior, I will swear under oath that you have an unblemished character and a reputation for impeccable conduct."

Apart from nodding every now and then, I kept silent. Ota and Franta had three beers while I was still sipping my first glass. I was afraid to finish it. I could not appear at the Ministry with a beer smell on my breath. And I must have a sober mind because I would need a hearty dose of self-composure and logic to pass the cross-examination that was awaiting me. I thanked my buddies for their moral support, got up and left.

It was raining, lightly but tenaciously, typical Prague weather in autumn. I took shelter under the arch of an old tenement house on the corner of Spalena Street and National Avenue. I was bilious. The world seemed to me unbearable, my future an impasse. I must think about something cheering and pleasant, I decided; so I recalled that when I first came to Prague there had been a sign on that very house announcing YOU TOO CAN DANCE LIKE FRED ASTAIRE. It made me rejoice because on the dance floor I was a wooden-legged bear at best. Here might be my chance in life to improve. Ten lessons of half an hour twice a week cost five hundred crowns, a whole fortune: it represented my monthly allowance. My teacher was a girl called Anna. She had extraordinary patience with me. After a month she succeeded in teaching me the basics of a bunny-hug. Then the director of the dance school, Mrs Zahorska, asked to see me.

"Well, young man," she said, "I suggest that we make a gentlemen's agreement. I give you your money back and in return you will give me your word that you never, ever mention to anybody that you attended my school." Afterwards, Anna volunteered to give me private lessons in my one-room flat. It was a narrow corridor crammed with a bed, a small table, a chair and a washbasin. One could do a number of things in it, except dance.

The tram was half empty. I sat down at a misty window down which streamed rivulets of rain. The tram turned off Spalena Street into National Avenue. I looked up: the second floor of the tall building on my left was where the Higher Institute of Languages used to be, where I studied English, French and Russian, after having been expelled from university. In my class, besides me, there were twelve girls, for at that time language studies were exclusively a female occupation. I felt like a pasha in a harem. I remembered many wonderful nights. I would play a Frank Sinatra song to my female classmates who visited me under the pretext of studying together: *Just One of Those Things.*

Tuition was one thousand crowns a month, plus rent, food, clothing, tram tickets and pocket money, which required another five hundred. All together my language education cost a minimum of fifty thousand crowns a year. My father's wages as a woodcutter might have amounted to some fifteen hundred a month at most. This is why mother went out to work. In hindsight I gratefully appreciate what they had done for me without ever saying a word about it. But I have never figured out how they managed.

The tram stopped at the National Theater, the Golden Chapel, as people would call it. The impressive building was as black as a chimney from soot and exhaust gas pollution. It had an unwelcoming and grim look. I used to dream that one day I would enter through the side gate reserved for artists. "Goodbye theater," I whispered to myself, "farewell youth's ambition." But I felt no heartache and sorrow. Hanicka was right: I had become a down-to-earth realist. And what was wrong with it? Life is not yesterday, nor tomorrow. Life is here and now…

We crawled through the narrow streets of the Little Town. Prague Castle appeared on our left. I did not appreciate its postcard aspects. All my attention, as every time I passed by here, was attracted to the Old Castle Stairs. From the tram window I could see only the rampart and the wall. The stairs were hidden between them. There, the communist militia had beaten us with blackjacks. We were several thousands, all students, who wanted to go to the Castle, the residence of President Eduard Benes, to tell him not to yield to pressure from the Communist Party leader Klement Gottwald. The militia drove us down the stairs. A panic ensued. I can still see a girl next to me falling on her knees. I pulled her up and put my arm around her shoulders to protect her. Dana Wolf…she might be in America by now. If I ever get there, I shall try to look her up. And then the tram rattled me away from my past.

I got off at Dejvice Square and directed my steps toward the Ministry of National Defense, not far away. I shuffled like an old man. I was overwhelmed by a vision of what was bound to happen when I appeared before a court. The truth must come out during the proceedings that I was an imposter. I could see the prosecutor pointing his index finger at me and saying: "The accused has changed his name, covered up his bourgeois origin, suppressed his exclusion from the university, falsified his personal file, sneaked into the Party. But more than that he writes in the newspaper only about the seamy side of life in our country. He denigrates all our achievements, which is why he was disciplined several times and called to account. In short, he is an enemy of our Party and our socialist society." Once discovered, and I didn't see how could I avert it, I would have to join my father and fell trees in the forest. When I have served my time in the jug, of course.

When I announced myself as a visitor at the gate, a duty officer accompanied me to an empty office furnished only with a table and two chairs. The bare walls were painted green, and even the otherwise ubiquitous picture of the president was missing. All this depressed me. I was sure I was facing an interrogation. I waited maybe ten minutes. It seemed to me an eternity. At last, the door opened and a slim officer entered. He extended his hand to me and said in English:

"I am Major Zapletal. Glad to meet you. Please sit down."

I was perplexed hearing him addressing me in English. But it immediately flashed through my mind that he was a counterintelligence officer and that Franta was right: I am being suspected of collaboration with a foreign espionage agency.

"Sir, if I am here because of my service card, I would like to assure you right away that it was lost or stolen. It's as simple as that."

Now it was the major's turn to be confused. He switched into Czech:

"I don't know what you are talking about. This doesn't concern some damned lost papers. Were you not told why we asked you to come?"

Then he added in English again: "This is about your possible assignment to Korea, and you are here to undergo a language test. Sit down, please, and relax."

I almost collapsed in the chair with relief. An immense burden fell from me. No interrogation, but just a stupid language test! My fear changed to euphoria. I felt like embracing the Major and kissing him on both cheeks. It was hard to contain myself. Just a simple, bloody language test!

The Major began to interview me. He asked about my family background, the schools I attended, my past and present occupations. Then we discussed the result of the autumn football league, and a British film, *Great Expectations*, showing at the time in Prague theaters. After this hodgepodge conversation the Major said:

"Now, I want you take some short dictation."

He took a recent edition of the London *Times* out of his briefcase and handed me a sheet of clean paper.

"Do you have a pen?"

"Sure, that's my working tool."

The Major opened the newspaper on the editorial page and dictated three or four paragraphs of a commentary. Then he took the sheet of paper with my handwriting and started to read the text aloud. When he ended, he nodded approvingly and said:

"That should do. Wait here for me a moment, I'll be right back."

"Could I have a glance at *The Times*, meanwhile, to see what's in it?" I asked. "I haven't seen it for ages."

The Major handed me the newspaper and left. The last time I read *The Times* was before the Communist takeover in 1948 when I regularly used to visit the British Council in Prague. I had no access to the foreign press in the Czechoslovak News Agency, and at *Obrana Lidu* we received only two American weeklies, *Time* and *Newsweek*, which I could borrow only with the approval of the Editor-in-Chief. I had just skimmed through *The Times* when the major returned.

"Come with me, I shall introduce you to Colonel Skopal who wants to have a word with you about Korea and your assignment there in the Neutral Nations Supervisory Commission," he said. "And give me the paper, please."

He took me to an office on the second floor. Inside, sitting behind a large brown desk, was a hefty, gray-haired man in a blue aviation uniform. Three rows of colored ribbons on his jacket told me that I had before me a unique specimen, a flier who fought in the British Air Force during the Second World War, and who miraculously had survived the purges in the army. Skipping all preliminaries he fired a question at me:

"What do you know about the Neutral Nations Supervisory Commission in Korea?"

"Not very much," I admitted. "I only know that it was set up after the war…"

"It was established by the Armistice Agreement," the colonel interrupted me because he guessed, rightly, that I knew practically nothing. "This agreement was signed on the twenty-seventh of July nineteen fifty-three. It stipulates that the Neutral Nations Supervisory Commission will be composed of Sweden and Switzerland for the American and South Korean side, and of Poland and Czechoslovakia for the Chinese and North Korean side. Its mission is to see to it that neither of the warring sides increases its armed forces, tanks, airplanes, ammunition and other war material beyond the level that existed at the signing of the agreement. Both sides, however, have the right to rotate units and replace destroyed or used up war material under the supervision of the Commission. This task is assigned to its inspection teams in the major ports of entry on the border, a sort of checkpoint through which the two sides are allowed to carry out rotation and replacement. The inspection teams should report their observations and findings to the headquarters of the Commission in Panmunjom."

"Pardon me my lack of education, but where is Panmunjom?"

"It's a conference area in the Demilitarized Zone on the 38th parallel dividing Korea into two, a place for regular meetings of the Supervisory Commission as well as the Military Armistice Commission. These bodies meet as may be necessary but at least once a week…"

"Sorry, you are losing me again," I interrupted. "What is the Military Armistice Commission?"

"It is composed of ten senior officers, five of whom are delegated by the American and South Korean side, and the other five by the Chinese and North Korean side. These military representatives discuss and deal with the reports of inspection teams of the Supervisory Commission. In certain cases they are empowered to request additional investigation and controls. In short, the Military Commission is the top watchdog," smiled Skopal.

"Where are those ports of entry you mentioned?" I asked, not so much out of interest but rather because of malicious anticipation that he would not be able to give me an exact answer. I was right.

"Hmm," said the Colonel thoughtfully. "Offhand I would not know…At the beginning there were ten ports of entry, five in the North and five in the South. Later on the Military Commission decided to reduce their number to three in each part of the country, altogether six. I would need to consult reports from Panmunjom to see which of them are still open. Further questions?"

"How do the inspection teams learn about the movements of units and material through the ports of entry?"

"Each side must submit documents reporting and listing such movements well in advance. The teams check and verify the information on the spot."

"And what if one side cheats and fails to report a movement?"

"The teams have the right to carry out unannounced inspections at any time, day or night...You know what, I can lend you a copy of the Armistice Agreement for you to study at leisure at home."

I left his offer without a reply in the hope that he would forget it because I disliked the idea that I would have to read a dull document full of diplomatic and legal loopholes.

"I would like to know," I added in an attempt to divert the discussion, "how come that the Ministry of Defense takes care of the Czech delegation to the Supervisory Commission? Why not the Ministry of Foreign Affairs?"

"In fact it falls under the competence of both ministries. We support it not only materially and financially but also as regards personnel. We provide officers for the inspection teams and soldiers for technical services such as radio operators, mechanics, medics and even cooks. We now have seventy-two men in Panmunjom. The Ministry of Foreign Affairs appoints the Chief of the delegation and some diplomats for secretarial services."

"I am not an officer, I was a mere sergeant," I said. "What would I do there?"

"Major Zapletal says that your English is excellent. We would need you as an interpreter at first and later on as an inspection commander. Which is why we would confer on you the rank of Captain."

The colonel paused, expecting astonishment or joy. But getting neither, he continued: "You will receive the same salary that you have at *Obrana Lidu*. It will be deposited into a bank account in your name. In Korea, you will have board and lodging for free, of course, and when serving on inspection teams you will receive a per diem in US dollars or Chinese yuans. Moreover, your time in Korea will be counted as an extraordinary

143

military assignment, which means that you will no longer be called up for any regular training for reservists in future. We are putting together a group that should leave at the end of the year, after Christmas. I would like to make up your mind soonest."

"Preferably by yesterday, right?"

"No. Tomorrow will do."

"I must think it over."

"Sure. Maybe we shall work together."

"Where?"

"In Panmunjom. I am supposed to become the Deputy Chief Delegate, but only as from next June. Call me up tomorrow."

He accompanied me to the door and shook my hand. His grip was strong and firm.

Outside of the ministry building it still was drizzling. The drops of rain on my face cooled me off. I still failed to grasp fully what had happened to me. I felt an immense relief mixed with a joy of being alive as if I had just escaped mortal danger. I leaned against the wall of the ministry and began, in a fit of hysterics, to laugh aloud.

An elderly man passing by looked at me, stopped for a while, and rolled his eyes. He must have thought I was drunk or crazy.

IN THE UNITED STATES THE KOREAN WAR is almost forgotten...It somehow disappeared from memory after the Vietnamese war. But it should not be forgotten. So much blood was spilled during this conflict, especially of civilians. Their total number cannot be established fully but historians tend to agree there were roughly three million. In fact it should be known as the Korean bloodbath.

The statistics about military losses differ depending on the source. According to Western data the Chinese lost 900,000 men. The Chinese People's Army reports 144,000 killed and 220,000 wounded. The North Korean losses are still top secret. No number was ever revealed, but it must have been worse than the South Korean losses, given as 228,000 dead, and 720,000 wounded or missing, and these are, most likely, a gross underestimation. The price US soldiers paid in Korea was comparable to that in Vietnam, where there were 47,364 killed in action and 21,741 wounded, missing or captured. However, the attrition rate was even higher given the Korean War lasted only from 1950 to 1953, while the US was in Vietnam from 1964 to 1973.

Civilian inhabitants were deliberately massacred following General McArthur's order that the Air Force should obliterate, by all available means, every town and village south of the river Yalu between the Chinese border and the fighting front. Daily bombardment, particularly by napalm, led to the death of at least 250,000 North Koreans. Official American sources show that, under the orders of General Matthew Ridgway, during just one raid more than 697 tons of bomb material, including 10,000 liters of napalm, hit the capital city of Pyongyang, killing some 8,000 civilians. The Commander of the 35th Infantry Division, Major-General William B. Kean, issued an order to his troops that "all civilians should be considered as enemy." The records show at least forty cases in which tens and even hundreds of fleeing women, children and old people were shot dead by machine guns on the pretext that there might be enemy soldiers among them.

The North Koreans and the Chinese also committed crimes against humanity as well as war crimes. Senator Charles E. Potter assembled the evidence in a report to the American Senate proving that the North Koreans and Chinese violated almost all terms of the Geneva agreement regarding prisoners of war. It states that almost two thirds of US servicemen died as a result of cruel and inhumane conditions in the POW camps (though there were remarkably very few—a sign of the viciousness of the conflict). Moreover, the two hundred page report listed 34,459 war crimes committed against the civilian population, causing the death of uncounted millions of innocent people.

The unlucky, ill-fated, battle-scared Land of Morning Calm was flattened twice by the steamroller of war! From its 38th parallel to its southernmost tip. Then up again to the river Yalu in the north, and back to where the conflict started. The open wounds were still evident everywhere when I arrived.

A TICKING TIME BOMB

Our camp was on a little rise. Below stretched unfarmed rice paddies in the direction of the Peace Pagoda and behind it up to the conference area of Panmunjom. The paddies were unfarmed since they were located in the Demilitarized Zone and full of booby-trapped mines. Our living quarters and offices were low one-storied buildings made of wood. They were well insulated to keep us warm even when the outside temperature dropped to minus twenty Celsius. In summer, when the thermometer rose to more than thirty degrees, they became as hot as a poker. We opened all the windows and doors but there was no relief: the air was stiflingly motionless. But we enjoyed also a great number of beautiful, pleasant days, especially in the spring, early summer and autumn.

Major General Odrich Chyle, the Chief of the Czech delegation, lived in a bungalow on the top of the rise.

He was a professional diplomat and the military rank was a courtesy, like mine. In contrast to the poor and spartan quarters in which we lived, his bungalow was furnished with carpets, upholstered easy chairs and couches. It had a real bathroom, while we had collective showers and washbasins.

To the left of the bungalow entrance stood a pole with a Czechoslovak flag which most of the time did not fly proudly but hung droopily, faded by the sun and rain.

A sand-covered pathway led down from the bungalow towards our living quarters and a mess. On the right stood a building in which there worked and lived not only the Deputy Chief of the delegation, but also a cipher cum intelligence officer, the commander of the signal unit, and our quartermaster. My office and my den, composed of a small living room and a bedroom, were located in the building on the left. Adjoining it were two office rooms for my secretarial staff officers whose job was to handle business in the Panmunjom conference area. The other part of the building contained a large meeting room that also served as a dining room for diplomatic receptions, staff meetings and film screenings.

I had a powerful army radio receiver in my living room to keep in touch with the outside world. I could tune in to BBC London or the shortwave newscast from Moscow. But mainly I listened to the Korean Forces Network, a radio station produced by the American Army. Night and day it broadcast news and jazz and country music.

Down below was a long barrack building that housed the living quarters of the other members of the delegation, including a doctor, interpreters, radio operators and administrative staff. Next to it was our mess hall, a barber's shop and rooms for auxiliary services carried out by Korean soldiers.

Our military commander and Deputy Chief of delegation, Colonel Skopal, tried his best to maintain an army schedule. He woke us at seven every morning with loud military marching music from a loudspeaker at the center of the camp. Limbering-up exercises were voluntary. Breakfast was served at half past seven, and work began at eight. We had a lunch break from twelve to two. The afternoon's work finished at half past five. Dinner was served at seven, then we had free time until lights out at eleven. Skopal was a gentleman who never checked who went to bed at what time. After all, there was no place to go. We could not leave the camp since it was hermetically sealed by Korean soldiers night and day.

From my office window I had a view of barren rice fields stretching out toward the conference area on the 38th parallel that entered into history unpredictably by chance. After Nagasaki and Hiroshima had been annihilated by atomic bombs Japan surrendered on 15th August 1945. At that time the Soviet Army had crossed the river Yalu and advanced rapidly southward. Nothing could stop it from liberating the whole Korean peninsula from thirty-five year long Japanese occupation because American forces were still tied up in the Pacific theatre. Strategy planners in the Pentagon frantically sought what to do to counter the Soviet threat. Colonel Dean Rusk, who later on became Secretary of State, had a brilliant idea: to divide the country into two spheres of influence separated by the 38th parallel. To everybody's surprise Moscow agreed. The first American forces landed in Korea only in early September.

On the wooden wall above my desk hung a map of Korea. I drew a line in red pencil on it along the 38th parallel. Six pins marked the six Ports of Entry under the control of the Supervisory Commission. Each of them had two small flags indicating which inspection teams were in action there. The Swiss, Swedish, Polish and Czech flags were approximate, but they gave us an overview of the inspection activity at a glance. The composition of inspection teams changed regularly to make sure that the representatives of the four neutral nations took their turn at each of the checkpoints. We were now teamed with the Swiss in Sinuji in the North, while the Poles were in Manpo with the Swedes and in Chongjin with the Swiss. We had a team, together with the Swedes, in Inchon in the South and another one working with the Swiss in Pusan, while the Poles and the Swedes were in Taegu. Next month the teams would play musical chairs according to a prearranged rotation plan.

A pile of reports from the inspection teams were on my desk. I was to analyze them and prepare a monthly summary for the next day's session of the Supervisory Commission in Panmunjom. I ploughed through them slowly and with difficulty because of my lack of sleep. Last night it had been so unbearably hot under the mosquito net that after midnight I got up and went to the showers outside, where I lay down under streaming water until dawn.

The door flew open and General Chyle came rushing in.

"Stay seated, Comrade Captain," he said, uselessly, since I had no intention of rising, let alone saluting him. "Are you done with the summary?"

"I have all reports from the South and now I am trying to put together all activities in the North. We had a communication hitch there and the report from Sinuji is still missing because of a radio failure that is being fixed now…"

"I know," the General cut me short. "How many inspections without prior notice have you received?"

"There were four in each Port of Entry," I said, consulting my notes, "which makes one control per week on average, and altogether twenty inspections without prior notice, not including Sinuji, of course. There were forty-eight inspections with advance notice, but again without..."

"Sinuji," the General filled in with some amusement. "When you come to drafting the conclusion I would like you to stress that the Czechoslovak delegation feels that it would be advisable to increase the number of inspections without prior notice...I have learned that the Swiss Delegate may submit this kind of proposal and I want to beat him to it. Draft me a short introductory statement to this effect."

"Certainly, Comrade General."

"Have you heard something of interest on the BBC newscast this morning?"

"Not much...except, perhaps, a commentary by Walter Lippmann. He is a most influential and reliable..."

"You need not to lecture me, Comrade Captain! I know very well who Lippmann is since I read him in the States long before you probably heard about him...What did he say?"

"It concerns the situation in Korea. According to the BBC, Lippmann wrote in yesterday's *New York Times* that...wait a minute, I took a couple of notes," I said, searching for a sheet of paper. "Here it is...Lipmann says in conclusion this: the truce in Korea created a volatile and potentially explosive situation. The presence of inspectors of the Neutral Nations Supervisory Commission may help to defuse this ticking time bomb, provided that they carry out their mandate faithfully and objectively. If they fail in their mission they will also be responsible for the explosion."

"This is excellent, to the point and exact!" exclaimed the General. "It comes just in time. Put this quote into the opening paragraph of my statement."

"I am not sure I took it down verbatim…"

"It does not matter. Just paraphrase it."

The General made several other observations regarding the monthly summary. I listened but I did not hear him because I thought hard about the advice he once gave me, namely that a good diplomat sets a clear goal for each encounter and prepares a scenario of how to achieve it. He must think through how to direct the discussion towards the subject of his interest, what he can say, what he must hide, and eventually what false information he wants to seed. My goal was absolutely clear: to con the General into sending me on an inspection mission, preferably to the South.

"I have yet another important piece of information," I said gravely, to get his attention. "During his recent visit to Seoul, American Secretary of State John Foster Dulles spoke with President Syngman Rhee about the possible withdrawal of our inspection teams from the South. Reportedly, they concurred that it could take place within a six-month period. I received the tip from my Swiss counterpart, Captain Hagenbuchler. He read it in a commentary in Tokyo *Asahi News,* written by their diplomatic correspondent in Seoul, who cited an undisclosed source from within the President's cabinet."

"Well, that we are a pain in their ass is old hat," said the General. "You know what Stalin used to say? If the enemy lauds you, it means you are doing something wrong. No one commends us, not even our side, so I think that we must be doing something right. But it is an interesting piece of information anyway…Dulles was in Seoul last Friday, how come that it makes news only now?

"According to Hagenbuchler, it was leaked on purpose," I said. "*Asahi News* was chosen among all other papers because it appears in English and is a source for international news agencies. Syngman Rhee tries to manipulate public opinion."

"You're shooting from the hip," said the General.

"I beg to disagree. From what I hear on the English language broadcast from Seoul and Tokyo there is a concerted campaign against us, red spies as we are branded, that is louder and more aggressive every day." I tried to press my point.

"I would like to read it to make my own opinion," said the General. " Could you arrange it?"

"No problem," I said obligingly. "I'll ask my Swiss colleague to lend me the paper. I can do it this afternoon as soon as I finish the monthly summary." When the General nodded, I added hastily: "Since our inspection activities will be terminated sooner rather than later, I would very much like to go to a Port of Entry for the last time before we are chased out. Lieutenant Krejca could stand in here while I am away."

The General looked somewhere beyond me for a while. Then he made about face and started for the door.

On the threshold he stopped and turned back. "I will think about it," he said. "By the way, you shall go to a Korean dinner tonight at seven to replace Colonel Skopal, who is down with the flu."

I wanted to object as I had attended a Chinese dinner the day before, and two others last week, and that I was sick of social events, but I swallowed all resistance because I realized that I should not antagonize the General if I wanted him to do me a favor. I rose and stood to attention. "Yes, sir!" I said.

IN THE FRONTLINE

I was waiting in front of my office for a jeep to take me to Panmunjom. I wore a pair of grey trousers - my parade uniform - that were lighter than the green fatigues, an army shirt with soft brassards, an officer's cap and oval McArthur sunglasses. It was four o'clock in the afternoon but the sun beat down mercilessly like at high noon. The thermometer must have shown at least 30 degrees. It was mid-July, and the rainy season ended two days ago. Forty days and nights of downpours. The earth was still soaked with water and steaming. It felt like being in a sauna. In a short while the shirt got stuck to my back. In January we experienced minus 30 degrees and shivered in heavy winter coats and Russian fur caps. Korea has extreme climate. The most pleasant days are in October. They are best described by a folk-saying: *The sky is high and horses get fat*. Before the war it used to be a month of popular harvest festivals called 'chasok.' No longer. Even *joie de vivre* became a victim of war.

There was a short ramp with a dozen steps leading to a driveway. I went down slowly because every rapid movement required a great effort and a lot of sweat. An old Willys arrived and its brakes squealed as the war trophy car stopped. A bodyguard in green uniform jumped out and put down the front folding seat so that I could climb onto a bench in the back. I would have preferred to sit next to the driver but this was forbidden. I knew that should I break the regulation, the guard would be held responsible and severely punished.

Two soldiers with automatic weapons, the omnipresent Kalashnikovs, guarded the entry to our camp. One of them lifted a wooden bar and we drove out. After one hundred meters we hit a dusty road, we made a sharp left turn in the direction of the conference area. We were right in the middle of the Demilitarized Zone, a no-man's land, which cuts through the Korean peninsula along the 38th parallel: it is two hundred and forty-eight kilometers long and four kilometers wide and represents the most dangerous frontier in the world. On the northern side stands an army of one million two hundred thousand battle-ready North Koreans, while on its southern side are eight hundred thousand South Korean soldiers and fifty thousand American GIs, also armed to the teeth and ready to fight. The two Koreas are technically still in a state of war.

We arrived at a little river that is half-dry most of the year. As the tires of the jeep hit the rollway of a wooden bridge I recalled that it was here where a massive exchange of prisoners of war, called Operation Switch, took place from April to September 1953. During that period this narrow bridge was a road to freedom for eighty-nine thousand four hundred and ninety-three North Korean and Chinese prisoners, as well as for thirteen thousand four hundred and forty-four South Koreans and Americans who returned from captivity. Repatriation of prisoners was the thorniest issue discussed at the Armistice negotiations in Panmunjom and constituted the main reason why it took two long years to reach an agreement. On approaching the bridge most of the North Korean and Chinese soldiers tore off the clothing and underwear they had received in captivity and threw it all into the river. They wanted to show their patriotism and disdain of the enemy. The bridge still carries the name The Bridge Of No Return because whoever crossed it at that time could not come back.

Right behind the bridge was the conference area, an

eight hundred meter wide, oblong enclave, guarded jointly by the North Korean and South Korean armies. It is often referred to as Armistice Village. In fact, there used to be here a small rural settlement named Panmunjom that was razed during the war. Instead of thatched-roof huts there were six long, box-like buildings covered with corrugated iron. They were US army barracks, originally green but repainted in blue, the color of the United Nations. It was here where the Armistice marathon talks took place in 1951–53. Now we shared the buildings with the Military Armistice Commission. Our secretariat was located in the first two and the third one was our meeting room. In its center was a large round table with seats reserved for Heads of the four Neutral Nations Commission delegations, their Alternates and Secretaries. The other buildings belonged to the Military Armistice Commission. In its meeting room there was a long table positioned in such a way that the 38th parallel ran down the middle of the desktop. American and South Korean officers sat on the southern side of the table and North Korean and Chinese officers on the northern side. So they were face to face while verbally aggressing each other by accusations of violations of the Armistice Agreement.

In our secretariat I found only Lieutenant Petr Krejca, and even he was about to leave.

"Hi, Peter, are you on strike? You should be at work until five," I said, looking around. There were four desks in the room. Each of them had a little national flag of one of the neutral states. "Where is everybody?"

"Well, we had a nasty, hectic day. So the guys beat it earlier," said Krejca. "What brings you here, Honza?"

"I need to make a call to the Swiss camp."

"No problem. Who do you want to speak with?" he asked on his way to the Swiss desk in the corner of the room.

"Captain Hagenbuchler."

"That little bastard? Why?"

I told Krejca briefly the purpose of my visit. He lifted the receiver of a Swiss Army telephone on the desk and turned its handle three times. Then he handed me the receiver and said, "Here you go."

"Captain Vitek from the Czechoslovak delegation," I presented myself to the telephone operator. "I would like to speak to Captain Hagenbuchler, please."

The Swiss came on in a jiffy.

"I am so glad you call, it's a pleasure to speak with you," he said in his usual polite manner. "What can I do for you?"

"I told our general about the commentary in *Asahi News* you mentioned to me, and he would appreciate it if you would be so kind as to lend us the paper. He would like to read it."

"Of course, with great pleasure! I am going to send somebody to bring the paper to you immediately."

"I'll return it without delay."

"There is no hurry. You can give it to me on Thursday when our Commission meets for its weekly session. Please give my compliments to your general."

When we had exchanged routine pleasantries, I hung up.

"I know that Hagenbuchler is a nitpicker par excellence, but you have to hand it to him, he is well-polished and respectful."

"Bullshit! You should have seen him this morning," said Krejca. "He rushed into the secretariat like a wounded tiger and raged and roared for half an hour, screaming that we are a bunch of incompetent lazy-bones who should be fired on the spot. Then he threw copies of minutes and reports on the floor that we had mimeographed for the Military Commission meeting tomorrow, and that we submitted for his approval because he is our boss this week. 'You are a disgrace on the good reputation of this international body,' he screamed, because some of the pages of the copies we made had ink stains...you know what our mimeograph machine does, it is a miracle of miracles to do a decent copy....But explain it to that little bastard! He said we should try to copy it again and again until we do a perfect job. When we had a third go at it this afternoon the other guys said to hell with Hagenbuchler, enough is enough, and they disappeared."

"What about the copies?"

"We sent them to his office, hoping he will get a heart attack when he looks at our work."

While Krejca was pouring out his frustration I looked at a strange little flag that stood next to the Swiss national flag. It had the form of a rectangle divided crosswise into four uneven triangles in different colors.

"Is this a cantonal flag?" I asked.

"No, it should be ours," said Krejca, "a symbolic flag of our Supervisory Commission reflecting the colors of our national flags. Red on the top represents Switzerland, white on the left Poland, yellow on the right Sweden, and white down below Czechoslovakia. The Swiss propose that this masterpiece should become our official flag."

"Fat chance," I said.

"Much greater stupidities happened," observed Krejca.

At the same time the door flew open, and a Swiss lieutenant entered. He directed his feet towards me holding a brown envelope and a sheet of paper. He handed me both.

"With Captain Hagenbuchler's compliments," he said. "Please sign here," he added, putting a finger on the sheet of paper.

That was vintage Hagenbuchler. I bet with myself that the brown envelope will be sealed. I won.

"By the way," I said to Krejca, "I asked the General to send me on an inspection mission, and I suggested that you could replace me as his sidekick."

"Fine by me," said Krejca. "Where will you be going?"

"My preference would be Inchon. I have not been there yet," I said. "More importantly, I would like to see the port in which McArthur landed with fresh forces in early September 1951. Having conquered the port he force-marched his troops across the peninsula to cut off supply and retreat routes to the North Korean Army, which laid siege to Pusan in the southernmost tip of Korea, defended only by the First Brigade of Marines."

"I have read somewhere that it was the bloodiest bloodbath of the war," said Krejca.

"Yes, for Kim's army. The threat of encirclement forced them to a headless flight north along the eastern coast. The North Koreans were bombarded by American planes all the way day and night. This was a turnaround in the war. In a few weeks McArthur stood on the bank of the river Yalu." I looked at my watch. "It's quarter past five, let's close the shop."

Outside the heat hit us hard and fast. For a while we breathed heavily opening our mouths like two carps on dry land. There was no relief in sight until late in the night, and even that was not for sure.

"Got a minute?" asked Krejca. Without waiting for my answer he added: "I want you to see a show that you will never forget. Let's go and hide over there behind a corner. It's better that they don't see us."

At the end of the building stood a South Korean sergeant with spread legs and hands behind his back in the American way. He was facing his North Korean opposite number, who stood upright to attention in the Soviet way. If looks could kill, both men would have been dead. The men changed every two hours, but the atmosphere of unquenched blood-thirstiness did not.

They stood only two meters apart, with the 38th parallel in between. If either of them overstepped this invisible line, it would be an aggression and *casus belli*.

All of a sudden, the South Korean pursed his lips and spat spittle right in front of the feet of the North Korean, who immediately sent spittle to just in front of the feet of the South Korean.

"They always miss their toe caps by an inch," observed Krejca. "My guess is they must undergo a special drill in spitting."

"As long as they don't start shooting, it's their problem", I said.

"Now they will rest a couple of minutes amassing saliva for an other performance," said Krejca. "Let's go home."

While driving over the Bridge of No Return it occurred to me that Lippmann was right: there was a time bomb ticking on the 38th parallel, a time bomb of implacable hate stoked by conflicting ideologies.

"Petr, has it ever crossed your mind that we'll be right in the frontline if something happens here?"

"Sure. But I am a fatalist. What will be will be. To be frank, I think that it will be our side to start again at daybreak...did you notice that wars usually begin at dawn?...And I hope that they will have the decency to evacuate us during the night so that we will be in safety."

"Are you kidding? Don't you realize that we shall be much more useful to them dead than alive?" I asked. "Can you imagine what political capital our corpses would represent for them? I can visualize the headlines:

Neutral nation's peacekeepers murdered by capitalist aggressors! First innocent victims of a criminal war! Their death will not go unpunished, our Dear Leader says!"

We spent the rest of the trip to the camp in contemplation and silence.

THE SECRET OF COLONEL WANG LI

The expression 'gambe' was a garble of the toast to your health in Chinese. On Tuesday, we had a 'gambe' at the Swedish camp. Yesterday at the Chinese HQ. On Friday at our camp. And so it went every week, month after month. Therefore, we would flip a coin to choose who goes and who stays. The losers put on their best uniform and kissed the next day goodbye, since it would be sacrificed to curing their hangover. No one called it a reception or a party, although this would have been a more suitable name for the dinners at the Swiss or Swedish camp, since there were far fewer bottoms-up toasts than in the Korean and Chinese HQs, where we had to participate in toast marathons.

"To our friendship, gambe!"

"To peace in the world, gambe!"

"To peaceful co-existence, gambe!"

"To the cooperation of our nations, gambe!"

The hosts laboriously searched for new reasons to raise glasses. On one occasion, a Korean major who considered it his patriotic duty to get me drunk, sat sullenly because he had run out of politically correct toasts, and then exclaimed: "To the health of your parents, gambe!"

"Both my parents are dead," I said to discourage him.

The major mulled it over. He was not a man to give up easily. Suddenly, his broad face beamed and in a

160

divine inspiration he said:

"To a happy meeting with your parents in heaven, gambe!"

The Koreans served their national poison, 'ginseng,' and the Chinese 'mao-tai.' We called it 'Mao Tse-Tung's revenge.' Both tasted like slop. On a number of occasions my attention attracted a Chinese Colonel, Wang Li, who made a lot of toasts and downed a lot of glasses of mao-tai and was never one bit tipsy. The Colonel was a short, very slim, frail-looking chap, but the way he tolerated alcohol intrigued me. Did he have a silver valve on his head to let out its vapors like the legendary Baron Munchausen? Or has he got five livers?

I decided to solve the mystery and began to cultivate him. Since he was a political officer we discussed social and economic developments in China, where a political relaxation was under way, inspired by Mao-Tse-Tung's slogan 'Let a thousand flowers bloom.' Indeed, new, unorthodox ideas did blossom all over the country and the press even carried some very critical remarks about the Party and government. I read about this political ferment in Hong Kong newspapers that I received courtesy of my Swiss colleagues. Wang Li often invited me to the Chinese camp and in addition to 'mao-tai' served up cuttings of articles that had recently appeared in Peking in English or Russian.

We befriended each other to the extent that I, at long last, ventured to pop the rather delicate question of how it was possible that he drank so much and stayed as sober as a judge. I had to swear to be as silent as the tomb and never breathe a word about it to anybody, not even in pillow talk, before he revealed his secret: you have before you a little glass of hard alcohol and a big glass with water. You make a toast, empty the little glass in your mouth, but you don't swallow its contents.

Then you take the big glass, pretending to drink water, while in fact you spit the alcohol in it. From time to time, when the big glass is full, you ask the waiter for fresh water. It's easy, so long as you are not an alcoholic.

There was no 'gambe' on Saturdays and Sundays, not for any religious reason but out of sheer pragmatism. Every weekend our Swiss and Swedish partners left their camps for rest and recreation, or as we used to say with envy, to 'get laid.' Those who watched their money drove in a jeep to Seoul. Apart from being near, its bars and girls were a bargain. Others, with money to burn, flew to Tokyo to be entertained by geishas whose rates were substantially higher. The Poles had two 'kubetas,' female warrant officers whom they guarded like national treasures. We played volleyball or football and watched for the umpteenth time an old film, *The Best Citizen*, starring a popular comic actor, Vlasta Burian. We knew it by heart. When I returned to Prague and guys asked me to tell them how Korean girls were in the horizontal position I had to admit my total ignorance—and how could I have known? On every outing, rare as they were, I was accompanied by a Korean bodyguard. Since the guys did not believe the truth and accused me of hypocrisy, I began to describe in some detail as personal experience what I had learned from my Swiss and Swedish friends about whorehouses in Seoul and geishas in Tokyo. As a result I exaggerated my sexual proficiency and gained the reputation of being a veteran philanderer.

The seating arrangements at a Korean 'gambe' were made in military fashion. There were seven round tables in the dining room. At the head of each of them a seat was assigned to a senior Korean officer as host. On his left sat a Polish representative, and on his right a Swedish one. Opposite the host sat a senior Chinese officer, who was flanked by a Swiss on his left and a Czech on his right. On that particular evening I sat next to Major Bertil Andersson with Colonel Wang Li on my left. Both were pleasant, enjoyable company. Bertil was a typical descendant of the Vikings with fair hair and blue eyes. When he smiled he reminded me of the famous Hollywood actor Richard Widmark. For a Swede he was a talkative man. He liked to listen to his own voice, and most of the stories I told to my friends in Prague about Korean and Japanese girls I heard from him.

We were twice together as commanders of inspection teams, first in Pusan in the South and then in Manpo in the North. Besides the two commanders, each team had a cipher officer and a radio operator. The teams would work a month in one place before rotating to another checkpoint. It meant that Bertil and I spent one hundred and twenty days and nights together, during which we emptied an untold number of bottles of aquavit and vodka.

At Pusan we were carried to the port in a helicopter, the windows of which were blackened to prevent potential spying. This mistrust made Bertil mad. He decided to hit back. When we monitored incoming or leaving American soldiers, Bertil stood on the ship ramp with a pocket counter, a small gadget resembling a watch. Each time a soldier passed by he raised his hand, pushed the button on the counter, and let his arm fall. It was as if he was counting cattle in a corral. Clearly, this provocative attitude was disliked by both the soldiers and the liaison officer who accompanied us. I hid my counter behind my back.

At Manpo we checked a military night train consisting of thirty wagons carrying infantry ammunition. The wagons were sealed, but we had them opened to make sure that they contained boxes of ammunition as declared in the transport documents. We randomly chose one wagon to inspect its contents. We opened one box and counted the wax-sealed cartons. We opened one of these and counted the number of shells. Bertil's eyes fell on a black letter inscription saying in Czech 'Made in Brno.'

"It looks like Soviet ammunition," he said tentatively.

"Do you think so?" I suspected that as a career officer in the Swedish army he would know something about the difference between Cyrillic and Latin script.

"Sure, Soviet ammo," decided Bertil. And he put that in the inspection report since that particular week he was the joint team commander, a role we alternated at weekly intervals.

While preparing for the Korean 'gambe' I ate a box of oily sardines and a big piece of lard to steel my stomach against the alcohol. Thus fortified, I turned towards Bertil and he turned toward me, so that we were facing each other, ready to perform our pre-gambe ritual. We slowly raised our glasses, held them to our left breast, then raised them to eye level, looking over the brim at each other.

"Skol," said Bertil.

"Skol," I echoed.

We drank the glasses bottoms up. We had a whole evening of fun before us. We were young, carefree, and the world was our oyster.

As I was leaving, when the 'gambe' ended towards midnight, a Korean liaison officer stopped me at the door. He told me he had found another old storyteller of folk fables and fairy tales for me. I collected at least three dozen, filling a thick notebook. But I never got down to transcribing them into a printable form. The notebook is god knows where, maybe lost forever, most likely destroyed. All I recall from memory is just one fable, which goes like this:

Once upon the time two young boys, Kim and Li, ran out of their native village into a forest on a hill. They stopped at a sunlit clearing, sat down facing each other, and laid a game board on the ground. They began to play Go, an Asian version of chess. It was an arduous battle of minds and Kim and Li were so absorbed in it that they lost completely all notion of time. When they finished, the sun, to their astonishment, was already setting. Slowly they got up and started to walk back to their village. The journey seemed extremely long and tiring, as they shuffled along, step by step. When at long last they arrived at their destination, they almost fell backwards in surprise. The village looked different and strange. They did not recognize a single house or face. Dogs barked at them as if they were foreigners. In the twilight of the dying day they looked at each other. Kim saw Li had a craggy face, furrowed forehead, thin, gray hair and a long white beard. Li noticed the same change in his friend. They were two old men staring at each other in utter disbelief, unable to understand what had happened to them.

Isn't life like a game of Go?

A NORTH KOREAN SHOW

The inspection that might have created an international incident took place at Sinuji, the main checkpoint on the Chinese–Korean border. General Chyle fulfilled my wish to send me on a mission as commander of an inspection team, but there was a hitch: he sent me to the

North and not to the South as I wanted. We arrived at Sinuji in a special train composed of two wagons. In the first there was a kitchenette, a little eating room, two cooks and six North Korean bodyguards. My radio operator, Sergeant Siska, and I travelled in the second wagon

My counterpart was Swiss captain Alex Schindler, nicknamed Mafioso, since he wore dark sunglasses all the time. He was an odd fish who spoke little and did not fraternize. Over the whole month we spent together he invited me to a drink only once, and that was after that bizarre inspection almost at the end of our stay in Sinuji.

Our activity consisted of two on the spot checks a week. We received an advance notice from the North Korean side that a train from China will arrive at a certain hour containing this many soldiers or this much military material, corresponding to rightful rotation as stipulated in the Armistice Agreement. The notice was handed over by the liaison officer to either Mafioso or me, depending on which of the two of us was the team commander that week. Then we announced that we wanted to inspect the train and asked for a convoy to take us to the railway station. Two jeeps were waiting in front of our quarters at the appointed hour. One was for the liaison officer and two bodyguards, the other for us. On arrival at the railway station, consisting of a couple of makeshift shelters and a dilapidating building, we found the train ready for inspection on a side track with wagon doors open. An armed soldier stood at each door. He handed us a list of the contents of the wagon he guarded. We climbed aboard and started counting and checking. When we were finished with the last wagon we signed a document to the effect that the train was inspected and found in order. Back in our quarters I wrote a short inspection report that

Sergeant Siska radioed through to Panmunjom. In addition to advance notices we also received a daily railway schedule. Out of it we chose haphazardly a train for an unannounced inspection. This means that without prior notice we went to verify whether a given freight train does not carry any military contraband, or a passenger train any unreported military personnel. Again, I wrote a short report for Panmunjom. And that was all.

One afternoon, after having a long siesta, I found on my desk the following message written in capital letters in broken English: NEVER MAKE INSPECTION OF TRAIN AT 23.30 TONIGHT CONTAINS CHINESE COMRADES!

The message was unsigned but I knew it was from our liaison officer, First Lieutenant Kim-Son-dju. My gut reaction was to tear it into pieces and throw it into the wastepaper basket, or better still, burn it. However, I immediately rejected this thought as a wave of rage got hold of me. Who does he think I am? His bus boy? That he can boss me around? That I jump when he whistles? Fuck him!

I saw red. I lost all self- control and rushed out of the office without coat or fur cap. It was late November and the thermometer showed some minus 15 degrees. A nasty wind was blowing from Manchuria and intensified the feeling of bitter cold. I began to run toward the Swiss quarters some two hundred meters away. Nonetheless I managed to think through what I would say and how.

When I stormed the Swiss quarters I found Mafioso and his radio operator in their office reading newspapers.

"Sit down," invited Captain Schindler. "Would you like a cup of tea or coffee?"

"No, thanks," I said. "I am sorry to parachute myself on you like this, but I have an urgent matter to take up with you." I made a dramatic pause, and then I started to spin my story. "I have received a highly confidential message from my general that our team has the worst record of inspections without prior notice. We carried just two of them, and there is only one week left until our departure. My general advises that we do something about it, and quickly. That, of course, is up to you to decide since you command the team this week."

"How nice of your general that he thinks of us," said Schindler with undisguised irony. "I do appreciate his concern. However, as you surely know, we have here in Sinuji a limited, winter railway traffic. Please, take a look at today's schedule," he continued, handing me a sheet of paper containing a report of train arrivals and departures he received from the liaison officer. "As you can see there are only three incoming trains today. One of them came in this morning, a freight train from China will arrive at 17.15 hours, and the last one is a passenger train, again from China, due to be here at 23.30 hours. But I am open to all suggestions. We can go and look at either of them. I invite you to choose to make your general happy."

It was an awkward situation. I needed him to choose the night train. And I needed it badly because it would be my alibi.

"We can flip a coin," I said. "It's all the same to me."

"What do you think, Franz?" asked Schindler of his radio operator, who just shrugged his shoulders and continued reading his *Neuer Zurcher Zeitung*.

We fell silent for a while. Schindler got up and started pacing the office. This, for some reason, unnerved me and boosted my tension. I could not endure the silence any longer. I was about to break it and make the desired proposal myself, when Schindler suddenly stood still and said:

"If it should be a surprise, we should inspect the night train. I am sure they will not expect that we come so late and that we brave such cold weather."

"That's a brilliant idea," I said.

"I'll tell them to provide transport as late as possible to catch them napping," said Shindler, warming to the idea. "Do you agree?"

"Absolutely!" I said. "Please call me as soon as you order the convoy."

"It won't be before half past eleven."

"OK by me. I'll be waiting."

It was a long afternoon and a far longer evening. I wiled away the time on my bed, trying to read a detective story. If somebody asked what was I reading I would have to say, like Hamlet: "Words, words, words."I put the book away and closed my eyes. To banish worrisome questions about potential consequences of the inspection we will carry out tonight, I attempted to focus on a mental picture of my secret hero General McArthur. I imagined him standing not far from here on a hillock, looking through the field glasses over the river Yalu, and waiting for a nod from president Harry Truman to conquer China. Instead, more than three hundred thousand Chinese soldiers attacked his forces on the first of November nineteen fifty, driving them back to the thirty-eights parallel...fade out...and I visualized him depressed, yet proud and pompous as ever, when in early April 1951 he was relieved of command because he wanted to stop a massive Chinese offensive by deploying an atomic bomb, which could have triggered off a nuclear war with China's ally the Soviet Union...fade out...and no other scene emerges since the mental escape gimmick broke down. Instantly, my mind became captive of an irrepressible fear of what would happen when we discovered a train full of Chinese soldiers being smuggled into Korea. Various scenarios, each of them ominous and dreadful, obsessed and frightened me. Only now did it dawn on me what I had done. What will the powerful Military Commission do when it takes cognizance of our report? This will be something the Americans and South Koreans have been waiting for: the reds caught red handed. They will jubilate. They will crucify the North Korean and Chinese because of grave violation of the Armistice Agreement. They will call for retaliation. How far will they go? Will they boycott the Military Commission for some time, or will they leave Panmunjom for good? Will they use our report as a pretext to declare the Armistice Agreement null and void? And what about me? Of course, I will defend myself tooth and nail that the culprit is Captain Schindler. He decided to inspect the train. He was the team commander. I had to obey. I couldn't do otherwise, could I? How will General Chyle react? Or rather, what will he do to me? Send me home by the first plane? Not so easily, because my deportation would become known to our western partners in the commission, who would accuse Chyle, publicly and privately, of punishing me for doing my duty. He would completely lose his face and credibility. He would show that he is not neutral, but tributary. So he will have to think thrice before he moves against me. Most likely, he will let me languish in the camp for a month or two, or until my case evaporates a little with the passage of time, and then, only then will he act. He will send me home with a confidential file that will mean the end of my journalistic career. More, I shall be blacklisted for life.

After dinner I played a card game with Siska to make sure that he stays in our office room and hears the telephone ringing. Siska did not speak nor understand English well, which was an advantage. He will not know what I shall say to Schindler. But he can testify that the Swiss called me up and that we spoke.

Schindler rang me up at half past ten sharp.

"I've just requested a convoy to the railway station," he said.

"How did the liaison officer react?" I asked.

"He was evidently taken aback and so perplexed that he stuttered," said Schindler. "To be frank, I did not think much about this inspection, but when the liaison officer began to shower me with all sorts of excuses, claiming that it was too late and that his men and drivers were already asleep, I got an impression that he does not want us to inspect the train. I found it fishy. So I gave him an order to provide cars and escort and I hung up."

"How is the weather?" I asked to prolong the call so that Siska would remember it.

"I don't know," said Schindler. "I have not stuck my nose outside yet."

"It must be very cold." I tried to keep the conversation going.

"That's for sure. Take warm underwear," smiled Schindler. "There's no hurry, the cars will come at eleven at t
he earliest."

I put down the receiver and exclaimed: "Fuck it. This Swiss geezer wants us to make an unannounced inspection at midnight!"

"But not me, I hope," pleaded Siska. "Or do you want me to come along?"

"No. Hit the sack," I said.

I indeed put on all the warm underwear that I could find, a thick woolen pullover and my winter uniform. There was an unfinished bottle of Chinese vodka on the dinner table. It occurred to me that I should take it with me. But I resisted the temptation, though not altogether. I poured myself a full glass and emptied it in two gulps. Then I completed my antifreeze outfit with a long warm overcoat, a muffler, a fur cap and a pair of thick army gloves. Once again I hesitated about the bottle of vodka. But I just had a hearty draught and put the bottle back on the table.

"When I return, I'll knock out a report," I told Siska. "You will send it to Panmunjom first thing in the morning. And don't dare to wake me up!"

"Roger," said Siska. "Have fun."

We were warming up and kicking our heels, yet we still felt like we were in an icebox. Two feeble follow spots from the headlamps of our Gazík illuminated part of the deserted platform. There was no electric light, like all over Korea after the war, where electricity was in short supply and outages commonplace. Nights in winter were pitch-dark because moon and stars hid behind clouds. We were some twenty meters from the station building but all we could see of it was a small yellow rectangle of a window behind which evidently shone a bulb. It certainly was minus twenty degrees, possibly more. There were occasional gusts of icy wind that tried to blow us away. I bitterly regretted that I left the bottle of vodka on the table.

North Korean bodyguards formed a clump and debated something noisily. First Lieutenant Kim-Son-dju stood alone at a distance. From time to time he looked in my direction but avoided any eye contact. He totally ignored me. I understood him, for I could imagine how he must feel and what inner torture he must be experiencing: he received orders to ensure that the night train pass unnoticed and he failed. Failure to carry out an order is punished in every army, and all the more severely in Kim's army. I could not help feeling pity for him.

"I think I hear something," said Schindler with a faint hope.

"I hear only Korean mumbo-jumbo," I said. "What time is it?"

"Eleven forty-two," said Schindler. He had a Swiss watch with a luminous face, which my Czech make lacked. "Such delay is not normal."

"You are not in Switzerland, Captain," I said. "Here a railway schedule is a wish list."

"I don't like it," growled Schindler. " I really don't like it. I am frozen like an icicle. We can't hang about here until dawn."

"Well, why don't you ask the liaison officer?" I suggested. "You command - give him an order."

"First Lieutenant! Come over here!" shouted Schindler.

Kim-Son-dju started toward us. He limped as a result of a war injury.

"I order you to find out immediately why the train is late and when it will arrive," Schindler told him. "There must be somebody in the station building," he added, pointing in the direction of the yellow rectangle in the dark. "Find out what's going on. And on the double!"

The Korean officer saluted, turned around and limped away.

I was beginning to suspect some foul play, or rather that a strange game was being played behind our back. But I kept it to myself.

"We'll see what the liaison officer will find out," I said after a while.

"He is already gone five minutes," said Schindler.

"Maybe he must telephone somebody, or send a telegram somewhere," I said vaguely.

Another five minutes passed before Kim-Son-dju appeared in the follow spots of Gazik's headlamps.

"Sir, the train is in Dandong. It cannot move. Something broke down on the locomotive. It will be here tomorrow. No exact time of arrival is yet known," reported the Korean officer. Dandong was a railway station on the other side of the river Yalu, not far from the frontier.

"And this you are telling us only now!" exploded Schindler. "You didn't know about it? Explain why!"

"I have failed to check the time of arrival before, sir. So sorry, sir. Please accept my humble apologies. It will not happen again. I fully assure you, sir."

It sounded like pre-learned phrases, or so it seemed to me. I grasped what must have happened. As soon as we asked for the convoy, the Koreans alerted the Chinese, who had ample time to hide the train on the other side of the frontier. Then the Koreans sent us cars and bodyguards as if everything was quite normal. They even let us freeze on the platform until we lost patience and sent the liaison officer to find out what's wrong. It was all just a well-managed show. It was also clear to me that once we leave the train with Chinese soldiers could clandestinely pass the frontier.

Captain Schindler's thoughts must have run a similar course. For some time he was silent as we drove back to our quarters. Then suddenly he said: "I fucked up."

"I don't see why," I said truthfully, not just to console him. "We did everything according to standard procedures. We did not make any mistake."

"It's all my fault," said Schindler. "I should have asked for the convoy at the last moment when the train was already on Korean soil, and not an hour earlier."

"If you had, it might not have changed much. I am afraid that they would have come up with another trick," I said.

"If you really think so, then please tell me, why are we here?" asked Schindler.

"To obstruct," I said.

"Whom? And what?" Schindler wanted to know.

"Both sides," I said. "Obstruct their rearmament."

"Don't be a fool," said Schindler. "You must know they are rearming anyway."

"Sure. But they must do it secretly bit by bit; they cannot do it openly and wholesale. That's a damn difference," I said. "If we did not obstruct them, their armies would be at full strength and equipped with the latest weaponry and technology. Most probably, they would already be at each other's throat because both sides are brainwashed by venomous propaganda and mutual hate."

"Do you really believe that?" asked Schindler.

"More or less," I said. "Anyway, I have not thought up anything better."

TOOTHLESS IN PANMUNJOM

It was the first of August. Our Swiss colleagues brought to the joint secretariat in Panmunjom a batch of champagne in magnum bottles, as well as sandwiches, peanuts, pieces of Swiss cheese, potato chips and other delicacies that they spread out on a round table in the conference room where the Supervisory Commission met every Thursday. Captain Hagenbuchler, my Swiss counterpart and *bête noir* during negotiations, gave a short speech and a toast. Thus for the first time I learned something about the Swiss Confederation and about the significance of the 1st of August for its citizens, who celebrate it as a national holiday.

175

Hagenbuchler was a lawyer by profession. His rank, like mine, was bestowed on him for the duration of his service in Korea. He had a freckled face, was as thin as a pole and his tongue was as sharp as that of a nagging mother-in-law. We took turns in chairing the secretariat at weekly intervals, a Swede followed by a Pole and a Swiss followed by a Czech. When Hagenbuchler was Chair everyone was fearful of his biting irony. His gray eyes spotted even the tiniest error or inconsistency in the documents we presented.

Today, however, he was a quite different man. He was very sociable, he joked and even took a sip of champagne, to my surprise.

"I hope you are enjoying the party," he said and smiled.

"Very much," I said. "Especially your champagne. It's a welcome change to our vodka and beer diet."

"I would like to have a chat with you," said Hagenbuchler. "Come with me, please."

We left the noisy secretariat and entered into the adjoining conference room. Hagenbuchler brought along a magnum of Veuve Clicquot and two glasses. He put them on the round conference table, at which we sat so many times opposite each other during the commission's meetings. After another toast to the Swiss national holiday Hagenbuchler said:

"You were in Pusan when the Military Commission suspended our inspection activities. I should be grateful to you if would tell me how did it go in there? I mean, how were you evacuated and what did you experience?"

"It was sudden and fast," I said. "I shall never forget it, nor the day when it happened, Wednesday 6th July 1956. We had arrived at the compound only two days earlier, on Monday, to replace a Polish team, and Swedes replaced your team, as you know. On Tuesday

Major Bertil Anderson and I carried out an inspection in the port without prior notice. Result zero, as usual. The next day the American liaison officer Lieutenant Brown asked me to come into his office. He had me standing there while he read out to me a declaration that the American and South Korean High Command abrogates forthwith compliance with paragraph thirteen letter D of the Armistice Agreement, in which the inspection mandate of our commission is anchored. 'You have two hours to prepare for evacuation,' he added. His arrogance exasperated me. So I said, 'You know, Lieutenant, we in the Czechoslovak Army are trained to scramble in five minutes. Which leaves us one hundred and fifteen minutes of free time to comply with your ultimatum. What about taking me to your PX? I would like to buy a Swiss Omega wristwatch as a souvenir.' Brazenness pays. They took me to the PX and I bought the watch. See for yourself." I rolled up the sleeve of my shirt to show him my new Omega Seamaster. "Our team, my alternate, radio operator and I, were transported to the airport at five in the afternoon," I continued. "There we were put into an army Dakota plane that landed in Seoul. On the airport we were paraded before a TV crew and a bunch of journalists with cameras. Then a 'copter with blackened windows took us to Panmunjom. End of story."

"Did they tell you why inspections were suspended?"

"The liaison officer said it was because the North Korean and Chinese side was introducing illegally soldiers and war material, and thus violating the cardinal provision of the Armistice Agreement stipulating that the number of men and weapons should remain the same as at the time of signing the truce."

"There is an important nuance," said Hagenbuchler, the lawyer. "The actual wording of the abrogation says

177

that inspection activities are suspended until the balance of armed forces and military material is restored. It means that our mandate *de jure* continues and that inspection activities may be resumed in the future."

"Well, meanwhile things happened," I said. "The North Koreans and Chinese have shed a couple of crocodile tears over the regretted inspections but they lost no time to chase out our teams as well. It's my guess that they did it with great relief. What do you think we'll be doing now?"

"We shall continue to carry out our mandate in Panmunjom," said Hagenbuchler. "We remain the watchdogs of the Armistice in Korea."

"Watchdogs maybe, but toothless," I said.

"That is not true. We still have an important job and mission," said Hagenbuchler.

"You still believe in Father Christmas?" I asked.

"No. But I reject primary pessimism," said Hagenbuchler. "I am an optimist by nature."

"Well, I do envy you," I said. "You know we have a joke about the difference between a pessimist and optimist...The pessimist says, the situation is bad, really very bad, it cannot be worse...Oh yes, it can, says the optimist."

Hagenbuchler's face became stony. His pronounced Adam's apple went up and down twice as if he was trying to swallow something. I grasped that it was not a good idea to tell a Czech joke in English to a Swiss. To make up, I raised my glass and said:

"I drink to your optimism, and I sincerely wish that the future will prove you right."

When we finished the bottle of Veuve Clicquot, Hagenbuchler invited me to go with him to the Swiss camp to see a Panmunjom first-night showing of an

American film entitled *High Society*. I had to report the visit by phone to our general and to the North Korean liaison officer. In the meantime, Hagenbuchler did the same on his side. On the demarcation line we were given two American MPs as guardian angels to accompany us to the Swiss camp, which was only about a kilometer away from the joint secretariat. The path there was muddy as a result of the rainy season.

The lead role in *High Society* was played Bing Crosby, together with Frank Sinatra and Louis 'Satchmo' Armstrong. I knew the lyrics and melodies of their hit songs from my youth when their faces peered out at me from the sleeves of their records, but I had never yet seen them onscreen. When Bing played a little accordion on board his sailing boat and sang the song *True Love* to Grace Kelly, I thought of the love of my life, for whom I still waited, and would surely meet somewhere someday. When Satchmo blew his magic trumpet and sang in his hoarse voice, *I found my thrill on Blueberry Hill*, I was so mesmerized and bewitched that I wished the film would never end.

And when it finished, I followed Hagenbuchler as in a trance. He led me to his living quarters, a low American army building with a concave roof. Two South Korean houseboys stood in attendance to serve us drinks and food, because Hagenbuchler wanted to show off the prestige he enjoyed because of his position and rank. We had shrimp on toast with a white wine whose label read *Fendant*, which I learned came from a place called Valais.

At one point the host remembered it was the national holiday, put a disc on the gramophone and played me the Swiss national anthem. I have never heard anything so melancholy and difficult to sing in my life. As I did not understand all the words in German, Hagenbuchler recited the first lines slowly in

179

French: "*Sous nos monts, quant le soleil annonce une brillant réveil et prédit un plus beau jour pour le retour, les beautés de la Patrie...*" It was a poetic hymn about the beauties of the motherland in comparison with which our *Where is my Home?* seemed like doggerel.

Hagenbuchler sang the remaining lines in his native dialect of Schweizerdeutsch, which is a somewhat deformed version of ancient German. Its sound reminded me of a recent occasion when the Chinese liaison officer approached me and wanted to know if I understood German. When I nodded, he said that they had recorded a message sent from the Swiss camp to Berne, and they would appreciate it if I would translate it. They played me the recording and I heard sounds resembling German, but I did not understand a word. Play it again, I asked. Zero. After the third try, I had to admit that I had not the slightest idea what it was about. I could just about guess the approximate meaning of every tenth word, but even that was not sure. The Chinese officer looked at me with suspicion. Most likely he thought I did not want to co-operate. And he was not wrong, which is why I was happy that it ended that way.

Hagenbuchler lost me after a couple of words in Schweizerdeutsch (which itself is pronounced Switzerttütsch). I listened to the rest out of sheer politeness. Then I raised my glass again—I did not know for how many times altogether—in yet another toast to the Swiss Confederation.

After midnight Hagenbuchler had the brilliant idea that we should exchange the jackets of our uniforms as a gesture of lasting friendship. Which we did, baptizing the newborn Czech–Swiss brotherhood with a successive number of toasts.

Brothers or not, however, Hagenbuchler could not

help challenging me. He just could not overcome his nagging nature.

"You are a Marxist," he said. "So I shall prove to you that spirit is stronger than matter." With that, he climbed on the table and stretched out his hand holding an empty glass. "Here we have matter," he said raising the glass above his head. "And here we have spirit vanquishing matter," he added and dropped the glass. It shattered into pieces on the floor.

I applauded dutifully, though I did not know what to think about that, or what Hagenbuchler meant. Neither did he, most likely. But none of this mattered; we felt closer to each other and were in heavenly harmony. I switched on automatic pilot and let myself be carried by it into yet another of those wonderful flights of weightlessness, lightheartedness and a devil may care mood.

Somehow I was delivered, courtesy of the American MPs and North Korean bodyguards, back to our camp. I had a short sleep. Then I got up, staggered under the shower, switching between hot and cold water several times. I tried a cigarette. It tasted like rotting hay. My mind was foggy. I did not remember much of what had happened last night. The only thing I could recall—and I still do—was that, supposedly, at the beginning of August 1291 the representatives of the cantons Uri, Schwyz and Unterwalden met on a small meadow and concluded a solemn pact that from thence forward they would join forces to repel all foreign enemies. It was some years before I learned this was a legend that was promulgated as fact only during the Second World War.

Having been summoned to a routine briefing the morning after the night in the Swiss camp, I stood in front of General Chyle like a boxer waking up from a knockout.

"*Guten Morgen, Herr Kapitän,*" said the General icily. "Are you in the wrong camp, or army, or both?" he added seeing my surprise and confusion.

Something dawned on me. I looked furtively at my right shoulder and then to the left. I saw epaulettes with two thin golden stripes. I was wearing Hagenbuchler's military jacket.

The Peace Pagoda, in which the truce was signed, stood in the middle of unfarmed rice paddies in the Demilitarized Zone halfway between our camp and the Secretariat of the Supervisory Commission in Panmunjom. On my way back from meetings I often asked my Korean driver to take a narrow road leading to the Pagoda. Inside, there was a long table and a couple of chairs. I sat down on one and imagined to myself tall, bulky General William K. Harrison walking to the table from one side, and small, slim General Nam Il from the other. Their subordinates hand them a paper to sign. They do so without saying a word. The historic act takes a minute. After that they leave without a salute or another gesture...

I would go to the Pagoda and sit for a while whenever I asked myself the question: What am I doing here?

VI. THAT'S HOW LIFELONG LOVE
BEGINS

I had a sneaking suspicion of being part of a fiasco. Maybe I had not explained my idea clearly and convincingly enough, to judge from the cool reaction of the man sitting behind the big desk in front of me. His face was as if cut from granite, expressionless. His gray eyes were like two round lenses of a microscope.

I was facing Karel Kalivoda, a police colonel, who from his large office in Bartolomejska Street in Prague commanded all the detectives, inspectors and interrogators in Czechoslovakia. Obviously, he did not fancy uniforms. He was dressed in a blue jacket, a white shirt and a dark tie. I had phoned him several days before to ask for an appointment, saying I would like to discuss a proposal of how to make the work of the criminal police better known among the public at large. That was why we were now sitting opposite each other. I decided that I needed to approach it from a different angle.

"All crimes, small or big, are never publicized and never appear in the press. They are taboo," I suggested. "However, criminal activity does not disappear from society if you keep mum about it. This is wishful thinking. The purpose of the series of true crime stories I would like to write is to end this ostrich policy. I want to show that we have a crime problem in this country, and that we have competent, efficient criminologists to fight it. Bluntly put, I want to kill the taboo. This is my first objective. The other is to make clear the difference between the criminal police, who protect citizens, and the State Secret Service, who defend the regime. Most people put you and the SSS in the same bag, which is not only wrong but also unfair."

I did not mince my words and put it to him bluntly, hoping against hope that I had before me an ordinary man, not a Party hack.

"It does not strike me as proper, or prudent, to indicate a marked difference between the two services," objected Kalivoda calmly. "It could create undesired problems and lead to jealousy......"

"Excuse me for interrupting you," I butted in, "but I do not want to differentiate between the two services or highlight the differences in their mission provocatively. I just want to report true crime stories and describe the ways and means your people use to solve them. It is as simple as this."

"Hmm, and what would you want from me?" asked Kalivoda after a brief reflection, causing my heart to jump with joy.

"Two things," I said in one breath. "I need access to criminal investigation files and to talk to the inspectors who cracked the cases concerned. I would like to kick off with some spectacular criminal, for instance the serial killer Mrazek."

Kalivoda shook his head and said:

"The bulk of our work by far is not murders, let alone serial killers. Most cases concern a variety of offences such a stealing of national property, robbery and fraud. For starters we could find you something from this kind of crime. Later on we could take on some capital crimes."

It sounded reasonable and I agreed. Before parting Kalivoda promised to call me up once he found the first case that was suitable for the opening of the true detective series.

Our discussion filled me with great expectations for the challenge of working on new subject matter and in a new genre. I badly needed a moral boost. Vinohrady Theater had rejected my play *The Isle of The Damned*.

It was a political play, as everything I wrote. Its message was a warning against accidental nuclear war between the USSR and USA. When the theater's dramatist invited me to discuss my magnum opus, I did not expect that he would embrace me as a new Shakespeare. Nonetheless, I went with a frail hope that he might give the piece a half-approving nod. The dramatist was a very charming man, considerate, he weighed every word on diplomatic scales, and gave me a lot of good advice—on how to rewrite the play from scratch. I worked on it during my stay in Panmunjom to while away time rather than out of inspiration. And it showed. I could see now that it was filled with clichés and paper heroes. It would have to be completely rethought and redone. However, here in Prague I did not have time or the motivation to embark on such a long haul. On top of that I was heavily pregnant with a collection of short stories about the civic courage of people who say what is what and whom no one can force to say what is not. I wanted to give birth to my new child as soon as possible.

The editorial offices of the daily *Obrana Lidu* were located in an ancient building dating back to the last century at Jugmannova Street 42, within walking distance of Wenceslas Square, and, more important, two hundred meters from our favorite pub, 'U Pinkasu.'

When I entered our quarters on the third floor it was filled with cheap cigarette smoke and the boisterous voices of Jiri Horsky, Ota Brozek and Frantisek Kejik. They were sitting at a low, square conference table, playing the popular card game 'Marias.' They must have been at it for some time, since the tobacco fumes were thick as fog.

"Take a chair and join us," Horsky invited me.

It was not necessary to repeat the invitation. In a

jiffy I was dealt excellent cards and announced I had a "big hand."

"First let's have a toast," said Ota. He fished out a bottle of vodka from under the table and poured each of us a full glass.

"Whose birthday?" I asked.

"Nobody's," said Horsky.

"So what are you celebrating, guys?"

"The sixth of October…The Day of the Army, stupid," explained Horsky. "Bottoms up!"

Almost all the editors of *Obrana Lidu* were career officers in the army. Ota and I were among the few exceptions. Since we were civilian employees, we counted as sort of second-raters. We received lower salaries and had no special perks, such as long vacations in army recreation centers for free, or, of course, uniforms. However, we liked things as they were, because we were not subject to army discipline, and did not have to jump to attention or salute when passing some higher-ranking blockhead.

I won my 'big hand,' a bit later a 'red one hundred,' and then 'two sevens.' In an hour I enriched myself by about thirty crowns.

The door opened and Major Gusta Hruby entered. He was a tall, handsome man wearing golden-framed round spectacles. It took him a while before he saw me through the fog. He approached me with a smile, lowered his head, and whispered in my ear in a conspiratorial voice so that the others could not understand a word.

"I have a date with Milena on Charles Square at seven o'clock. Milena will bring along her friend. With you we'll be four, and we'll go to the Pleban's and have a ball. I am inviting you all. I am loaded, I got a pay bonus today."

"So you are inviting me on a blind date?"

"And why not?"

"Do you realize the risk I'll be taking? What if Milena's friend is cockeyed, red-haired and bow-legged?"

"Don't worry. Milena wouldn't have a gorgon as a friend."

"That's what you are telling me. But what shall I do with some slowcoach? I am now on a winning streak, I don't want to go anywhere."

"Do as you please. But if you change your mind, give me a tinkle at my office. You can catch me there any time. I'll be sweating out an editorial for tomorrow's edition."

Gusta was a lady's man if there ever was one. He had a lot of charm and he knew how to use it. I remember one late evening in the hotel Europe in Pilsen when we were in a lift with an elegant woman in maybe her early forties. Gusta cast his spell on her, talking to her softly, and when we stopped at the second floor he remained in the lift with her. We saw him again in the morning at breakfast. It was the fastest pick-up I have ever witnessed. In the newspaper Major Gusta Hruby was responsible for the ideological education of our readers. He accomplished this task with nonchalant frivolity. That's perhaps why his editorials and Marxist analysis were almost digestible. He had to pay a hefty alimony for his two children, however, and therefore was moonlighting at another Prague newspaper as sports editor to earn more money.

My luck began to desert me because I was not focused on the game. I suffered a couple of heavy losses and decided I should quit before losing everything. So I picked up the phone, dialed Gusta's number and told him I was going to take a calculated risk with the blind date. But as soon as I put the receiver down I heard an inner voice warning me that I had made a grave mistake. It occurred to me that I should find somebody to replace me. Without hesitation I called up my friend Ivo Dostal, with whom I spent almost a year in Korea. I told him we were planning a marvelous evening at the Pleban's and that he was cordially invited to join us. Ivo said he was on his way to attend a reception at the Swedish embassy, but once it was over we could count on him. Ivo had dinner and cocktail parties as part of his job description since he worked as Chief of Protocol at the Foreign Ministry.

My concentration on the card game dropped to less than zero because I was searching in my memory for something that eluded me. Suddenly I had a chilling premonition that something fateful was awaiting me tonight.

"Count me out," I said throwing my cards on the table. "You guys robbed me of fifty crowns. I am broke and done with you."

"Unlucky in cards, lucky in love," said Ota.

"Don't you pull that one on me," I retorted, "I am not superstitious."

We walked leisurely; it was only half past six, no need to hurry. As we strolled toward the entrance of the park on Charles Square Gusta was telling me about a practical joke he and Major Vavra pulled off the day before. When the workers who were repairing the courtyard in front of our building finished their job and left their tools and overalls in a shed, the two majors changed their uniforms for the workers' outfits, took a pickaxe, a shovel, four poles and paper signs with the inscription 'Repair work in progress.' Thus equipped they set out at around midnight for the thoroughfare of Narodni Avenue. There, right in the middle of the road, they tore up cobblestones and dug out a large hole, surrounded it with the poles and the paper signs, and disappeared.

"The hole is still there and the avenue is congested," laughed Gusta.

"I don't see what's so funny," I said.

"Well, the funny thing is that no one did anything about the hole and no one complained about it," said Gusta. "People are just sheep."

"Right," I snarled. "But has it occurred to you where the roots of this herd behavior and sheepishness come from?"

"No. Why should it?"

"It's a systemic syndrome."

"Translation, please?"

"If people are so meek and compliant, it is because the oppressive system makes them behave like that."

"As Marx said: everything is intertwined with everything."

"You sure he said it?" I wondered, knowing that Gusta is far from shy in inventing a quote from a classic when he needs to drive a point home in his editorials.

"Pretty sure," smiled Gusta. "If not Marx, who else? Engels, maybe?"

We reached the end of the park. Across the street stood an ancient two-storied house with a peeling facade and an arched entrance with a wooden door in the middle.

"Milena shares a sub-let studio over there," said Gustav pointing to a window on the first floor.

A silky fog was descending from the cloudy October sky. I turned up the collar of my Montgomery coat and waited. Subdued light from a street lamp fell on the arched entrance, creating the impression of a stage scene. The street was padded with fallen leaves that glittered like old gold sprinkled with drops of blood. I had a strange feeling of unreality, as if I were in a dream world.

A squeak of the door awoke me and I saw two young girls coming out. One of them had brown hair and wore a green storm coat. When my eyes fell on the other girl lightning struck. In its blinding, burning flash I saw a sparkling firework of images…from the film *Golden Helmet* with Simone Signoret, but younger and frailer…from the fable *Princess Dandelion*…and more than that: a youthful dream of eternal love personified. It was a '*coup de foudre*' that happens to you once in a lifetime if you are lucky. I was totally overwhelmed, as groggy as a boxer after an uppercut. In my stupor I only faintly registered that the girls stopped, whispered a while, and began laughing as they walked towards us.

Their carefree, joyful laughter brought me back to reality. My god, you stupid jackass, this beautiful blond must be Milena. How could you, even if just for a split-second, imagine that she would not belong to Gusta. You can only dream about a girl like this! I was overpowered by helpless jealousy and anger. Why can't I be Gusta, at least once, just once in my life, and let it be now. But no, that will never happen. Luckily, I was foresighted enough to invite Ivo to join us. As soon as he comes I will take a powder. I stepped backwards into the shadow so that no one could see my disappointment and the gloom I could not suppress or hide.

Gusta opened his arms.

"Milena, my little darling," he said, embracing the dark-haired girl.

"Meet my best friend, Ruzenka," Milena introduced the blond beauty.

I was dumbstruck and speechless. I could not move. I was standing there like a man of marble cemented to the ground. Gusta had to push me forward.

"Vítek," I managed to mumble. "Jan Vitek."

I was mesmerized by the sight of this girl in a light pink coat: a filly, as we called teenaged cuties. How old is she? Seventeen? Damned young for an old fool like me. I decided, using my rights of seniority, that we should be on a first name basis from the start.

"You can call me Honza," I said, "everybody calls me Honza."

But that was the limit of my courage, for I did not dare to offer her my arm. I tried to adjust my bearish footpace to her tiny steps as we walked through the park.

"What do you study?" I asked after an awkward silence.

"I graduated more than a year ago."

"So what did you study?"

"Pharmacology at an institute in Brno. I now work as a laboratory assistant."

"Where, which pharmacy?"

"In Hloubetin, almost at the far end of Prague."

"How old are you?"

"Are you not too inquisitive?"

"You should not have a problem telling me your age, and you need not lie about it yet. So how old?"

"Twenty."

"Oh, that much!" My silent groan was not ironical though it might have looked like that. It was a sigh of realization of the age abyss that lay between us. I needed to change the subject, so I pointed to the old gray building we were just passing in Jugmannova Street.

"Here is where I work. This is our editorial office."

"Doing what exactly?"

"I am a wordsmith, I put words on a string," I said because I did not want to elaborate on what I write, to avoid giving the impression I was a blowhard. "One of these days, Ruzenka, you could come along with me on a reportage trip and you would see for yourself what I have to do for a living. We could go to Karlsbad or Pilsen, which are my favorite places."

"If this is an invitation, I have to decline it. On weekdays it's impossible because of my work. And weekends I spend with my parents in Moravia."

"Where in Moravia? In Brno?"

"No, but nearby, in a small village named Olbramovice."

"Do you have any brothers or sisters?"

"Yes, I have two sisters and a brother, Zdenek."

"Are they younger or older than you?"

"Marie and Zdenek are older and Emilka is younger."

"What's Zdenek doing for a living?"

"He works at a big tractor factory in Brno."

"And your sisters?"

"They are both teachers...Why haven't you asked about my parents since you are already vetting me like a personnel manager?"

"OK, so what's your parents' occupation?"

"Father was previously chairman of the people's committee at Olbramovice but he was dismissed because some big-shot in the county council did not appreciate that he defended the politically persecuted farmers. Now he is a traveling salesman. Mother is a teacher at the village kindergarten."

We were walking on Narodni Avenue past the hole Gusta and Vavra had dug out last night towards an intersection where we turned right. I glanced at the building on the corner and wanted to say: Look, Ruzenka, there was once The Institute of Modern Languages, my refuge when I was purged from the university because of my bourgeois origin and political unreliability. But I suppressed the temptation, because I realized that at that time she was only seven years old. She would have no idea of the purges and persecutions after the Communist takeover. Instead I asked:

"How come that you did not become a teacher also, like your sisters and your mother?"

"My father advised me to study at pharmacological school because he thought that working in a pharmacy is an easy, clean job. He did not know that it means standing on your feet the whole day and mixing gunk for long hours."

"So you don't like your job?"

"Well, I rather like it but it's very exhausting. But maybe I will get used to it."

"Do you go to the cinema? Which movies have you seen lately?"

"It was a French film…"

"*The Country I Come From* with Gilbert Becaud?"

"I think so…yes. He sang a nice song…"

"What books are you reading now?"

"Look, what's this all about? A cross-examination?"

"No way, but just a little depth probe by a curious journalist. Inquisitiveness is my professional malady."

The bar at the Pleban's was a hangout for underground artists, poets and writers who lived in a strange co-existence with Communist Party officials. For us, it was a launching pad from which we blasted off into orbit on our drinking nights. Therefore, we had a table reserved in a corner where we could enjoy at least some privacy despite the usual noisy crowd. The corner was sort of protected by a fake Chinese screen made of wooden sticks and paper which separated our table from the rest of the room. The headwaiter Frantisek struck a match to light the half-burned candle on the table, and asked if we wanted to drink wine. He offered us the standard choice: Ruland or Blue Portugal.

"We are celebrating the Day of The Army, so it will be vodka for Honza and me," decided Gusta. "This young lady will have Blue Portugal, if it is fine with you, Milena. And what's your pleasure, Ruzenka?"

"Mineral water, please."

"Come on, you will not sit here without alcohol," insisted Gusta.

"I want mineral water or juice," said Ruzenka.

They bickered with each other a while and I followed their duel of willpower with interest, betting to myself that the frail girl would have her way.

"Bring this young lady a bottle of mineral water and a glass of Ruland wine," ordered Gusta finally to cover up his defeat.

When toasting, Ruzenka put the glass of wine to her lips but did not take a sip. I was sitting opposite her and tried my best to hide that I was stealthily devouring her with disguised glances. She had a high, smooth forehead. The tips of her eyebrows were turned slightly upwards which gave her eyes a kittenish look. I was not sure of the color of her eyes, but in the twinkling candlelight they appeared greenish with tiny golden glitters. There was no make-up on her face, just a touch of rouge on her lips. Her teeth were dazzling white. She wore a light pink dress with a low oblong cut that emphasized her swan-neck and revealed her delicate collarbones. The only ornament on her neck and breast was alabaster skin. I felt an irresistible craving to put my head on her shoulder and to breathe the intoxicating sweet smell of her body. The table hid her slim figure and well-modeled legs but I had them enshrined in my memory from the first moment I saw her coming toward me in the park.

All was lost on me—words, jokes and laughter—and I was lost to the world. From time to time I registered a sentence, but its meaning eluded me. I experienced Ruzenka with my entire being, nothing else but her. Her shining eyes resembled two small kettles where childish confidence mixed with female mistrust, hesitancy with decisiveness, tenderness with toughness, joyfulness with authority, doubt with resolve. At times, her eyes became deep fountains that reflected the innocence of her soul and goodness of heart.

I was totally bewitched by her smile and spellbound by her eyes.

I realized that I had fallen in love with her, desperately, hopelessly, and forever. This shocked me profoundly.

Gusta was saying something to me, but I did not understand, I did not listen, I was not even there, I was in a trance.

"Are you bored?" Gusta's question finally woke me up.

"No, why should I be bored?"

"You are so silent, I don't recognize you."

"I was on another planet."

"Then come back to earth, please, and talk to us."

"I must go and call somebody," I declared. "I'll be right back."

With that I got up quickly and started walking towards the bar followed by three puzzled looks. I felt Ruzenka's eyes penetrating like a dagger under the left blade bone into my heart. It was silly, but that's what I felt.

On the left behind the bar there was a short and narrow corridor. A coin-operated telephone was fixed on the wall, but I passed it and walked to a door with the inscription GENTS in block letters and a figure of a little boy pissing in a pot for the benefit of those who could not, or were too drunk to, read. There were two urinals, a washbowl and a water closet, and a sour stench of piss and vomit. A mirror hung above the washbowl. When I looked into it I did not like what I saw: the strange face of a man on the threshold of middle age with chestnut-colored hair that once was abundant and curly, a deep furrow between the eyebrows, a big nose, fan-wise wrinkles around the bleached, once blue eyes (which after a couple of vodkas were becoming bloodshot). The bitter smile revealed teeth that were white a long time ago. No, I really did not like what I saw.

Then for a second I visualized the lovely, young and clean face of Ruzenka. I uttered a four-letter word. And swore again and again. This helped me to get a hold of myself. No, I will not become a laughing stock! Not me! We used to ridicule middle-aged men who dated fillies to show off, or rather to prove that they were still attractive and young. They paraded their trophies in theaters and bars, and were the joke of the town. Such romances always ended in disaster.

What's the age difference between us, how many years? Thirteen. My God!

I splashed my face with cold tap water and dried it with my handkerchief since I did not trust the scrap of moist cloth hanging on the wall as a towel.

When I returned to our table Frantisek was serving rounds of vodka. I told him to also bring me a glass of plain water.

"I have heard that you saved castaways on the high seas," said Gusta casually. I immediately grasped his intention to give me a chance to talk. When I did not take the bait he insisted by asking whether the story was true, although he must have known better, because I had written it up for our newspaper. "Why don't you tell us how it really happened?"

"That was more than a year ago," I said, getting mad at Gusta. Why is he forcing my hand? I hated to talk about myself because I did not want to create the impression that I was a clever Dick. "It really is history."

"I would like to hear it," said Milena.

"OK, but don't blame me if you're bored," I warned them, deciding that I'd shorten the narrative and make it plain, no frills. "Our ship's name was Dukla. She was a freighter of sixteen gross registered tons. Funny thing is that her homeport written on the bows was Prague. The Captain was Chinese, but all other officers and ship engineers were continental Czechs. Here I must explain that our national maritime company has twelve freighters owned jointly with the Chinese. This is sort of a fig leaf because if the ships flew a Chinese flag they wouldn't be permitted to use port facilities of the countries that do not recognize the Chinese People's Republic. And this is still the case for most countries."

I broke off, as I was not sure that I had succeeded in explaining complex ship company ownership, but since no one raised a question I continued.

"It was already the beginning of the stormy season but the strait between Borneo and Indonesia was relatively calm. I was standing behind the bar in the officers' mess and watching the forecastle going up and down to the rhythm of waves. I was sipping a glass of whisky following the captain's advice that the only tested way to prevent seasickness is to focus on the pitching so as to allow the stomach to anticipate the seesaw movements, and at the same time to steady it with whisky. So I was enjoying the cure when suddenly when the forecastle went down I caught a glance of a far away, tiny line like a hyphen. After a couple of ups and downs I distinguish something like two dots on that line. Then the dots become elongated and look like exclamation marks. Finally they grow into two figures waving a white cloth. I run to the bridge and cry: "Two

197

castaways ahead!"

The waiter interrupted me. He lit a new candle on the table and put in front of me a glass of plain water. Instantly, I drank half of it so that I'd be ready to employ the trick that I learned from Colonel Wang Li in Korea.

"This recipe against sea-sickness sounds great," said Gusta. "The question is—does it really work?"

"Marvelously! In the Indian Ocean we hit a storm lasting ten hours, with waves like a tenement house, maybe eight meters high. With every wave the ship swung upright as if she was about to capsize, but in the most critical moment she fell down with big thump into the maelstrom. I had to hang onto the bar counter like a crab with all my force otherwise I would have been a flying saucer, alternately hitting the ceiling with the top of my head and then the floor flat with my face. The whole crew got seasick. They were, pardon my expression, puking like crazy. The captain and I were the only upright men on board."

I noticed with satisfaction a faint smile from Ruzenka, although I tried hard not to look at her often, just throwing an occasional glance in her direction. Milena wanted to know what happened with the castaways. It was good that she asked me because I could turn towards her, look in her eyes and continue the story as if I were telling it just for her. This helped me to implement my tactic to lure Ruzenka: pretend that you pay no attention to her so as to attract her attention to you. That's what Stendhal counsels his hero in *Red and Black*, so I followed his tip.

"The captain ordered us to raise a flag signaling 'rescue operation under way.' When we got closer to the castaways he ordered the crew to put down a lifeboat. That was a task completely new to the crew, so there was chaos on board. The first lifeboat was wrecked. The men attacked another one while the ship circled around the two unfortunate sailors. Finally, after almost an hour, a second lifeboat reached the surface with four men aboard, all of them very well nourished, with more fat than muscles, and impressive beer paunches grown in Prague pubs. They began to paddle, encouraging themselves with shouts of 'hej rup, hej rup!' The sea was choppy but its waves seemed to represent an insurmountable obstacle to our four rescuers. There was quite some sea traffic in the Strait, and several other ships sailed by, but when their captains saw our flag 'rescue operation under way' they sounded their horns, saluting our effort, and continued their route. Our four men in the lifeboat did not give up; they sweated and strained their flabby muscles. It took them about two hours to reach the castaways, who were standing on a capsized junk. When at long last all of them climbed on board our ship, the rescuers were more exhausted and in a much poorer condition than the castaways."

"Who were the castaways?" asked Gusta. "Fishermen?"

"Well, we tried to communicate with them in English, Chinese and the captain even in Malaysian, but they clammed up and did not say a word. We took them to the nearest port, where the police were already waiting for them. As it turned out, they were smugglers transporting raw rubber from Malaysia to Australia. The captain made an entry in the ship's log that—and I quote—today, four men of our crew risked their lives to save two Malaysian citizens. The only sign of the risks our heroes endured were cracked blisters on their palms from paddling, which took several days to heal."

"How did you get on the ship?" Milena asked.

"Well, I climbed aboard on a companionway in Shanghai."

"What I want to know is what you were doing on the ship...apart from taking a cure against sea-sickness?"

"I was purser, which means ship treasurer."

"Don't tell me that they entrusted you with money," said Gusta.

"No way. That was a cover. I wanted to make a reportage trip around the world on a ship. From Shanghai to Haiphong in Vietnam, then to Singapore, Djakarta in Indonesia, across the Indian Ocean, through the Suez Canal to the Mediterranean and Gibraltar, onward to Rotterdam, Hamburg and Stettin in Poland as my final destination. Well, it was not really a trip around the globe, but almost. To be permitted to leave the ship and visit all the ports where we anchored, my passport would not do. That's why I had to have a Seafarer's Book. Since I was not an able-bodied seaman, I was enlisted as purser, but only on paper, of course, without pay or other allowances. I had to save my dollars while I was in South Korea to have some pocket money to buy a glass of beer in port pubs. But board and lodging on the ship I got free...well, to be straight with you, I had promised to write a couple of promotional articles about the glorious Czechoslovak Maritime Company."

"I don't know about you but I need a drink," said Gusta, who evidently thought I had talked too much and that it was time for him to take center stage. "Cheers! Bottoms up!"

We raised our glasses. While toasting I drowned in Ruzenka's eyes, and it was exactly at this very moment that I fully grasped the meaning of Nezval's line: 'Her beauty was beyond all belief.' And it occurred to me that such beauty could never fade away, that it would stay untouched by the passage of time, as we grew old together...Together? You are dreaming, wake up to reality!

I emptied my glass but I did not swallow the vodka and kept it in my mouth. Then I took the half-full glass of plain water, put it to my lips and spat the alcohol in it, just as the Chinese Colonel Wang Li had told me was his practice. I wanted to stay sober since I was all too well aware that this evening was unique and unrepeatable, and that I must not spoil it, nor waste it, which is why I had to keep my mind sharp and undimmed.

Milena inquired about Korea, why I went there and what I did there, but before I could open my mouth Ivo turned up. I realized that I had originally invited him to come as my stand-in and that, meanwhile, the situation had changed dramatically. What should I do about him? Ivo was evidently in high spirits already. He made a showy bow and introduced himself:

"The name is Dostal, Ivo for friends."

With his usual grace he kissed both girls on the cheek. Then he pulled an empty chair from a nearby table, put it next to Ruzenka and sat down as if he belonged to her. Ivo's taste in lovely women was his hallmark. I must neutralize him somehow, I decided.

"You are late," I said, "and merit a punishment. How many rounds did we have without him?"

"Four," said Gusta.

"Five," Ruzenka corrected him.

"I could not make it earlier," said Ivo. "After the Swedish reception two colleagues of mine stuck to me, so I had to shake them off first before coming here. I see your poison is not rum but vodka. What's the occasion?"

"The Day of the Army," Gusta informed him.

"Also a good occasion to get loaded," acknowledged Ivo. "The Swedes were serving aquavit. Vodka will be a good company."

I waved for the headwaiter, Frantisek.

"This gentleman would like to have five vodkas," I said pointing to Ivo.

When Frantisek put the five little cups in a row on the table, Ivo emptied one after the other in a manner that revealed great experience and determination. I immediately ordered another round. The more the better since I entertained a faint hope that alcohol would overpower Ivo and render him harmless.

"Let's have a toast our way," suggested Ivo.

We raised our cups, looked over the brim straight in each other's eyes for a second, and then put the cups to our hearts.

"*A nos amours*," said Ivo.

"*Quelles sont au four*," I completed the toast.

We drank the cups at one gulp.

"Nail check," said Ivo.

We both put the cups on our left thumbnail bottom up to show that there was not even one tear of vodka left in them.

Milena and Ruzenka followed our performance with a puzzled look.

"Pay no attention, forget it," said Gusta sneeringly. "The boys from Korea are showing off before you, they will grow out of it one day."

"What was the toast you made?" asked Milena. "To whom?"

"To our loves the devil took away," smiled Ivo.

"How many?"

"That, Milena, is a state secret."

Meanwhile the Pleban's was throbbing to a feverish late-night rhythm, its large room resembling a barn full of tobacco smoke, tinkling glasses. Somebody accompanied a party singing a popular song that soon was drowned by a hurricane of cries and explosions of boisterous laughter. I felt I was on the film set of an Italian neo-realistic film in which a lonely, sad man tries to make his way through a crowd brimming with a lust for life. Ivo was whispering something in Ruzenka's ear and she smiled and nodded. I had grossly underestimated the function of his liver. He took the drink like an old sea wolf. Gusta was embracing Milena. And I sat there feeling a sod.

No one missed me, certainly, when I slipped out into the corridor behind the bar. A drunkard bumped into me as I entered the GENTS room. I splashed my face with tap water to freshen up. My mind was a beehive. I needed to sort out the mess in my head. In the mirror the ugly middle-aged man yawned at me and asked: What now, wise guy? You have two possibilities: take a powder, or make a fool of yourself. I chose the first option and went to the telephone hanging on the wall in the corridor. Whom do I call? Jarmila is in Slovakia doing reportage for her magazine…Hana does not have a phone…Anicka is sleeping soundly in her matrimonial bed…Sarka! Of course. Sarka is like a Good Samaritan, always available…I put a coin in the slot and started to dial her number from memory. Suddenly, I saw in my mind the angelic face of Ruzenka. I realized at the same moment that it was not only her beauty, but something else, some magic power, which attracted me to her irresistibly…A voice in the earphone sleepily said "Hello?"…and I rudely hung up.

When I returned to our table, Ruzenka looked at me and asked maliciously:

"She did not answer?"

"Who?"

"The girl you just called."

Down my spine slid a bitter cold suspicion that Ruzenka had a witch's gift of seeing through me.

"I did not call anybody," I tried to defend myself.

"To finish the story," Ivo butted in, "Panmunjom was for us…"

I stopped listening, flooded by the blissful recognition that Ruzenka had noticed my absence, had even wondered about it, and her suspicious reaction filled me with utmost happiness.

Ruzenka rose while Ivo was still trying to charm her.

"Now it's our turn to make a tinkle," she said. "Come, Milena."

As they were leaving the table Ivo followed them with a thoughtful glance.

"You know, Ruzenka's Moravian genetic heritage is undeniable," he observed with satisfaction because he was also born somewhere in that part of the country. "How long have you known her?"

"Three hours fifty-one minutes," I answered with purposefully overblown exactitude.

"She has got personality," admitted Gusta.

"She has got class," added Ivo, and abruptly changed the subject. "By the way, Jan, I met Oldrich Chyle the other day, he sends you his best regards and congratulations on your book *Green Laughter*. He liked it very much. Chyle returned from Panmunjom last month but he will not be working at the Ministry any longer, he is taking an early retirement."

"Chyle was the chief of our delegation in the Neutral Nations Supervisory Commission in Korea," I explained to Gusta. "I am surprised that he ever thought of me, we did not part on good terms when I left Panmunjom."

"In any case, he spoke well about you," said Ivo.

"We had, let's say, different opinions," I mumbled.

"About inspection activities?" Ivo asked.

"Not about that, but I wrote a regular monthly

analysis of the political, economic and social situation in South Korea for the Ministry, and we often quarreled about the conclusions. Trivia, as I see it now."

"You guys, as Korean veterans, should know who started the war there in nineteen fifty?"

"Well, that's a rather complex question," said Ivo cagily. "As you know, the Korean peninsula was divided along the thirty-eighth parallel after the Japanese defeat. The USA gradually armed the South and the USSR the North…

"You can be frank with Gusta," I interrupted him. "There is no question that it was Kim Il-sung who fired the first shot with the blessing of Moscow and Peking. It was a dirty, bloody war which cost uncounted millions of lives, both military and civilian."

"That much I know, too," said Gusta. "But tell me something else…Since you were there to prevent illegal introduction of weapons and men, I want to know if your border controls were effective or just pro forma? I mean, did you catch anybody red handed?"

"I did not carry out inspections," said Ivo, "but Honza did, he can tell you."

"Show-off," Gusta goaded me.

His remark and its tone irritated me. Why the hell should I waste my time and breath telling him what happened at Sinuji. He does not care, and why should he? It's done and gone anyway.

"It would be a long story," I said, having taken hold of myself. "And that's not what we came here for."

"You're damn right," smiled Gusta. "Just one last question: How long did you stay there, Honza?"

"Eight hundred days and nights."

"Looking back, any regrets?"

"Frankly none. As the saying has it, it was wonderful, but enough is enough."

Gusta yawned and looked at his watch.

"Past midnight, closing time for me," he announced.

"But the evening is still young," protested Ivo.

"When the girls return, I'll pay and we'll go," decided Gusta. Then he whispered in my ear: "Ruzenka has promised to give Milena and me shelter. I hope that you do not disappear and will stay with us to accompany Ruzenka, if you are the gentleman you try to impersonate."

I nodded quickly and gladly.

"Let's have one for the road," implored Ivo, on whom it dawned that he was the odd man out. His brown melancholic eyes filled with sadness but I felt no pity for him, not a bit.

The taxi that was waiting for us in front of the Pleban's was a battered Soviet-made Dzigulik. The girls and Gusta squeezed somehow on the back seat. I sat next to the driver in the suicide seat, so nicknamed because people occupying it were often killed in car accidents as car seatbelts had yet to be invented.

"What's the address?" asked the driver.

"Na Plzence number one," replied Ruzenka.

The suspension of the car was lousy. We jerked along the bumpy cobble-stoned Prague streets that were dotted with potholes. Soon we passed the National Theater and crossed the bridge over the Vltava River in the direction of Smichov.

"You are good company, boys," I overheard Milena saying to Gusta, "but you drink too much."

"My dear Milena, you can't even imagine how wrong you are and what an injustice you do us!" protested Gusta.

"Oh, stop it, Gusta, we counted the vodkas you downed! Say, Ruzenka, how many did they swallow?"

"Twelve. I would bet they had some more behind our backs when we weren't there."

I sat there deaf and dumb, relying on Gusta's eloquence to defend us.

"My dear ladies, you are totally misled and mistaken," he started, "for you should know that God has allotted to every human being, both of you included, an equal quota of beer, wine, rum, vodka and other bug-juice that he or she must consume per year and per life. Now, if everybody was honestly drinking his or her apportioned quota, all would be fine and in perfect balance. But here is the catch: the world is full of dodgers and even teetotalers who subvert the planned divine harmony. Luckily, however, there are self-sacrificing volunteers like ourselves who unselfishly and disinterestedly try to stand in for the slackers and saboteurs. The moral, my dear ladies, is that we are not alcoholics but altruists and benefactors of mankind."

The driver laughed like mad, but both girls maintained an icy silence.

"Did you say something, Ruzenka?" asked Gusta.

"Nothing," replied Ruzenka but then she changed her mind and remarked with emphatic irony: "I note with great satisfaction that you have a religious explanation for your drinking."

The taxi stopped in a short, blind alley at the end of which I spotted in the dim light of headlamps something resembling a growth of bushes or a disfigured little park. The house with number one stood at the left-hand side of the alley. Its facade and entrance were cracked and flaking like all pre-war tenement houses in Prague.

"Keep the change," I said paying the driver.

"Thank you, sir," he bowed his head and then whispered: "Would you like me to come pick you up in the morning?"

"Forget it," I replied angrily because I imagined the

dirty mental sequence in his calculating mind: two bucks, two cuties, cuckoldry, fat tips at dawn. "Scram!" I said.

It was already past midnight. It started to drizzle, and no more trams, if one ever came this way. So my only hope was that Ruzenka would not chase me out before daybreak. Maybe, I will get a chance to tell her what she means to me, if I find the courage and right words.

On the second try Ruzenka succeeded in unlocking the entrance door, which opened with a squeak.

"Mind the step," she warned. But it was too late for Gusta. He stumbled and would have landed flat on the floor had Milena not held him up. He lost his officer's cap and tried to find it in the dark corridor lit only by the shimmer of a far-away street lamp. Then a key rattled in a lock and I heard the click of an electric switch. Suddenly a stream of bright light penetrated the darkness. Ruzenka was standing in the open door of her studio and asked us to come in.

The room had a bizarre shape and was no bigger than forty square meters. A large wardrobe on the right-hand side of the entrance masked a folding couch behind. One had the impression of entering a small, narrow hallway. A cupboard with a gramophone and a lamplight on it stood on the opposite wall. In the left corner was a sink with two faucets. There was no kitchenette. A white curtain covered the window. In the middle stood a coffee table with two little fauteuil chairs and a reading lamp. To me this simple abode appeared homey and welcoming. I looked around with the faint-hearted feeling of a heathen in a church.

"Nothing to drink here, I guess," said Gusta with slight hope in his baritone voice.

"You guessed right," smiled Ruzenka. "You can have tap water. My father says it does not dim intellect."

"Nor does it make one brighter," snarled Gusta. He yawned. "Time to take up a horizontal position." He took off his uniform jacket, threw it on the coffee table, kicked off his shoes and as a matter of course stretched on the couch.

Ruzenka and Milena held a hushed-up conference. As I did not want to seem to be eavesdropping I switched on the radio and tried to tune in to my favorite American Forces Network in Munich. But the set was prehistoric and the only station I was able to get was Radio Prague broadcasting a late night concert of classical music.

Meanwhile the girls made some changes to the set. The coffee table was pushed to the window and the couch unfolded with Gusta's help. The two little fauteuils were moved into the would-be hallway between the back of the wardrobe and the wall.

"This is all I can offer you, "said Ruzenka pointing to one of the fauteuils in the corner formed by the wardrobe and the door.

"It's more than I merit," I accepted with false modesty. I took off my Montgomery coat, rolled it up and arranged it as a cheek rest on the backboard of the fauteuil. When I managed to squeeze up in the fauteuil, I stretched my feet towards the wall to be more comfortable. From the radio, string quartet music filled the room. I would have preferred some love song, say Bing Crosby singing *True Love*, but in the final analysis any tune would do, since it served as a musical curtain.

Ruzenka switched off the light and sat down next to me. I immediately blurted out a question that was on my lips ever since I saw the folding couch.

"Do you live here alone?"

"No. With my best friend Gabina."

"Do you know her a long time?"

"We studied together in Brno. Gabina also works in a pharmacy."

"How come that she is not here today?"

"She took a day off and went home. Gabina lives at Velke Mezirici and we usually travel home together on Saturday afternoon."

"By train?"

"No, we hitchhike."

"Wow, and are you not afraid that something unpleasant may happen to you, that you might get into a car with a rough driver?"

"Well, we are careful...You see, a great many cars drive from Prague to Brno on Saturday afternoon, so we have a choice. It's more complicated when I have to go from Brno to Ostopovice, but luckily I can take a train which does not cost much."

"May I ask you, how much is your monthly pay?"

"Eleven hundred crowns."

"Net?"

"No, gross."

"And can you live on such pocket money?"

"I must. Mother always prepares a food package for me. Often I get a roasted rabbit because father breeds rabbits, and with all this I can survive a whole week."

"Tomorrow...actually, today already, this afternoon you will be traveling alone without Gabina."

"Sure, but not alone because there are always other hitchhikers waiting for a ride to Brno."

"What if you stayed here for the weekend?"

"I can't. I have to help Mother. There is a lot to do, we have to prepare the garden for winter, make jams and bottle fruits. My parents need my help, I cannot disappoint them."

My right hand lay on the armrest of the fauteuil which touched that of Ruzenka, and it seemed to me that I felt a fluid streaming out of her hand that lay on the adjoining arm rest only some millimeters away. But I did not dare to close the distance. Her flat refusal of my proposal to stay in Prague—with me, of course— discouraged me.

"Would you mind, if I put you some questions for a change?" asked Ruzenka.

"I don't mind questions but sometimes I mind answers. Try anyway."

"Why did you go to Korea?"

"For two reasons. One, this was my first and only possibility to get out of the cage. I would have preferred to go in the opposite direction, westward, but that was impossible because I am not politically reliable, so eastward it was. I certainly do not regret it. We traveled the slow way by train from Prague, via Moscow, Irkutsk, Peking, Pyongyang to Kaesong, and then by car to Panmunjom. There were eight of us: seven soldiers on active service—radio operators, cooks, medics—all of them auxiliary personnel, and I was interpreter with the rank of a captain. We set out shortly after Christmas and celebrated the New Year in Moscow. We spent a whole week traversing Siberia. A train conductor pointed out to us a big bust of Stalin carved in a stone cliff overhanging Lake Baikal that was done by long-term state prisoners from a near-by gulag, or concentration camp, if you like. The transition from China to Korea was a shock. Instantly, we found ourselves in a devastated land. Two years had elapsed since the end of the war but everywhere you could still see craters caused by American carpet-bombing. Most houses were still in ruins. Rice paddies were frozen over, not a living soul around, so the picture of desolateness and ugliness was absolute. I'll never forget it."

"And what was the other reason?"

"This is more complicated. Whenever I try to explain it, words desert me, because I am afraid of sounding high-flown and pompous. The essence of it is that I firmly believed that the work in the Supervisory Commission had a sense...From our camp we could see the Peace Pagoda, a low, wooden building standing practically right on the thirty-eight parallel, in which the truce was signed after a murderous insanity lasting three years and ten months. The loss of human lives and limbs was apocalyptic. It all could start again if the precarious truce is broken. We were there to help make it last. We could not be all over the country but our presence and inspection activities represented a sort of buffer so that neither of the warring sides could rearm to be able to start a new conflict."

"Why did you go there once more later?"

"Oh, I see, Ivo told you...Ivo is a windbag...OK, the reason for accepting a second tour in Korea was not the inspection activity—this was finished when Americans chased our teams out from the South...My motivation was China. You know I was very much fascinated by China, which has a great history and perhaps an even greater future. I accepted the second tour to save money for a two-month study tour in China."

"Ivo says you wanted to circumnavigate the world."

"That was icing on the cake. The cake was China. I traveled through the east coastal part from Peking down to Nanking, Shanghai, Canton, Guangzhou and the Hong Kong border. I visited factories, universities, communes and research institutes. The Chinese Ministry of Foreign Affairs helped me with the itinerary and program. I had an interpreter, of course. Well, I don't want you to bore you with a long account, so here are just a couple of snapshots. Number one: our train stops at a small railway station. From the window

I observe a long double line of bent backs, people in blue jackets. They are working but I cannot recognize what exactly they are doing. After five minutes as the train begins to pull out of the station the double line opens and now I see a kilometer of brand new railway track. Number two: the scene is a small communal workshop with about twenty women sitting in a half-circle on the ground. They have some simple tools with which they peck at the surface of copper pieces, base wafers and some other materials, handing pieces one to each other. The final products are relay switches resembling those that were used in the production of the first generation of computers....In a book I wrote about China I asked this question: what will happen when, and that time will come, over a billion capable, hard-working and quick-to-learn people lay their hands on and apply their brains to up-to-date technology and advanced techniques? They will make a giant leap forward and overtake all other nations."

"I would like to read it."

"Why not? If it ever appears on bookstalls."

"Why should it not be published?"

"You may not know about it but there is a rift now between Moscow and Peking. The censor at the publishing house subjected the book to a very unfavorable critique, branding it as unbalanced, unfair and politically mistaken because I predict in the conclusion that the next century will belong to China. Therefore, I called it *A Sleeping Giant*. The censor sent my manuscript to the cultural department of the Central Committee for a decision. That was two months ago and the final judgment is still pending...Come to think about it, maybe the Soviets came to the same conclusion and that's why they cancelled all technical co-operation with China and recalled their experts and advisers..."

I left the thought unfinished. Stop babbling, I told myself. When you start telling your stories as a Korean veteran, you lose all sense of appropriateness and consideration. What can she think of you? That you try to dazzle and flummox her? I indignantly rejected such an idea, although deep inside I knew it was true. If it were possible, I would fill every word with love, dispatch an intoxicating little cloud with every sentence, and turn every thought into Cupid's arrow aimed at her heart. Is it possible that this frail, gentle girl is my *'femme fatale'*? One day I shall have to confess that I had married out of youthful stupidity, that my marriage died while I was in Korea, and that I am separated but not yet divorced. Not now, however. Some other time, when she knows me better, when I have won her trust and convinced her I really love her. If I confessed now, she might think I am a fusty, philandering married man in the sheep's clothing of a misunderstood, injured husband.

All of sudden I had a feeling that my life was splitting in two. One part had finished and another was starting.

I decided that I'd tell her what she means to me squarely and directly.

"Ruzenka is a name that suits you…My Little Rose…Ruzenka," I repeated with all the affection I felt for her.

"I have never liked it," Ruzenka sighed.

"But I like it very, very much. I like everything about you. Your lips and teeth and eyebrows and hair and skin and voice, and how you shake your head when you disagree, and how you walk, simply everything. I love you as you are enormously. You are the loveliest girl I ever met…"

Embarrassed, Ruzenka kept silent.

"I will confide to you what has happened to me

today," I continued. "But first of all I'll tell you an old Indian fable.…It says that among the countless trillions of stars each one is meant for another one. This is why there is an eternal movement of stars wandering about the sky since they are searching their predestined partners. Such an encounter is extremely rare. But when it happens we see a shooting star in the night sky…Human beings share the same fate. We also are wandering about the world seeking our predestined mate, but most of the time without success. But if, through the mercy of the goddess of love, we do succeed in finding that person, then it is as if we were struck by lightning, scorching everything that was before and cleansing our soul so that we feel reborn. It happened to me when I saw you in front of me on Charles Square."

"This is…too sudden…so unreal that it cannot be true."

"It is true, never in my life have I felt so heavenly."

"But we've known each other a couple of hours…And you did not pay any attention to me the whole evening."

"I was afraid to betray myself. That if I looked at you I'd blush and start to stutter like a smitten student. But you must have sensed that I was crazy about you."

"Not at all, you hid it well."

I took her little hand into mine. It was soft, tender and frail in my paw and it trembled slightly like a trapped bird. I felt how its touch radiated an enormous strength that vibrated my whole body like a bowstring when the arrow is loosed. Oh, please let Ruzenka be mine, I begged Jehovah, Allah, Buddha, even the Great Spirit. I promised, I swore that I would change, lead a better life, kiss all my mistresses goodbye, and that I would divorce. I'll do all that and even more, if I can marry Ruzenka, and then I'll never ask God, whoever he may be, for anything more, ever.

"I don't know…" whispered Ruzenka, leaving her doubt unvoiced.

"What do you not know?"

"If I can believe you or not."

I understood that she has a problem with me. To convince her I must crawl out of my shell, lay myself bare and surrender to her mercy.

"Please listen to me, you need not say anything, just listen to me for a while," I began. "I am thirty-three years old, Christ's age. This is a turning point in the life of every man and all the more so of a dreamer such as I. Schopenhauer says that all dreamers should die at thirty-three because they have nothing good to expect any longer…When a man reaches Christ's age, all things lie before him stripped and bare, without embellishment, warts and all. He thinks of all his failures, though he does not regret what he has done but rather that what he could have done and did not…from lack of opportunity, feebleness of will to act, or because of a missed chance, or that he was too weak. And then he does not sleep at night and ruminates over what errors he has made, how many times he slid down and rose again, and he tortures himself with hope that in the other, remaining half of his life he will live more fully, when there is no more time for trifles, games and pretense. I met you at the right time. My batteries were low, I vegetated from one day to another. I was burned out. But now everything is different. In your presence I feel young. I want to live, to fight and to love. The odometer shows zero again. Life begins with you, and you are my future."

Meanwhile the music broadcast had stopped. The radio-set fizzled quietly and its scale radiated a faint bluish light. We were couched in the fauteuils next to each other in a small space between the wardrobe and the wall, a space of no more than two square meters, but to me it seemed that we had the whole universe just for ourselves, and that we were floating through it on a magic carpet of yearning and dreaming. I was still holding her hand from which the reinvigorating force was streaming into my body. My bliss reached its summit when her thumb gently caressed the back of my hand. I was sure that if now I embraced and kissed her she would not resist. But I was telling myself not to be in haste, to be patient. Stendhal advises that after a declaration of love one should not rush the next rendezvous and wait at least three days before meeting again. That would be Tuesday. But I cannot hold out so long. I'll call her Monday, invite her to dine with me in the Chinese restaurant, the only one in Prague. I'll buy her a bouquet of red roses, accompany her home and then, and then only, I'll kiss her for the first time. On Tuesday I'll take her to the Vinohrady Theater to see Chekhov's *Three Sisters*....I will go one step at a time. I must savor to the full the dazing, miraculous birth of our love, for it is so unique, it will not happen again in my lifetime.

I lowered my voice to a faint whisper, trying not to sound sibilant but keeping my voice at a deeper, melodic tone. I whispered slowly, thoughtfully, and beseechingly.

"When one loves it must be the whole way, fully and forever, on sunny days as in stormy weather, in good times as in bad. I have only two paper suitcases with worn-out clothes and underwear. I cannot promise you riches, or that our life together will be a walk in the rose garden. I cannot promise anything but love. Love that is majestic like the Himalayas, profound like an abyss in the Pacific, solid as titanium, clean as a fountain in the hills. If you allow me to love you, I will love you the whole way, from here to eternity."

217

I covered her fingers and palm of her hand with butterfly kisses. With each one I repeated:

"I love you, Ruzenka."

"Ach, Honzicku," she said softly and lovingly. For the first time she called me by a diminutive of my first name, like my mother used to do when I was not a naughty boy.

This was the beginning of our great and lifelong love.

VII. THE COSMONAUTS OF PRAGUE

I thumbed rough pipe tobacco onto thin round paper and rolled it in my usual way into a thick product resembling a cigar more than a cigarette. I took a long sip from a big tin cup filled with coffee so strong that it would even revive a corpse. I lit yet another nail in my coffin, inhaling nicotine in a deep breath and then puffing out the first cloud of smoke of the new day. It was Saturday, five o'clock in the morning. I had slept fitfully because a short story I had started to write several days before kept awaking me. It was about Lieutenant Tichy, serving in an out-of-the-way garrison commanded by a careerist major and his political officer, an ear-bender. Tichy struggles against whitewash, falsified progress reports, harassment of rank and file soldiers, and the rewarding of bootlickers. At the division HQ he is known as 'The Last Apostle' because they consider him as an idealist who preaches and sermonizes in the desert. Therefore, he is unpopular and transferred from one rotten job to another. Tichy finds out that the situation is the same everywhere: moral decay, hypocrisy, demagogy, and degeneration of human relationships. This comes about because of a system created by the omniscient and omnipotent Party in order to keep itself in power. To make the system more human, concludes Tichy, one would have to humanize the Party, which is, like the Church, unchangeable and immovable. In this lies its strength. When do you finally grasp it? he asks himself. Gradually, he realizes the futility of his efforts. How naïve of him to believe, or even to hope, that the Party might be reformed from the inside! There is a limit to tolerance of a corrupt regime, and to continue beyond that red line is unacceptable. You must say no. No to what you preach, comrades, and no to what you represent. Tichy knows what the implications of such refusal will be. Hence his hesitation and doubts about whether he really has the guts to say no.

I glanced at the last sentence. I wrote: "It will take courage. You will have to vanquish fear and cowardice."

My fingers started running over the keyboard, putting on paper what I wrote during the night in my mind, and subsequently polished it a number of times.

When a man is in dire straits, when it seems to him that he is losing his mind, and when he does not see a solution or an escape, he thinks about the ordeals he has gone through, about the people whom he knew and respected, and what advice they gave him. "Well, my lads, the way to get ahead is to study and get an academic degree," Tichy hears his professor saying, "then build your career so that you may become a success in life." But what is success? What is the yardstick to measure it? Is it money, rank, a fancy car, a villa? An old wound opened up, a feeling of the disappointment and failure returned that he had experienced when his application to the university had been rejected. After that he stood a whole year at a drawing table in a furniture factory. Then he was called up to the army. Having finished his two-year duty he joined the Communist Party because it was a condition for gaining access to the Military Academy. "And here I am," he said aloud. As he threw his arms wide in a gesture of helplessness, he knocked down an empty bottle of vodka he had finished alone last night to celebrate his thirtieth birthday. He shook his head. "So here I am," he repeated with disbelief. Suddenly he saw his room with the eyes of a stranger, a pitiful dump of a room, with a bed, two chairs and a table, a wardrobe, a sink. All junk. Icy air penetrated through loose window frames. An inventory on a piece of paper pinned to the wall stated that the Garrison Administration leased him the following items...rubber-stamped and signed by an unknown bureaucrat. Leased for his lifetime, it occurred to him. No way, I must put an end to it, I must stop being scared. I have reached my end station. I must get out of here and now. With this resolution he fell onto an iron bed in his uniform and boots. But sleep escaped him...

Just at the moment when my imagination was gathering steam, the telephone rang. Shit, what stupid asshole is calling at this ungodly hour! I hesitated whether to answer. Then I said to hell with it, what if it is a friend in need? I picked up the receiver.

"You know what time it is, man?" I told the unknown caller.

"Quarter past five," said a voice I knew well. It belonged to Antony Pospichal. "Sorry to wake you up."

"Far from it, I have already been bashing my typewriter."

"Glad to hear it. I have a little problem. I am sitting in the restaurant at the Masaryk railway station and I have had something to eat and drink. Would you mind coming over because I am broke?"

Mother used to say that my buddies dangle me on a string. How could I refuse something to Tony, a kindred soul? We met, or rather we discovered each other, in a bar, and what began as drinking companionship turned into a rock solid, deep friendship. We had much in common: theater, literature, alcohol, and women. Not always in this order. We faced the same problem: our marriages broke down and in the ruins we were not the innocent party.

We got married too soon, too young and inexperienced. Our lust for life was too great to be satisfied with slippers, TV and bottled beer at home. We each found our *femme fatale:* for Tony it was Vera, for me Ruzenka. We wanted to marry them, but first we would have to divorce and drink the full chalice of bitterness and trouble. Small wonder that we postponed it for another day, week, month or year. From indolence and cowardice.

"How long will you take to get over here?" asked Tony.

"Ten minutes to get dressed, after that it depends on tram connection. There are not many trams running now."

But luckily a tram came along as if to order and took me to the Masaryk railway station in only half an hour. Tony sat strategically near to the entrance of the restaurant, waving at me to make sure I saw him. He had before him a cup of black liquid that was billed as espresso, a half-empty bottle of mineral water, and a crumpled box of cigarettes.

"You are a real buddy," he said, "coming to my rescue. I owe you big. It's worth pure gold."

I sat down on the next chair and asked a sleepy waiter for a coffee. Tony ordered a box of Chesterfields. His blue eyes looked at me lovingly and his sotto voice assured me of eternal gratefulness.

"Skip the preliminaries," I said, "and confess your sins. I may give you absolution, but don't hide anything from me."

Tony lit a cigarette and began to tell me that a colleague of his at the Ministry of Foreign Affairs was appointed as ambassador to Kabul, which is why he gave a farewell party yesterday. Champagne, caviar, cognac and all kind of delicacies—nothing you would want to miss. When the host threw them out after two

222

o'clock in the morning, Tony and a couple of other joyful gentlemen stood facing a problem: what to do with the rest of the night? They decided to solve it by going to their favorite nightclub, 'Barbara.' They stayed there until the closing hour of four. By that time Tony was penniless. The other gentlemen went home, while Tony directed his feet to the Masaryk railway station where he was sure to find the restaurant open. He knew what he would do: send an SOS to me.

"Why didn't you take a train to Kolin?" It was a place near Prague where his girlfriend, Vera, lived.

"That's not so easy," sighed Tony. "The trouble is that I promised Vera to bring meat for the weekend. No money, no meat, but if you lend me two hundred crowns, all will be fine."

"How do you explain Vera that you didn't come to her on Friday evening, and where you spent the night?"

"Leave it to me, I'll find something plausible. But say nothing to Ruzenka, because you know they conspire behind our backs. We must be careful what we tell them."

I nodded. Tony had dark circles under his eyes, and when he lit a cigarette his hand trembled. Clearly, he had a terrible hangover. I felt sorry for him.

"The butcher's opens at eight," I said. "But the Pinkas pub opens at seven, which is in half an hour. If we start right now on foot, we can be there easily in time. What you badly need is a strong goulash soup, a croissant and a beer to raise the level of alcohol in your blood. Not a Pilsner, but some weak brand."

We had plenty of time so we took a longer route to the pub past the Powder Tower and across a completely deserted Old Square. In that early May morning Prague seemed to me even more charming than usual. The slight breeze was perfumed with chestnut blossoms. Tony asked me what I had been writing when he called.

I knew that it was not simply a courtesy question, and that he really wanted to know. So I began to recount the story of 'The Last Apostle,' an officer serving in an outpost garrison where the only way to pass your free evenings is to watch a black and white TV set. The nearest village is eight kilometers away with a population of two hundred souls, a small chapel and a pub. The soldiers leave after two years of service, while the officers stay and are easy prey to boredom and 'submarine syndrome.'

"In essence, I am writing a story of a man who searches for a moral force inside himself to revolt against a system in which the winners are sycophants, yes-men and hypocrites. Honest and decent men have no chance," I explained. "My wavering hero realizes that the only thing he can do to be able to look into his own eyes without shame is to say no to the power that created the system. No, comrades, I stop right here and now…I am not going to lift my hand in support of your regime again."

"I don't like your story," said Tony.

"Why? It is true. The man called 'The Last Apostle' exists. His real name is Vaclav Cermak. He is currently assigned to a border regiment at Tachov. All the officers in the division know his case. For some he is an off-putting example, but there are many others who secretly admire him."

"It does not matter whether it is a true story or not, this is irrelevant. The crux of the matter lies in how it will be interpreted."

"What are you trying to say?"

"That they will accuse you of attacking and smearing the Party."

"But there has been some political relaxation…"

"Oh, come on, that's cosmetic. The root problem remains: the Party! This story is like preaching in the

Vatican that God is dead. You will be excommunicated. Purged! In the end, your efforts will be wasted anyway because no one will publish it. You want to bet?"

"You may be right…I am not going to bet, but I must write the story all the same. It's inside me, consuming me. I cannot get rid of it unless I do."

By this time we had already reached our destination. The brown door of the pub was still closed but a group of working men were already waiting outside. From behind the corner emerged Gusta Hruby accompanied by several drinking buddies. When the door opened, everybody wanted to be the first in. A rough struggle ensued. Within a few minutes the pub was full of smoke, boisterous laughter and the tinkling of glasses. Some voices sang a popular song about Prague—that we would rather tear down than cede to foreigners. It was a start of another beautiful drunkard's day.

Gusta approached our table and said:

"Honza, come and join us. We are celebrating Josef Polcar's birthday."

"Sorry, but I can't, Gusta. I am here on a mission of mercy. I must nurse this old boy who is a bit tired, so that he gets sober and then put him on a train to Kolin."

"OK, but come afterwards," said Gusta. "We are planning a party that will last until Monday morning."

Man's nature is a frail thing, and one should not listen to a Siren song because it's easier to succumb than to resist. I paid and we quickly left. Although we were walking slowly, we reached the butcher's in Jindriska Street shortly before eight. We had to wait a while until a tall, skinny saleswoman rolled up the roll-shutter and let us in.

"Welcome, Doctor Pospichal," she said, "I was expecting you yesterday. I had put two beefsteaks aside for you, but I had to sell them since you did not come."

"I could not make it, dear Vlasta," said Tony. "Maybe you can find something else for me. I'll owe you big time. It's worth pure gold," he promised.

Vlasta disappeared behind a curtain and returned with a small package.

"Here's a kilo of pork for Wiener schnitzel. I am sure you will like it. And please don't forget my theater tickets."

"How could I forget you, dear Vlasta?" said Tony with a voice of reproach. "I'll bring you the tickets to the National Theater on Tuesday afternoon."

Tony was a lawyer employed in the ministry's Press Department. This is why he could get tickets to all major Prague theaters that were usually sold out. He used them to barter for scarce goods and services like meat, oranges or repairs to home appliances. He gave Vlasta two hundred crowns instead of the one hundred and fifty she asked. It's easy to be generous with other people's money.

I accompanied him to the train. We shook hands.

"I owe you big time. It's worth pure gold," said Tony climbing on the first step of the wagon. Then he turned backed. "Would you like to go to Geneva?" he asked with big smile.

"Where?"

"To Geneva. In Switzerland."

"I can't tomorrow. Ruzenka comes back from a visit to her parents and will bring a roasted rabbit. I wouldn't want to miss such delicacy."

"This isn't a joke, this is serious. The International Labor Organization in Geneva has advertised a competition for an editor's post. Come to think of it, you fit it like a round peg in a round hole. I should have thought about it earlier; the application form came some two months ago. Fill it on Monday, and off you go to Geneva!"

I did not take him seriously, since I knew Tony had a habit of promising people blue heaven, not deliberately to tease people but because he wanted to please them. I called him, therefore, Antony Promises Pospichal. Which is why I instantly forgot what he said.

For once, Antony Promises Pospichal was as good as his word. He appeared in my office Monday mid-morning and laid on my table a yellow form with green printing.

"First, read it very carefully before you start filling it in," he advised.

I looked a while at the yellow form. It had four pages with thirty questions and spaces for an answer.

"You should not have any problem with it," said Tony. "Meanwhile, I'll go downstairs to a bistro to have a sausage and glass of wine."

"Wait a minute, Tony...Here I read that I am applying for employment in the International Labor Office. But you spoke about the International Labor Organization. It looks like two different institutions to me. Am I right?"

"Well, you'll be surprised but it's the same thing. I would not know why...oh, yes, now I remember. That Office is the secretariat of the Organization. But for a precise explanation you'd better ask my colleague Pechacek who is a desk officer for all UN agencies at the ministry."

"Tell me something, Tony. International Labor Organization...this sounds like...isn't it some sort of a communist international? Not that it would matter..."

"Gracious god no! Definitely not," Tony assured me. "Pechacek says that the ILO stands for cooperation and is against class struggle. Moreover, I know it is listed at the ministry among capitalist institutions such as The World Bank and the International Monetary

Fund."

"Sure?"

"Cross my heart. I'll be running now…"

"Wait, Tony. I am all for fun but within a certain limit. For me, it is a shot in the dark to apply for a job abroad. As far as I know, to get this one has to have the nod from the ministry, if not from the Central Committee of the Party. I am not going to bother myself with an application form that some bureaucrat will throw into a wastepaper basket. And above all, I like it here, I don't want to leave."

Tony gave a mild sigh, sat down and began to tell me in detail that he had discussed my candidature with Pechacek as well as the Personnel Department Chief, and that he had succeeded in obtaining their go ahead.

"You see, the point is that the competition is open to candidates from thirty two countries," he added. "If you consider that it concerns a post for an English editor you, as a Czech, have not the ghost of a chance of winning."

"All the more reason not to bother," I said.

"OK. Let's look at it from the positive angle," said Tony. "You don't get the job. But since we are such a funny country that is under-represented in the ILO, they will invite you to an interview. It means a trip to Geneva. Get a glimpse of the capitalist world and come back. And that's what it is all about! See my point? Therefore, be so kind as to fill in the yellow thing so that it can be sent to Geneva by tomorrow's diplomatic pouch. And please, don't put in the date," he added.

"Why?"

"I'll tell you later," said Tony and was gone.

I decided that it was not worthwhile wasting time with the application form. I would be quick and succinct. I put the first page in my typewriter. Name, address, marital status…well…separated, mother tongue Czech, other languages English, French, German, Russian. Second page. For what work do you wish to be considered: assistant editor; period of employment which you would accept: one to five years; education: High School, Institute of Modern Languages, with a university degree in English; publications you have written: two books of short stories, one novel. Third page. Present employer: *Ceskoslovensky vojak*; description of duties: senior reporter; previous employers: Czechoslovak News Agency, *Obrana Lidu*, Neutral Nations Supervisory Commission in Korea. Fourth page. References: Dr Antonin Pospichal, Ministry of Foreign Affairs, Rudolf Franc, editor, *Ceskoslovensky vojak*; health disabilities: none. I wrote the entries without much thought and missed a question or two. The ribbon of my typewriter was used up and some letters were less legible than others. It did not look neat or tidy but I did not care.

"I have filled it in as best as I can," I told Tonda, "except for the date. What do I put there?"

"Say the twentieth of April," suggested Tonda.

"Today is the tenth of May," I pointed out. "Why should I pre-date it?"

"Because the closing date for the competition was the first of May."

"Gosh, that means my application is no good. Why didn't you tell me about it before?"

"Because you would not fill it in, as I know you."

"You bet! How are you going to explain the delay?"

"Bureaucracy at the ministry, or our mission in Geneva will take the blame…That's not your worry."

"You are right there. But starting from today, pray hard every evening that they do invite me. Otherwise you will owe me big time, in pure gold, as your favorite saying goes, for the rest of your days."

After lunch in an office canteen of fatty pork meat, dumplings, sauerkraut and a small beer, I took a nap on the couch in my office. I used my necktie as a light shade and my jacket as a cover. I did not need a long shuteye; half an hour was enough to make me feel as fresh as a daisy. I almost invariably woke up from my siesta with some new idea or thought or phrase, and even a word, emerging out of my subconscious mind that kept working while my body took a rest. Therefore, once I closed my eyes I would focus on a story plot or some other creative problem I was struggling with to stimulate my imagination. It was a method that I learned to use well, and it rarely failed.

This time I assigned it the job of solving the difficulties I was having with the end of the story *The Last Apostle*. I wrote and rewrote it a number of times but all attempts were unsatisfactory. Now, my subconscious produced several changes that made me jump up and hurry to my typewriter. I wrote:

Tichy threw his Party membership card into the oven fire and silently watched as flames consumed it. Afterward he closed the hatch and went to the table on which stood a bottle that had the label 'Carlsbad Mineral Water' to deceive intruders, since it contained a high-grade homemade slivovitz. He poured himself a full measure in a big glass jar that had once contained mustard.

It is damn difficult to do what you must, he ruminated, but it will be even more difficult to accept what will surely follow: accept humiliation and not eat humble pie. To keep my spine straight even if I had to leave the army, since they will kick me out for sure. And, above all, not to be afraid of anything any more. This is the most important thing in life: fear nothing, kowtow to nobody, be your own master. It seemed to him that probity was crucially important, more important than anything else. Of this he was certain.

And so what: as long as I fight, I am, and I know that life has a sense. Am I right? He smiled at the fellow in the mirror on the wall, who smiled back at him. He raised his glass. Down the hatch? Sure, but to what?

That you did it! Cheers!

When he emptied the glass a thought struck him, or rather a question that will keep coming back to him and to which he would have to seek an answer time and again:

And what did you actually achieve?

Re-reading what I had written I realized that the title *The Last Apostle* did not fit. It did not correspond to the message I was trying to pass on. So I crossed the title out and wrote a new one: *Say No*.

Later on, it became the title of a book of my short stories introduced by a quotation from the ancient poet Flavius: 'Glory to the man who says what is. And I say, therefore, glory to the man who cannot be forced to say what is not.'

The book was published in 1965 but its distribution was forbidden at that time. It appeared on the bookstalls only during the so-called 'Prague spring' in 1968, when our country experienced a short spell of freedom.

GOING INTO ORBIT

On that ominous Monday in August 1965 I appeared in the editorial office after lunch. That morning I had knocked out a report about the suicide of a rank-and-file soldier, and then I packed a few things in my carry-on for a short stay in Geneva. I was supposed to fly there the next day at eleven. I had received an invitation from the Director of the ILO Press Department, Snow Herrick, to come over for an interview that was scheduled to begin on Wednesday morning. I was intrigued that it should take two whole days. What do they want to talk about for such a long time? Two hours, in my opinion, should do amply for a chat. Maybe they want to give me some time to see the town, which I would appreciate, of course. The Ministry of Foreign Affairs paid for the air ticket that I was to collect at the airport counter of Czechoslovak Airways. Mr Pechacek from the Department of Intergovernmental Organizations did not hide his surprise at the invitation, which came like a bolt from the blue. Being a diplomat and a well-educated man, however, he nonetheless wished me a good trip and much success. The National Bank, on the strength of a ministry certificate, promised to let me draw twenty Swiss francs in exchange as pocket money.

The office was quiet, usual at that time since my colleagues had not come back from the Pinkas pub. I answered a couple of letters from readers, rejected one feuilleton, and wrote to Jiri Krenek that we would publish his short story. Entitled *A Sunday To Kill*, it described the mortal weekend blues of young officers rotting in a forsaken garrison outpost. I went to the secretariat and borrowed, against my signature, a copy of the last week's issue of *Newsweek*. I leafed through it and carefully read a commentary by Zbigniew Brzezinski about 'communist economic co-operation.' He wrote that the Soviets had made milk cows out of all their satellite countries, which we all knew very well, but he documented it with statistical data that were news to me because behind the Iron Curtain the facts were classified and guarded as state secrets.

I returned the copy of *Newsweek* to be locked away. Then I shut my desk drawer and ran down the stairs leading to the building entrance in Jugmanova Street where the sultry August afternoon hit me like a sledgehammer. Originally, I planned to return home and have a good night's rest before departure. But, suddenly, I visualized a misty glass of beer with a white foam cap, and my throat became as dry as the Sahara.

I'll have just one beer and not a drop more.

With this noble-minded and, I thought, firm decision I entered the Jelinek pub. I saw Franta Kejik. Oh hell, I said under my breath. I felt a panicky urge to run away. But it was too late. He had spotted me, too, and waved at me to join him. Franta sat alone at a table drinking away money borrowed from friends. How he spent his salary was a mystery. Some say he supported his parents financially, others that a woman was sponging off him. In front of him, beside a half empty glass of beer, lay a book. I recognized it on sight because I had wrapped it in ordinary brown paper so that it would look inconspicuous and would not provoke by its title.

No sooner had I sat down than a waiter put a pint of Pilsen beer for me on the table. He knew me well.

"Cheers," we chimed our usual toast in duet. The glasses clinked loudly but did not break. They were of solid material made to last.

"Franta, if you lose this copy of Orwell, I'll rip your balls off," I said. "Don't you know that it is on the list of prohibited books? Why did you bring it here? If you are caught with it, we both are in trouble."

Orwell's novel *1984* was a farewell gift I received from Hagenbuchler, the Secretary of the Swiss delegation in Panmunjom.

"While reading it last night, all at once scales fell from my eyes and I had a stunning revelation," said

233

Franta. "You know what occurred to me?" He paused dramatically. "That our Party hacks also practice doublespeak! They use it for a dual purpose: to obscure social problems and to pre-empt the rise of new, different ideas."

"There is more to it," I said, "because language, a tool for understanding, is perverted into a means of disguising thoughts and of confusing minds. The essence of doublespeak is duplicity, the arch-enemy of clear speech. Take any harangue by our masters and you will find long, worn-out phrases in which you get lost, which, in turn, enables them to substitute ideas. Thus evil is presented as good, dictatorship as democracy, and oppression as freedom."

"You should write it," said Franta.

"Why me? It's originally your idea. You write it," I retorted.

Franta chuckled and lifted two fingers as a signal to the waiter.

"Let's have one more," he suggested.

"I must be going," I objected. "I must be fit tomorrow."

"Just one for the road," insisted Franta.

"OK," I agreed. I made a grave mistake but I did not realize it at that moment.

When the waiter brought us two glasses of beer, the door opened and Ota Brozek entered, accompanied by his retinue. In came Zdenek Lavicka, who replaced me as Ota's alter ego, followed by Jiri Horsky, Jiri Janes, Jarmila Kratochvil and Jan Cerveny. All of them were already launched in orbit, as we used to call an all-night drinking bout. They pushed two tables close to ours. Ota sat at the center, being a recognized leader of the clan. He was of medium height, his dark hair was combed back, and he had bad teeth stained by nicotine. But his most remarkable feature were his brown eyes radiating high intelligence. When he spoke they sparkled like two precious stones and their glitter seemed to add special significance to his words. We were fixated by these eyes like religious maniacs. Ota was an inexhaustible source of ideas. Before we separated, or rather before I left the daily *Obrana Lidu* for the magazine *Ceskoslovensky vojak*, we did a series of articles together on the subject of scientific revolution. In the last story we wrote about a first-generation computer that was being born at the Institute for Mathematics and Physics in Prague.

Brozek and his entourage had started on rum and coffee at a bar called Sutera already that afternoon. Around five o'clock Ota felt an insuppressible thirst for a beer. That brought them here. They carried on an impassioned discussion about Ota's latest brainstorm: to launch an independent magazine. At the bar, they had agreed on its title: *Reporter*. Its target audience should be young people at school and at work. The readers would find in it investigative reports, analysis of topical, social problems, feuilletons, short stories, poetry, as well as news from the world of culture and sports.

"Don't forget style!" Franta cried boisterously. "We need a new style: short sentences, kill adjectives and modifiers, just facts and more facts."

I was on my third beer. The alcohol in my blood reached a level at which I felt free of shyness and inhibitions.

"You are talking about an independent magazine," I said, "but where do you find money?"

"We can count on a founding grant from the Union of Journalists that will be our sponsor," replied Ota, "but after five or ten issues we must be self-supporting."

"How often will it appear? And what will be the

press run?" I pressed him.

"Twice a month with thirty thousand copies as a starter," said Ota.

The editorial staff will be small: five or seven people. Ota will be Editor-in-Chief, but an equal among equals. The main source of copy will be a network of contributors, recruited from among the ranks of prominent journalists, writers and specialists. Second in command will be Zdenek Lavicka, while Jan Cerveny will take care of poetry and literature. Franta was assigned the post of chief of investigative reporting, and Jarmila Kratochvilova head of the cultural section. I was the odd man out. Ota had not forgotten my desertion.

Jarmila looked at me with a mocking smile, to let me know that as far as she was concerned I did not exist. But there were times when she had looked on me with tenderness and love. "It was just one of those things," as Sinatra sang, "one of those wonderful nights, a trip to the moon…but it was just one of those things…"

"I will now take a powder," I whispered to Franta. "I am going to the Pleban's to have supper. Will you join me?"

We left the pub and walked leisurely down Jugmannova Street to National Avenue where Franta wanted to visit the Monica nightclub. Another temptation pawed at him when we passed the Grizzly pub, but after that he followed me like a lamb to our destination on Bethlehem Square. Once seated at the Pleban's we ordered a venison steak with French fries and a bottle of red wine. It was almost midnight when the waiter brought us a third one. At the same time a small group of artists burst in. I recognized two of them: Karel Stedry and Waldemar Matuska, who performed at a theater nearby. Corks popped, wine glasses clinked, jokes were cracked, and songs filled the air. Matuska contributed his latest hit, 'All that the summer wind blew away…' I felt blissful and buoyant. I was in orbit and nothing could bring me down. I was ready for another of the thousand and one nights of floating on air, enthralled by my lightness of being, until the bitter end…

"I see Radovan Selucky over there," said Franta. "Let's say hi to him."

Selucky was a promising young economist who had the guts to say and write publicly that the Czech national economy was going down the toilet. I edited one of his treatises for our magazine in which he showed that our economic policy of wide-ranging development had brought about economic stagnation, and that we could get out of the impasse only by changing direction radically towards accelerated intensive development. From now on, emphasis must be on quality, not quantity. All the five-year development plans were fulfilled just on paper, Selucky noted. Had they really been carried out, we would have used up all our natural resources, from forests to uranium ore.

We clinked glasses with Radovan, who reported that he had returned from Switzerland the day before and could not get over what he had seen there. Hearing the word 'Switzerland' gave me a jolt. I looked at my watch: Jesus Christ, it's almost one o'clock in the morning. I must get going and have some sleep. But I decided to stay a while just to hear why the Swiss are rich, as Radovan began to tell us. It went like this:

"When our Lord created the most beautiful country in the world, he was not fully satisfied with his work. Something was missing. So he created a man and called him Swiss. 'Look, my son, what a wonderful piece of

Earth I am giving you to use and enjoy: white tipped mountains, green meadows and fertile valleys! Could you ever wish for anything more?' The Swiss looked around and said: 'Yes, my lord. I could use some cows.' So our Lord created a herd of black and white spotted milk cows and a couple of bulls. Wiping sweat from his forehead, he said that he was tired by all this effort and was thirsty. 'Please go and draw a glass of milk for me, my beloved son.' The Swiss complied and the Good Lord drank the milk. Returning the empty glass, he noticed that the Swiss was looking at him with undisguised expectation. 'I gave you the most beautiful and richest country in the whole world. I gave you mountain meadows full of cows. What more could you possibly wish?' The Swiss replied: 'One franc for the milk, my Lord.'"

It turned out to be one of the most famous stories that the Swiss tell against themselves. But it reminded me that in a few hours I must go to the bank to buy twenty francs for the trip. So I bowed out, paid my bill and started out into the night. I decided that I would hail a taxi on Wenceslas Square to take me home to catch some sleep.

I walked briskly back to National Avenue, passed a building on my right where I studied languages, went round the house on the corner where I failed to learn how to dance but succeeded in balling a chick whose name I had forgotten. Remembrances of things past swam into my mind as if I were bidding farewell and should never return. It gave me the blues and I felt like crying.

On Jungman's Square I slowed down. In an adjoining narrow street were two of my favorite nightspots, T-Club and Barbara. I hesitated only a moment. I need a nightcap. I'll have a White Lady at the bar, and then leave right away.

T-Club was a few steps nearer. The bouncer knew me and let me in with a respectful bow to a known barfly. At the bar, I did not find voluptuous Vera but grumpy Karl. He mixed the cocktail and, without a word, put a glass with a rim dipped in lemon and sugar in front of me. I was sitting with my back to the room, as I did not want to talk to anybody. Humming voices came to me as if from far away, unintelligible and muffled by alcohol in my head.

Then I felt a hand touching my shoulder. I turned around slowly and saw a female head with short-cut hair. It belonged to publishing editor Magda Hajickova. Her lips were painted shrieking red and as they moved I heard her stentorian voice. Magda said she wanted to have a word with me, and invited me join their party sitting at a table near the dance floor. Looking over there I recognized her husband, an influential literary critic, and a well-known author, Jan Otcenasek. There was a third man whom I did not know. I said I was sorry but I had no time, I had just stopped here on my way home, and I must be going because tomorrow, or rather today, I would have a hectic day.

"What exactly would you like to discuss, Comrade Hajickova?" I asked. We had known each other for several years but we still addressed each other formally as comrades and never on a first-name basis.

"I have had another look at your book on China," said Magda. "I think it's a shame that it is gathering dust in a drawer."

"Four years have passed since I wrote it. China must have changed enormously," I said, "but the comrades at the Central Committee are the same and they don't like the book."

"You are wrong. There have been personnel changes, and my husband says there is a certain relaxation of cultural policy," said Magda. "Now is a propitious moment for you to return to China to gather new material, which would make the book topical. Come to my office and we can sign a new work contract for you to submit to the Writers' Union with a request for a study trip. My husband will back you and I am sure you will get a grant."

I thanked Magda, promised I would think it over seriously, and left.

Outside I took a deep breath and started walking, with the inner conviction that my steps now were steady and straight. I had just passed the Barbara nightspot when somebody crawled out of the joint onto the stairs and through the opened door I heard the siren sound of the violin played by Maestro Settler. I could not resist.

On a tiny dancing floor two couples shuffled cheek to cheek. Before I could look around I heard a foghorn call:

"Honza, here we are!" Ludek Burianek rose from a corner, as big and stout as ever. He shouted: "Honza, come over here!"

To turn around and flee was impossible. So I went to Ludek, who embraced me firmly like a lost son.

"I have not seen you for a week, where have you been?" he asked.

By week Ludek meant the time we had not met with a glass in our hands. Otherwise we saw each other every day in the editorial offices, since Ludek, an academic painter, was our graphic artist.

"Meet my buddy from the Academy, Karel Vodicka," Ludek introduced his drinking pal, an architect. "What a coincidence, because just before you entered I was telling Karel that you would need a flat."

They both drank white Bacardi, and the waiter brought us three fresh glasses of this Cuban poison.

"Why don't you tell him all about it?" Ludek prodded his friend.

What the architect began to explain to me seemed as unbelievable as a fairy tale. Somebody at the Ministry of Industry had the idea of building apartment houses in Prague for our countrymen exiled in Canada and USA who were retired and might want to spend the rest of their days in their homeland. There was a political thaw going on, and the bonds of ideology and politics were starting to loosen. Therefore living in Prague might be tempting, even inviting, for elderly exiles. Their Canadian and American dollars, converted into the local currency, would give them more purchasing power. And the cost of living in Prague was incomparably lower than on the other side of the ocean. So a six-floor apartment house was built at Pankrac and another on the outskirts at Krc.

"The hitch is that our countrymen aren't hurrying to return," architect Vodicka said in his heavy lisp. "Therefore, it was decided to sell the flats to Czech citizens who can pay in cash. It's an experiment. They would be full and sole owners. It's yet another achievement of Socialism—private ownership!"

Of course, I wanted to hear details. Vodicka said that a two bedroom flat with a kitchen, a bath and a WC would cost ninety thousand crowns at Pankrac, while a similar apartment at Krc was twenty thousand crowns dearer because it was built more solidly and with better materials. I made a quick mental calculation: from royalties for the first volume of *True Detective Stories* I had fifteen thousand crowns, and the second volume would yield some forty thousand. I could sell my car, a Wartburg. Together I might be able to rake up ninety or even one hundred thousand crowns. The Wartburg was almost new. I liked it very much, but to hell with it, if Ruzenka and I could have our own nest. The question was, was this drunkard of an architect just shooting off his mouth?

"Mister Vodicka," I said solemnly, "if we close this deal, I'll pay for you to take a three-day long first-class bender."

"That's too generous, I am just an intermediary," Vodicka said with false modesty. But it was obvious that he liked my offer very much.

The alarm clock was ringing. Its rattling echoed in my head like a staccato machinegun. I mechanically reached out my right hand towards a chair near my bed, pushed the damn clock off, and sank back into a blessed quiet. Narrow sunlight penetrated the room through the worn-out Venetian blinds.

I lay on a couch and tried hard to think. The alarm clock…I must have set it in the night but I could not recall when. Why? I am to go to Geneva. This realization made me to sit up. The hands on the clock showed it was half past seven.

I pulled up the Venetian blinds. Bright sunlight blinded me. On the chair next to the alarm clock I saw the contents of the pockets of my trousers that I had thrown on the floor: money, cigarettes, a lighter and a piece of paper. It was a bill with several items and a total of two hundred and twenty-five crowns. There was no heading on it but it was not a bill from the Barbara nightclub. Was it possible that on the way home I made yet another stop? I did not know. I could not recall anything of what followed after I had parted from Ludek and Karel on Wenceslas Square.

I turned the bill over. On the back side, I deciphered a few words: 'a heretic in the regiment.' I had a habit of noting down thoughts that occurred to me when I was in orbit. Sometimes they were nuggets that yielded valuable story ideas when I sobered up. A heretic in the regiment…what does it mean, why the hell did I note it down? Oh, yes I remember! Orwell and brainwashing. Apparently I had a flash of hope that I could write it up. Maybe, if I put Orwellian ideas into somebody's mouth, a heretic who refuses to be brainwashed and who will have to pay an exorbitant price for his unorthodox thinking. That's the only way the story could finish. No happy end. I was pleased with myself that I was capable of recalling at least something.

I went to the bathroom and took a shower. Cold, hot, cold, again and again for ten minutes. I looked into the mirror. Seeing my face brought to mind the opening sentence of Krenek's short story *A Sunday To Kill*, when the hero looks into the mirror after a binge and says: "I am right in the shit, but it's a shit within the norm…"

I was alone in the flat. Blanka, whom I still had not managed to divorce, left for work at seven. Given the bohemian life I led we saw each other rarely, if at all. The flat consisted of two rooms. A smaller one was my den, and the larger one, originally a kitchen, was converted into a sleeping-cum-sitting room, with a tiny kitchenette separated by a curtain. When I was not at home, which was very often, Blanka had the flat to herself. Apart from the car my total possessions, if I can call them that, were a typewriter, a dozen books, two suits, two pairs of shoes, several shirts, a pair of pajamas, a few socks and neckties. All of which would hardly fill two suitcases.

I was right in the shit, but an abnormal, monumental and international piece of shit, I thought while shaving. In this form and condition I cannot appear before anybody. Flying to Geneva like this is out of the question.

I cooked half a liter of extra-strong coffee, lit a cigarette and started to think what I should do.

I must cancel the trip to Geneva. That's a priority.

Then I must pack and hightail it to Liben where Ludek owns an artist's workshop to which I have the key, and hole up there for the rest of the week. Nobody will be looking for me. Ruzenka and Tony, the only ones who knew about Geneva, will think I am gone. As for the office, I am officially on leave. Later on I'll find some better explanation for my disappearance but right now I must sober up completely, be myself again. I need a couple of days of peace and calm. I can use them to study the booklets Pechacek lent me about the International Labor Organization which I had not opened yet. All things considered, every cloud has a silver lining. I tried to comfort myself with these lyrics from a song.

I shall fly to Geneva on Sunday. Luckily, I have the free ticket from the Ministry of Foreign Affairs. I just need to call up the airport and change the date.

But first and foremost I must send a cable to Geneva.

I parked my Wartburg illegally right in front of the Post Office at Vrsovice. Inside, I found a blank cable form lying on a small desk and took out my pen to fill it in.

Address: Snow Herrick, ILO Geneva.

I hesitated before I began to write:

'Last minute bureaucratic problems. Coming next Monday, if you agree.'

On a second thought I crossed out 'if you agree.' Why beg for their consent? Simply parachute in on them, like it or not.

VIII. ILO: FIRST ENCOUNTERS OF A NEW KIND

A lanky man stood up behind a large desk made of dark mahogany wood. He stretched out a hand.

"Snow Herrick."

"Jan Vitek." We shook hands.

"Call me Snow and have a seat. May I call you Jan?"

"Sure."

The Director of the ILO Public Information Branch, Snow Herrick was an impressive man almost two meters tall, suntanned, with steel rimmed glasses behind which glittered gray, penetrating eyes. He must have been some four or five years older than I, and his handshake was firm and full of confidence. From the very first moment, I had a feeling of affinity with Snow without knowing why. Similarly, without knowing why, I was certain that this feeling was reciprocal.

"Could you kindly reveal to me," he asked with hidden pointedness, "what were the bureaucratic complications that prevented you from coming last Wednesday when we expected you?"

"Money. The bank did not want to change my crowns for Swiss francs. The bureaucrats stalled. Finally, they gave me twenty francs. The taxi from the airport to the hotel cost fifteen. So I am broke."

I knew I would have to explain the reason for my postponement, so I had my excuse ready, blaming the bank. In fact, they did exchange just twenty francs and the taxi did cost fifteen. That was right. I asked the taxi driver at the airport to take me to a hotel near the Bureau International de Travail. After a half hour ride through the streets of Geneva, which on a hot Sunday afternoon were lifeless, I ended up at the Hotel Eden, dead tired with five francs in my pocket. I could not fall asleep for a long time. The heat inside the room was suffocating. I had to open the window to let in fresh air—and with it the noise of speeding cars in the street as evening brought the town back to life. On top of that I was as hungry as a hunter because I had not enough money to buy a dinner.

"Did you have a pleasant flight?" Snow asked.

Since I anticipated such a standard opening question, I had prepared an eloquent reply depicting the breathtakingly magnificent aerial view of the Swiss and French Alps, with below me a filmset of houses surrounded by green gardens with blue swimming pools, golden sunlit fields, dark patches of forest, snaking country roads and arrow-straight highways. I told him my suspicion that all this must be a sorcerer's trick by the Swiss Tourist Office, because such beauty and tidiness and perfect harmony between nature and human settlement could not exist in reality; it was simply out of this world.

Before Snow could react to my ode on Switzerland the door opened and another lanky American entered, carrying two thick files in brown jackets.

"Mike, meet Jan Vitek...Jan this is Michael Clark, Editor-in-Chief of *ILO Panorama*," said Snow.

Mike and I mumbled "How do you do" and "Glad to meet you" while sizing each other up as we sat down in the easy chairs in front of Snow's desk. My impression of Mike was that he was as cold as a fish and poker faced.

"We have a little work program for you," said Snow in his New York drawl. "Mike will tell you all about it and you will work under his guidance."

Mike's voice indicated an excellent education, most likely Yale or Harvard. As he spoke, I stared dumbly and felt thunderstruck. The rest of this Monday morning and the whole afternoon until six o'clock I was to study the two files Mike had brought for me concerning an ILO project in Thailand, then write a feature story about it of some one thousand words. Tomorrow morning I would tackle a study on unemployment in the world and write a press release of six, seven hundred words. I would devote the afternoon to drafting a story on a subject of my choice, some one thousand words. All that they call a little work program! Jesus Christ! I was completely groggy and felt like a defeated boxer being carried out of the ring. My buddy Tony who had talked me into applying for an ILO job, assured me (swearing on his head) that the interview would be an urbane conversation, a polite encounter between civilized people. And now what a shock! As a surprise it was an unqualified success. The two Yankees had caught me with my trousers down. I swallowed drily a couple of times, but otherwise I tried my best to be cool.

"That looks swell. Let's get started," I said nonchalantly as if nothing was wrong.

Snow smiled, maliciously as it seemed to me, and I suspected that he well knew how I really felt. OK, smart guys, I thought, you are tough with me; I can be tough, too.

"By the way, Snow, I could use some advance for my traveling expenses," I said.

"OK, come back at lunch time. My secretary, Claude Passet, will accompany you to the cashier's."

Clark showed me to a vacant office with two desks opposite each other and two chairs. There was a typewriter on one of the desks with a batch of clean paper. A large window offered a view of the park with a statue and a partial glimpse of Geneva's Lake Leman. Clark handed over to me the two thick files whose

247

brown jackets were marked Thai PU 11 at the top, and below in capital letters the mystic title MAN/DEV.

"This is the most important management development venture of the ILO in Thailand," said Clark. He went on to explain that the files contained a description of the project as well as reports by ILO experts and evaluations of results achieved so far. In short, all the necessary information and data that should serve as the basis for the feature story. He asked me if I had any questions, but I was so floored my mind was totally blank.

I lit a cigarette, took off my jacket, hung it on the backrest of the chair, loosened my tie and sat down with a deep sigh. Then I opened the first file. I know where Thailand is, but what the hell is management development all about? I took it as a challenge. The file certainly has a logical arrangement, I noted. Most probably it is organized chronologically. If so I would not need to read all the papers entirely, page for page. First and foremost, I must grasp the economic rationale of the project, why it was launched, how it is financed, what its goals are, how it works, and with what success. Then I can just leaf through the pages and scan them. This was easily conceived but hard to do. I wrestled with the new notions, technical terms and ILO jargon that was mumbo-jumbo to me. The ashtray was soon full of cigarette butts. I jotted notes, facts and figures, and dog-eared the most important pages in the file.

I lost track of time. Somebody knocked at the door but I could not hear it, I was in Thailand.

"*Bonjour, Monsieur Vitek*," said a female voice. It belonged to Claude Passet, a willowy young lady who asked me if I still wanted to go to the cashier's to collect my traveling expenses and per diem. If I wanted money? What a question!

Within half-an-hour I was rich. Out of my new

treasure I should have to pay the Ministry of Foreign Affairs three hundred and fifteen francs for the air-ticket, but the rest, six hundred francs, would be mine. Well, not all, because I shall have to deduct two hundred and ten francs for three nights in the hotel, and, say, eighty francs for food, maybe less, if I eat frugally. Which will leave me at least three hundred francs I can take home. I did not dare to convert it into Czech crowns to avoid vertigo. My mood improved enormously. I felt great.

Clark invited me to lunch in the restaurant on the first floor. He brought along a copy of the latest issue of *ILO Panorama*. The magazine was printed on coated paper, richly illustrated with photos and totaled forty eight pages. As we sipped an excellent asparagus soup, Clark told me his plans to increase the frequency of the magazine from a bimonthly to a monthly. That was why he needed an assistant editor who would take over some of his chores, including preparation of manuscripts for the printer, co-ordination of translations into French and Spanish, supervision of production, and, of course, drafting original stories as necessary.

He is looking for a journalistic jack-of-all-trades, I thought, a junior underling. Well, my gofer years are past and long gone.

While downing a beefsteak with hash potatoes and cucumber salad I asked Clark how many candidates had applied for the job. A great many, replied Clark vaguely, adding that the Selection Committee chose three candidates to come to Geneva for interview, and I was the last of them. He pointed out that he was in no hurry to find an assistant, and should no competent candidate emerge from the present round of the competition, he would launch a new call for candidatures next year.

That did not sound too encouraging, but since I did not entertain any hopes of getting the post, I felt a great temptation to say: You know, Mr Clark, I am also not in a hurry to change my job. I have become an established author, with two books published, a third in the press and a fourth coming from my typewriter. But hearing that, Clark would certainly want to know why on earth I had applied. I could not possibly tell him the truth, namely that it was because of the paid excursion to Geneva. So I suppressed the temptation. Life under Communist rule had taught me to keep irreverent thoughts to myself. I silently munched the hard steak that must have come from an ox a hundred years old.

We drank tap water that was served free. I chose ice cream as dessert. Clark paid the bill. I thanked him with heartfelt gratitude. He had saved me at least twenty precious Swiss francs.

On the way down to the office I asked Clark whether it would be possible to talk briefly with the desk officer responsible for the Thai project, because I would like to quote him in the article to make it more readable. Clark said no, because that would give me an advantage over the two other candidates, who had not asked to speak with the desk officer. I objected that it was their problem if they did not think about this possibility.

"Forget it," said Clark.

I made my way through the second file until three o'clock and finished totally exhausted. I opened the window to let fresh air into the room and air my aching head. There was a knock at the door; this time I heard it and said "Come in." It was again Claude Passet, who brought me a cup of coffee on a tray.

"Merci mille fois. Vous êtes un ange," I said.

(*Thanks a million. You are an angel.*)

"*Je le sais*," she smiled, "*tout le monde me le dit.*" (*I know. Everyone tells me.*) Then she informed me that her husband, René, was a correspondent of Agence France Press at Geneva's United Nations main building, the Palace of Nations. That's why she knew that a journalist without cigarettes and coffee could not function. She added the valuable information that a bar was at the end of the corridor behind the entrance hall. I made the trip there several times in the afternoon. I paid one franc for each cup of coffee but I considered it a vital investment.

I was struggling not only with the subject matter but also with the typewriter, which had the same keyboard as my old Underwood, but with the keys z and y interchanged, a Swiss-French arrangement. As I am used to touch-typing this difference caused frequent typing errors. I was just cursing myself for that when Snow appeared in the door.

"How is it going?" he asked.

"Fine, I can see the end of the tunnel."

It was not true. I had finished only the first page. I tried to write short sentences, both to avoid stylistic errors and because they read better. I made a new paragraph for every thought to stretch out the story and fill the pages more quickly. It was half past five when I pulled the fourth page out of the typewriter. Altogether it should be seven or eight hundred words, by my estimate. I lit the last cigarette and carefully read every word and every sentence, making corrections by hand. They were many and the manuscript looked messy because of my hardly decipherable handwriting. It occurred to me that I should retype the whole thing, but there was not enough time. After all, I don't care about the job; I am here just for fun.

What should the title be? I debated for a while. Then

I wrote at the top of the first page in block letters:

WANTED: MANAGERS FOR THAILAND's FUTURE

On the stroke of six the door opened. Clark came to collect my masterpiece.

I left the ILO building and went into the adjoining park. There were a couple of giant sequoias and among them a sculpture of farm laborers in harness pulling a plough, or so it seemed to me. I was overdosed on nicotine and caffeine. I needed an antidote. A glass of beer or two would do nicely. When I thought of a pint of Pilsner, my thirst became unbearable. But I knew I must resist at any cost. I did not want to awaken a dormant demon. I knew myself too well. I must stay sober.

I decided to take a walk and began to study the City Plan that I picked up in the reception hall of my hotel. It showed the center of Geneva forming a sort of horseshoe around the lake. I decided to follow the path in the park that winds along the lake, continue as far as the Mont Blanc bridge, then turn right and go up to the railway station of Cornavin, then turn right again and walk along Rue Lausanne back to the hotel.

The path in the park brought me to an elevation from which I had a wonderful view of the lake. A strong wind was blowing, churning the water and making waves with white tops like coquettish nightcaps. The lake was dotted with sailing boats, and when you looked towards its far end where it melted into the horizon, you had the impression of being at the seaside. The air smelled good, a strange cocktail with the odor of water and trees and flowers and God knows what else.

I stood there a long while to let the wind air the poisons out my body. My mind was full of Thai managers and it was difficult to chase them away.

Think about something else, I ordered myself. Remember this is the first time and the last time you are here. Look around attentively, capture a picture of this place in your memory so deep that it will remain there forever. However, I was aware it was futile. I tried to do it in Korea and China, but my mental photographs never last, they fade with the passage of time until they disappear into a dark hole.

It was an early August evening and the park was quiet. Only a few people were strolling around. Most benches were deserted. However, the terrace of a restaurant, Perle du Lac, was full of life. I heard animated chatter, laughter, the tinkling of glasses. Not a single table was empty. I stood at a distance and observed the human hive. It seemed to me so carefree, light-hearted, feather-headed, and hedonistic. Maybe it was because I was hungry, thirsty and dried out like a lemon, but it was certainly also because I realized that I was a foreigner and that I did not belong here and never would. I felt an unbearable solitude.

To chase away melancholy and self-pity I started to march resolutely on the waterfront. In less than twenty minutes I already saw the tip of the lake crossed by the bridge of Mont Blanc. On the right I spotted the Hotel Richmond. A bit of history came to mind, which I had read somewhere. This hotel was the first refuge for Tomas Garigue Masaryk when he was in exile at the beginning of the First World War. He was sixty-six years old when he started the campaign for the recognition of an independent Czechoslovak Republic. The reporter in me prompted: Go there, do a story. But I had no energy; I was too exhausted mentally and physically. What I needed was to drink, eat and sleep, in that order.

I went up the rue de Mont Blanc and there, near the railway station, I stumbled on a self-service restaurant.

The menu was written by hand with chalk on a blackboard. The prices seemed reasonable, compared with those I had seen elsewhere. I chose beefsteak with eggs and a bottle of Badoit mineral water. All together they cost twelve francs, a fortune converted into Czech crowns. That would have paid for a binge in Prague.

But by half past nine I was fast asleep on the hotel bed.

On Tuesday at nine o'clock sharp, Mike brought me my morning menu in the form of a slim publication containing sixty pages and entitled *New Development Strategy to Combat Unemployment and Poverty*.

As he put it on my desk he told me that I had two-and-a-half hours to write a press release of six hundred words minimum. He added that at half past eleven I should go to the office number 34 in this corridor to see the Deputy Director, Marc Carriche, who wanted to speak with me. The name was French, so I deduced that he wanted to check on my French. This bothered me. When had I spoken the language of Moliere for the last time consistently? Oh, yes, it was at the Institute some fifteen years before.

I went to the bar to get a cup of coffee, lit a cigarette and opened the booklet. It depicted the evolving social drama of the second half of the Sixties. Worldwide 300 million people were unemployed or underemployed. Before the end of the century a billion new jobseekers would be looking for work in the developing countries alone. Therefore, the challenge is to create over a billion and a half new jobs during the next thirty five years, if currently unemployed and future jobseekers are to be able to earn a living. Some 800 million people live in absolute poverty and 500 million go to bed hungry every day. The social chasm between nations and within nations is growing larger with every day. An emphasis on economic growth has failed to bring about the needed development, which is why it is necessary to change strategy and direct national and international efforts to the satisfaction of the basic needs of large masses of people. The key to success is employment creation. I found the analysis and description of the problems precise and convincing. But the proposals for what to do consisted of generalities and wishful thinking.

I put a paper in the typewriter and tapped out the first paragraph:

Work for all. Far easier said than done, if we mean that everyone should have a satisfying job and one that is useful for society. It is an unending struggle that has become the central problem of our time…

I got used to the strange keyboard and made fewer misprints. Then once again I infested the manuscript with corrections, but this time I had enough time to retype it with a headline: 'JOBS, JOBS, AND MORE JOBS.'

Marc Carriche was a small frail man with a lively and pleasant face. His brown eyes mirrored intelligence and sensibility. He was a perpetual number two because the Director's post in the Public Information Branch belonged to Americans.

Carriche received me warmly as if we were old friends, but I remained alert not knowing what to expect. Since my French left much to be desired I admitted it right away saying "*Mon francais est rouillé.*" (*My French is rusty.*) Carriche took note of it, nodding his head.

"*Pourquoi voudrez-vous joindre BIT?*" he asked me off-hand. (*Why do you want to join the ILO?*)

What should I answer? That such an idea had never entered my head and that I am here to see Geneva and

255

get a glimpse of capitalism…No, I must come up with something constructive.

So I said that since the ILO was created to help improve the lot of working people everywhere, it would be an honor and privilege for me to work for the Office to the best of my abilities, and that I was sure to find personal satisfaction in making a contribution to the ILO's mission. Nothing better came to my mind. But my shot in the dark seemed to have satisfied Carriche. He nodded approvingly. Then he started to lecture me about the origins of the ILO at the Versailles Peace Conference, stressing that the French delegation advocated the idea that the ILO should not only set international labor standards but should also be authorized to impose sanctions on states violating obligations they had accepted. He went on to say that the British and American delegates defeated the proposal, and as a result the ILO supervisory activities are toothless, which is very regrettable.

I managed to interject that our Minister of Foreign Affairs, Eduard Benes, who later became our President, was among the founding fathers at Versailles, and that the Soviet Encyclopedia branded the ILO as an reactionary instrument taking the edge off the struggle of the working class because instead of class confrontation it stands for co-operation between the workers, employers and governments.

Carriche said something like "*C'est très intéressant, jeune homme*" (*That's very interesting, young man*) and continued his exposé, telling me that the first Director-General was a Frenchman, Albert Thomas, who initiated the adoption of the first international labor standards regarding forced labor and child labor, but that these problems were still with us.

Obviously, he liked to talk and delivered a long monologue. Which made me happy because I did not have to say much, just to utter from time to time: *Ah, oui...mais vraiment?* He would have gone on and on if he had not interrupted by Claude Passet, who came to tell me that Snow Herrick was waiting for me because he wanted to take me out to lunch.

"*Bon, bon,*" acknowledged Carriche. But before letting me go, he asked me how long would I want to stay in the ILO, if I got an offer.

"*Une année,*" I said without giving it much thought. (*One year.*)

"*C'est drôle, je suis également venu pour un an.*" (*That's funny, I also came for a year.*)

"*Combien de temps avez-vous passé au BIT?*" (*How long have you spent at the ILO?*)

"*Dix-sept ans.*" (*Seventeen years.*)

Wow, he had also wanted to stay for only one year. But how come that he had already served seventeen?

"*Vraiment? Comment avez-vous fait?*" (*Really? Why have you stayed?*)

"Easy," smiled Carriche. He added in English: "Geneva is a golden cage."

Snow Herrick's car was a big Lincoln convertible that seemed to float over the asphalt road leading from the ILO to the Palace of Nations, located on an incline above Lake Leman. There was no guard at the entrance, just a gatekeeper who sat in a booth reading a newspaper. Snow had a problem finding a slot in the parking lot large enough for his land cruiser.

During the whole trip I was trying to recall a story regarding a Czech connection with the Palace I had read somewhere long ago...Half forgotten, it emerged piecemeal to my memory...A daughter of our first President Masaryk, Olga, came to Geneva right after the First World War for treatment for tuberculosis...in a sanatorium she met a certain doctor

Revilliod....They married...Meanwhile, her brother Jan became the Minister of Foreign Affairs and was often in Geneva to attend meetings of the League of Nations, the predecessor of the UN...One day he mentioned to his sister that the League was looking for a suitable building site to construct its headquarters...The park on the lake was considered as an option but negotiations with the city fathers failed...Olga told him that her husband owned a huge meadow on the hillside above the lake...She convinced him to give it to the League for free...However, Doctor Revilliod had two conditions...that the cedars of Lebanon he had planted there must be preserved, and that there would always be a couple of the peacocks he adored in the park...I made a mental note to ask Snow if peacocks were still there.

From our table on the balcony of the restaurant on the eighth floor we had a unique view of the lake and the old town with St Peter's Cathedral. The lake below was calm, reflecting the blue sky. Far on the horizon was a panorama of Alps giants dominated by the snow-topped Mont Blanc and Aiguille du Midi. I had the same impression I experienced in the plane that this view was not real, that I must be looking at a kitschy mirage only nature could create.

"Do you like fish?" asked Snow. He added that a specialty of the restaurant is *perches du lac,* fresh perch from the lake, served with rice. "Some wine? Or would you rather have a beer?"

"Neither. Just water."

Snow ordered a salad for both of us as *hors d'oeuvre*, *perches du lac* and, for himself, a bottle of Fendant, the Swiss white wine I made acquaintance with at the Korean Demilitarized Zone. I asked for my favorite mineral water, Badoit. I was on my guard. I knew he had not invited me for the pleasure of my company.

"Do you see the mountain over there?" Snow pointed his hand in the direction beyond the lake. "It is Le Môle, but it is also called American Mont Blanc." He went on to explain that the real Mont Blanc is only visible on sunny, summer days like we had that day, while in other seasons the view was often blocked by clouds or fog. When American tourists come to town in winter and demand to know: "Where is Mont Blanc?" guides point to the snow-covered Le Môle, which is viewable every day. Hence the nickname American Mont Blanc. Probably by now every American tourist has heard the story. I laughed to be sociable, and waited to hear what Snow would bring up next to probe me in depth. For as the Americans say: There is no such a thing as a free lunch.

When we started eating our main dish Snow directed the conversation towards my stay in Korea and wanted to know what I thought of the Neutral Nations Supervisory Commission in which I worked for almost three years.

"Did it serve some purpose, or was it just a fig leaf?"

"To be honest, I must say that both sides cheated. Both were illegally, behind our backs, increasing their military potential," I said. "However, had the Commission and its inspection teams not been there, the pace of rearmament would have been much faster and the situation on the 38th parallel would have become far more dangerous and explosive. After all, the fact that the truce holds speaks for itself."

Snow brooded for a while, and then with a malicious glitter in his eyes he asked if I would take a blunt question.

"Just go ahead, shoot," I said.

"Tell me, Jan, do you belong to the Communist core

members?"

"Definitely not!"

"Then enlighten me, please," Snow drawled with a touch of irony, "How is it possible that you could apply for a job in the ILO?"

He had certainly done his homework. He knew how things worked in a communist country. I decided to level with him.

"I have a drinking buddy, Tony, who is the son of a Czech minister and, therefore, occupies a high position in the Ministry of Foreign Affairs," I said. "One day, well in early May to be exact, after having a beer in the pub Tony asked me if I would like to go to Geneva. I said not today, maybe tomorrow, when I get sober. Tony said he was serious, that he had on his desk a competition announcement from the ILO regarding the post of an assistant editor, and that I should apply. When your invitation came, there were last-minute objections to my trip to Geneva from a Party boss at the Ministry, but Tony succeeded in overcoming them."

I don't know whether he believed me or not. That was his problem, not mine.

After a prolonged, awkward silence, Snow asked:

"How do you like Geneva?"

"I love what see."

A banal question calls for a banal answer. Then in an effort to steer the conversation to a topic I had prepared I asked:

"Are there peacocks in the park?"

"Peacocks?" wondered Snow. "In fact, yes, how do you know?"

This gave me an opening to show off with the little-known historical background of the Palace of Nations and the role played by Olga and Jan Masaryk. I silently hoped that the story was true and that I had remembered it accurately.

"Jan Masaryk," said Snow. "He was murdered, wasn't he?"

"That is still a mystery. A friend of mine, Dusan Hamsik, has tried to write a book about it, but he was hampered by the police and by the Central Committee of the Communist Party. Most of the relevant documents, including the autopsy, are sealed as a state secret."

"How is it, to be a journalist in a communist country?"

I shrugged.

"You need not answer, Jan."

"OK, it is difficult and exciting," I said.

Snow remarked that he could imagine the difficulty of my profession, but that he failed to see what I found exciting in it.

Now I could have used a glass of wine to stimulate my eloquence. Instead I just tried my best to explain a complex problem. I started by saying that at the moment we were living in a benign period of political thaw and hope for change. A lot of my friends think that the regime can be reformed from within, and that writers and journalists must play a special role in sowing determination into the minds and hearts of our people to bring about the desired change. This is why we must fight every day for freedom of expression in the media and in public life. That, in turn, means we must battle censorship with wit and imagination.

"It is this challenge that makes my job exciting," I concluded.

We finished our coffee. Snow glanced at the bill and put a couple of banknotes on it.

"Let's go," he said.

We boarded his land cruiser and slowly floated back to the ILO.

"Do you believe that communism can be reformed?"

asked Snow.

"Not really…But what other option do we have?" I said.

It was the plain truth. I did not share the optimism of my friends. However, I did not see any alternative either.

Mike Clark was waiting for me in the office. I arrived half an hour late and could blame Snow for the delay.

"I know," said Clark. "You will have to hurry. I want you to finish at five."

"Fine by me," I said.

Clark explained rapidly that he wanted me to write eight hundred words at least of a treatise or reportage on a subject matter of my choice. The purpose of the exercise, evidently, was to test my stylistic abilities.

"Have you chosen your subject?"

"Sure."

"Good luck."

Three months ago, in the middle of May, I lived through a memorable week with a rescue party in the mining region of Ostrava in Northern Moravia. A fire broke out around midnight in one of the main pits and was rapidly spreading in the direction of a chamber where three tons of dynamite were stored. If they exploded all the adjoining galleries would be destroyed and the pithead machinery would be blown away. Rescuers had to work in heat that could reach 1200 degrees Celsius, but with courage and superhuman effort they put out the fire. I published a detailed report of the event in our magazine. Now I decided to rewrite it from memory in English.

I started with the headline:

THE NIGHT WHEN HELL BROKE LOOSE
It was no exaggeration. There really an inferno

raging underground at Ostrava as a result of the fire. Then I continued with a description of the scene.

The shrieking sound of a siren high above the pithead, men jumping on trucks and bikes, or just running, women standing in front of the main gate, muted by fear and bewilderment—the picture is still so vivid and sharp that it might all have happened yesterday...

True, I had the picture before my eyes as I was typing the story. I paused to recall that two weeks after my report had appeared I received a cable from the rescuers to come right away to Ostrava. I thought that I had spoiled the report or had made mistakes in it. Therefore, I feared the miners might correct me with their heavy fists. Instead I was welcomed as a celebrity. It turned out that no one had thanked the rescuers for saving the mine. They received a sizeable financial reward from the management only after my report appeared in the magazine. The miners knew how to be thankful, and it took me three days to recuperate from their hospitality.

I attacked the keyboard again:

I can recall quite clearly the sudden stillness in which, after a long wait, a rescue party emerged from the cage and plodded over the muddy courtyard. Stiff and weary, the men hardly uttered a word. Words were superfluous; they could add nothing to the ominous message written on the drawn faces that were smeared with coal and sweat. Their bloodshot eyes seemed to be burning white anger...

I had got used to the keyboard completely and made a minimum of typos. I was so immersed in the story that I lost all notion of time.

"Have you finished?" Clark's voice interrupted me.

"Here you are, the length should be all right." I pulled the fifth page out of the typewriter with the story unfinished. With a touch of irony I wrote by hand at the end: 'To be continued,' as in a TV series.

I handed over the manuscript to Mike Clark, who glanced at it and, apparently intrigued by the headline, started to read the first paragraph.

"Hmm, it reads like Zola," he said.

I did not know how to take his remark: as a compliment or condemnation? But I could not care less. I had done my stint, and so far as I was concerned, I had finished with the ILO.

I went to Herrick's office to say goodbye to him.

"It was good to know you, Snow," I said sincerely, with some regret, because I was sure never to see him again.

"My pleasure, "said Snow. "You will hear from us."

"I know, don't call us, we'll call you, as they say."

"This is ILO, not Hollywood," smiled Snow. "We don't call, we write."

I had supper in the same self-service as the day before. I chose beef Stroganoff but it was a sham compared with the real thing they serve at the restaurant Moskva in Prague. It cost me ten francs fifty centimes. I hesitated whether to indulge myself by ordering some beer as a treat. A small bottle of Heineken cost two francs. If I save the money, I can have at least four pints of Pilsner at home. I opted again for Badoit mineral water.

On the table lay a copy of the local paper *La Suisse* that someone had left behind. Out of professional interest I leafed through its pages of sober layout and print. A lead story on the first page caught my attention. It contained a report about a proposal to build a tunnel under the lake that would relieve the heavy traffic across the bridge of Mont Blanc. In the cultural section I learned that the cinema Rex was showing a new blockbuster, *Dr No*, based on the book of that name by Ian Fleming. I had several of his books that I had bought at an American army PX store in Pusan in South Korea, but *Dr No* was not among them. Now I could see it on the screen. That was an opportunity I must not miss.

A waiter explained the way. The Rex was within walking distance. In twenty minutes I found myself at the box office. It was shortly before eight and there was a long queue. However, the cinema hall was large and we all were seated. The ticket cost five francs, a fortune for me, but I spent them gladly. The plush seat I sank into was extremely comfortable, like a club chair. James Bond was portrayed by an unknown actor named Sean Connery. The camera loved him: he was charming, glamorous and gracious, and at the same time a real he-man. For me he immediately became the personification of James Bond as I imagined him. The picture lasted an hour and a half but it passed quickly in thrills and excitement. I left the cinema in a daze. As I walked through the sleepy town I felt as elegant, irresistible, witty and strong as James Bond. For a few happy, uplifting moments.

The receptionist at the hotel told me I had a message and handed me an envelope. When I opened it, I found a hand-written note saying 'Please call Mr Clark in the morning.' What does he want? Most probably, he has thought up an additional test! Oh, not me, Mr Clark, my cup is overflowing. With that I threw the note in the wastepaper basket near the lift.

I had a fitful night. The last two days haunted me, coming back to me bit-by-bit, topsy-turvy, keeping me half-awake. What else could I have said? What words could have been better chosen? The sentences I wrote now sounded hollow. I wished I had a second chance, to give it another go. When saying goodbye to Snow I should have made a more graceful exit, rather than resorting to that cheap Hollywood joke. But he took it well. I was sure he will write a polite letter that to his great regret my candidature was not accepted....So what: do you want to live in Geneva? No. Thus there is no problem.

While I was flinging myself about in the narrow bed of the cheapest room in the Hotel Eden, my mind was filled with images and scenes inspired by the piece I wrote yesterday recounting a contemporary social drama. In my dream state I saw the four horsemen of the Apocalypse on their fuming horses holding their reins in one hand and blazing swords in the other that carried bloody slogans: *unemployment...poverty...hunger...exploitation.* The swords were pointed at me and I stood there naked, armed with a quill pen...the riders drove over me, knocking me down...then they turned for another attack...and the nightmare started all over again. It was a weird sort of premonition, so forceful and impressive that made me sit up in the bed while cold sweat ran down my spine.

I got up, went to the window and opened it wide, standing there immobile, gasping for fresh air. Dimly-lit rue de Lausanne was deserted. In the darkness of the park the ILO building was hidden. Now part of the World Trade Organization, it seemed to me then like Kafka's Castle, maybe because it aroused in my subconscious a feeling of uncertainty and fear.

Back in bed I decided to focus on something associated with pleasant memories. I recalled the lovely face of Ruzenka and her shining smile. We shall be together again tomorrow in her little studio...and, perhaps soon, I shall buy a real flat for us, and we will get married and we shall be happy and live together forever. I finally fell asleep.

Boarding time was eleven thirty. I still had a half-an-hour to kill. On the spur of the moment I went to a telephone booth, put fifty centimes in the slot and dialed the ILO number. When the operator came on, I asked to be connected with Michael Clark.

"This is Jan Vitek," I said. "You wanted me to call you…"

"Oh, yes, Jan," said Mike in a warm, almost friendly tone. "You have forgotten your pen here…Do you want to stop by to pick it up?"

When I explained that I was calling from the airport, Clark asked whether he should send the pen to my address in Prague.

"It's a Parker," he added with some emphasis on the brand name.

In fact, it was a copy of a Parker. I had bought some two dozen of them in China for less than a dollar apiece as presents for friends, and I still had several of them at home.

"No, thank you, don't bother," I said.

"As you wish…Have a nice trip back home, Jan."

"Have a nice day, Mike. Goodbye."

That Mike wanted to send the pen to me in Prague, I concluded, means he does not count on seeing me again. Fine by me.

When I mounted aboard a Soviet-made plane of the Czechoslovak Airlines, I felt great relief. I am on the homestretch, hurray! The tension and stress of the past two days evaporated like hot air from a teacup. I was reborn.

My seat was at the window on the right-hand side, so I should see the Alps panorama one more time…for the last time.

"What would you like to drink?" asked a blue-uniformed airhostess.

"A beer," I groaned. "My kingdom for a pint of Pilsner."

IX. ORBITAL RE-ENTRY: MANACLED TO THE GOLDEN CAGE

My new office was on the ground floor with a view of the park and Lake Geneva. Its surface changed according to the weather, reflecting blue or filmy skies, playful cirrus or low thunder clouds. In late summer afternoons the setting sun produced a golden vault of rays arching over the water. The lake was vain and capricious like a vaudeville coquette. Sometimes it was calm and peaceful, then suddenly full of waves with white caps, and wild and throwing high surges of water over the pier and flooding the quay.

I arranged my desk diagonally in the room so that I sat with my back to the lake and facing the door. I wanted to avoid being distracted by the view when I was writing. Finally, I had an office for myself. What a relief, and what a difference compared with the small, crowded annex office in which Mike Clark put me on the 3rd of January 1966 when I joined the ILO. I called it our barn. We toiled there under Mike's constant and vigilant supervision: a French editor, Spanish editor, editorial secretary, two typists, and myself as an editorial factotum.

Clark was particularly strict about office hours. At half past eight we had to be at our desks, or come up with a plausible excuse like children at school. Punctuality has never been my forté. Nor have I been eager to submit to discipline at work. Moreover, I moonlighted. At five o'clock every morning I was already bashing away at my portable typewriter to finish the last chapter of my second volume of true detective stories. It covered the case of the serial killer

Mrazek. The benevolent Colonel Kalivoda, who loaned me the police files regarding this case, would certainly have had a stroke if he knew that I had smuggled such confidential documents abroad. I made slow progress in writing the story because of my lack of concentration so early in the day. And when I finally managed to focus, I had to stop, take a quick shower, shave, put on my best, and only, suit, and hurry off to be on time at the office. I had a small studio in Montchoisy Street on the left bank of the lake. As the ILO was located on the right bank, I had to cross Mont Blanc bridge, follow the quay past the Hotel Richmond and the restaurant Perle du Lac and then via the park Mon Repos to the treadmill in the barn. To get there took me about a half an hour of forced marching. I could use public transport but that would involve changing buses and it would not be any faster. On top of that, I would have to pay a fare, and I did not have that much money to spare at that time.

Clark and I were different in many respects. This difference slowly but surely degraded our working relationship. Most markedly, we differed in our conception of journalistic approach. Clark insisted that right at the beginning every article should have a mention of the International Labor Organization, which, like a *deus ex machina*, was arriving to solve a given problem. The conclusion ought to resemble a solo of kettledrums announcing the advent of shining tomorrows thanks to the ILO, of course. It was a propagandistic approach that I knew and hated from way back. I revolted against it at home, and was not willing to accept it here.

For instance, Clark asked me to write an article about a vocational training project in Tunisia. I began with the description of unemployment primarily afflicting young men leaving school. I instanced the demographic trend that showed the problem would become even more pronounced in the future. All this took the whole first page. Only then did I describe the role the ILO would play to help young Tunisians to integrate into the world of work. Clark forced me to start the article as follows: 'An ILO project in Tunisia is bringing hope to millions of young people in the country...'

When I was in the Ostrava coal basin to report a story about a rescue team in the mine, its members took me down to the deepest shaft, where we had to crawl flat on our stomachs in heat and coal dust that penetrated into my lungs causing fits of choking coughs. No money in the world would induce me to accept such drudgery, I said to myself when we left the pit and were in fresh air and the sunshine again. Now, sitting in the barn, I repeated this thought every day as an incantation against my pitiful lot.

The only respite from Clark's slavery I obtained was the possibility to improve my two working languages. Every day from two to three o'clock I was able to take alternately private lessons in English style and a course in French grammar. I never missed any of them. They represented both an escape from the present and an investment in the future, be it in the ILO or at home.

I became a miser, thinking thrice before spending a franc. As I could not afford to eat in the cafeteria, I brought a box of sardines, a half loaf of white bread and a piece of black cooking chocolate to the office. I devoured this daily menu hastily and secretly in the men's washroom at lunchtime when it was deserted, chasing my meal down with tap water. I dined at home on whatever cheap food I found at a Migros shop on my way home. Clark invited me for dinner only once. However, I was a guest at the Herricks' at least once a week. Snow and his wife led an ostentatious social life.

271

I had the opportunity to meet with practically all the high ILO officials and department directors. Several times I sat opposite the then Director-General David Morse, who made his mark on the history of the ILO when he enriched its traditional standard-setting activity by launching a new field: technical cooperation with developing countries.

I lived like a hermit out of sheer necessity. I had a small salary matching my low grade, since I started at the bottom of the ladder. ILO's bureaucratic structure consisted of five professional categories, each of them having from ten to fifteen rungs. Advancement was slow, usually one step a year, exceptionally two. To move from one category to a higher one was conditioned by a substantial change in job description, in which case you took on far more important functions and responsibilities. But such promotions were rare.

Being in the lowest professional category and on step one, I received a monthly salary of some 2,400 Swiss francs. However, I had to give almost one thousand francs to the Czechoslovak mission in Geneva. We called it the 'haircut.' Supposedly, it was a contribution to the social and pension insurance at home. But in fact it was a measure to fleece you and to make sure that you didn't become purse-proud and difficult. An inevitable and large expense was rent. I lived in a small studio with a kitchenette for which I paid 520 francs a month. This is why I decided to move into a sub-let room in a villa on the outskirts of Geneva. It was too far from the Office to go on foot, and there was no bus connection there at that time. The only solution was to have a car. So I acquired a second-hand Simca 1500 that cost 2,500 francs, to be paid in monthly installments. It was a rattlebox but compared with my old Wartburg at home I seemed to be driving a Rolls Royce.

At Easter I took a couple of days of leave and drove to see Ruzenka in Prague. She could not join me in Geneva because I still was not divorced. The procedure became complicated. My wife did not want to agree to a divorce, and also my lawyer proved incompetent, in addition to my absence. I will cope with it when I return, I thought, because I shall return home at the end of the year, once I have saved enough money to buy a flat. It turned out that architect Vodicka, although he was under the influence of alcohol when he offered me a two bedroom flat, kept his word when he sobered up. We went to see it. Ruzenka found that a lot of things were not properly finished or were missing altogether. Nonetheless, we took it and I had to pay half, some sixty thousand crowns, as down payment right away. This was all the money I had received for the two volumes of true detective stories. My savings in Geneva ought to cover the rest as well as the purchase of furniture. At long last we would have a place to call our own, a home and love nest. What a wonderful feeling of happiness! What great expectations!

The week I spent with Ruzenka and my buddies convinced me that Ota Brozek was right when he said:

"I don't know, Honza, what are you doing in Geneva when your life is here?"

On my way back to Geneva, Ruzenka accompanied me as far as Frantisek Spa not far from the frontier. We spent the night at the best hotel. We were the only guests at that time of year. When I was leaving in the morning, Ruzenka stood in front of the hotel like a statue a while, then she waved her hand, and the last thing I saw were tears sliding down her cheeks. At this moment I felt an urge to brake, stop, jump out of the car, and take her in my arms. My heart beat in my breast like an entrapped bird. This daybreak scene of parting will never fade from my memory.

After my return I endured another two weeks of slavery in the barn before I decided to submit my resignation.

"I would like to go home as soon as possible because to work under Mr Clark is extremely difficult," I told Snow. "But if it is necessary I shall stay until the end of my probationary year."

Snow nodded while listening to my outpouring.

"It looks like you and Mike are an odd couple who will not get on together…Mike is not happy either." It was clear that Clark had also complained, and from his point of view he had valid reasons. "But I don't accept your resignation," continued Snow. "I don't want you to leave, because I am convinced that you have talent and that you will be an asset. This is why I decided to make you editor of *ILO Information*. You will have your own playground to show your worth. Win, or lose, the ball is at your feet."

ILO Information was an occasional clipsheet edited by my French colleague André Lang, and I objected that I would not want to deprive him of a part of his job.

"André has enough on his plate as French editor," said Snow. "He retires at the end of the year anyway, and he is glad to get rid of *ILO Information*."

Well, if André agrees, I thought, it means that they made a deal behind my back.

"OK. When do I start?" I asked obligingly in an effort not to lose face since I grasped that I was being presented with a *fait accompli*.

"As of next week, if you finish the article you are writing for Mike."

I plunged into a new job by reading all issues of *ILO*

Information published so far. Altogether they were fifteen. André produced two or three issues a year. The clipsheet appeared on four pages of a newspaper size. Its layout resembled a railway schedule. André shoveled in selected press releases put out by our department about various ILO activities, including conferences, meetings of industrial committees, Governing Body sessions, adoption of new labor standards and technical co-operation projects. It was a hodge-podge of whatever press material was available.

It was clear to me that the first thing to do was to create a well thought-out editorial concept, one that would focus on three basic issues, namely the objectives of the magazine, its contents and its target audience.

I prepared a document entitled 'ILO Information: New Mission, Contents and Presentation.' I proposed that it should become a direct communication link between the ILO and its tripartite constituency—governments, employer organizations and trade unions worldwide. At the same time it should be a source of noteworthy information for the media about economic and social matters, and, possibly, also for the public at large. It should advocate the basics of the ILO credo: that a lasting peace in the world can only be built on social justice; freedom of expression and organization are the key preconditions for democracy and economic development; poverty anywhere endangers prosperity everywhere; economic growth by itself cannot ensure equality and social progress, and therefore it must be accompanied by a purposeful people-oriented policy guaranteeing the basic rights of working people. Its long-term mission should be to create an image of the ILO as a progressive contemporary institution that generates new approaches, proposals and solutions contributing to social and economic progress, and an equitable distribution of national wealth.

In the technical part I suggested that, for starters, *ILO Information* should appear regularly as a bimonthly. It should have a magazine format, a new layout with photo illustrations, and contain twelve printed pages, two of which would focus alternately on ILO activities one issue in Africa, South America, Asia and the next in developed industrial countries. I envisaged that these special sections would later on become regional and national editions.

When I submitted the new concept to Snow he mulled it over for a while with a thoughtful air.

"It looks OK," he said, "except one problem area…unemployment." He wanted to put an emphasis on ILO activities related to job creation, such as research on unemployment problems, new international labor standards, and technical co-operation for member countries. "And talk to Marc Carriche," he suggested, "pick his brain. He is a fountain of wisdom, he can give you excellent advice."

Marc was enthused that *ILO Information* would at long last have a clear-cut editorial policy. He made a number of comments, concerning especially the ILO's contribution to the improvement of working conditions, equality in the workplace, safety at work, and the protection of basic rights of working people. Had somebody told me at that time that I was preparing a new conception not only of a magazine but also of my whole life, I would have dismissed it with a smirk.

"It is an ambitious plan," said Snow when I brought him the finalized document for approval. "Do you think you can deliver?"

I did not answer. I was not at all sure I had not bitten off more than I could chew. I was aware that I could not rely on the work of my colleagues as André did and fill the pages of the magazine with their sterile products. I must write my own reports, articles and analyses. I also must introduce new forms such as commentaries, editorials and interviews.

All this implied that I must personally attend and cover conferences, meetings and Governing Body sessions, as well as read all the studies and reports and write them up myself. I would have to conduct interviews with authors of those studies and reports. The same went for experts working on technical cooperation projects. Over three weeks I must produce some forty to fifty pages of copy, and devote another two weeks to the coordination of translations into French and Spanish, while simultaneously preparing the layout and material for print. The production proper, including corrections, would take more than a fortnight, and a couple of days would be needed to organize and supervise distribution. Meanwhile I would have to gather material for the following issue and start drafting new copy. I did not know how I would cope with this Sisyphean labor but I was dead set on doing it.

I said goodbye to Mike's barn and moved to an office shared with Dave Skybar, who looked after the budget allocated to our department by the Governing Body. Dave was a Canadian who had already served in the ILO for fifteen years. Since he knew everybody in the secretariat he gave me a lot of precious advice about how to approach high-ranking officials and obtain their collaboration. He was also well acquainted with the printing business and, therefore, I could consult him when preparing the layout and manuscripts for the printer. In addition he volunteered to correct English proofs. He introduced me to the best Geneva photographer, Jean Mohr, who traveled to ILO projects around the world to produce picture reports. I used his photos almost exclusively to illustrate the magazine, since they were always special, inventive and true to life.

Snow asked a junior editor, Sandra Florin, to translate my copy into French. She was a very elegant young woman whose favorite perfume was Chanel No. 5. She considered the translations an unwelcome chore and did not hide this when she delivered them to me. She would throw the neatly typewritten pages onto my desk with obvious disgust.

"*Eh, voilà.*"

When on one occasion I ventured to remark that the French title of an article was too pedestrian and would need jazzing up, she retorted that we were editing an ILO publication and not *Canard Enchaîné*, a satirical French newspaper. I changed the title to suit my taste and asked Claude Passet to check that I had not desecrated the language of Baudelaire. After that I fought a silent war with Ms Florin that lasted until the magazine became the workhorse of all the public information effort of the department, and Snow assigned a new French editor to work with me full time.

My other part-time helper was Rudolf Selke, a polyglot who could work in English, Spanish, German and Russian. His life was like a novel. He was born in Odessa, his father was a wealthy Russian landowner and his mother the daughter of a Jewish merchant. After the Bolshevik Revolution in 1917 the Selke family went into exile and settled in Berlin, where Rudolf studied German literature at the university. Before the war he translated from Russian into German Sholokhov's classic novel *And Quiet Flows the Don* and Tolstoy's *Resurrection*. When Hitler came to power the Selkes concluded that they should emigrate as far as possible from Berlin. A friend recommended to them the Spanish island of Ibiza as an ideal place where a Jewish exile could open a small but profitable coffee shop. "Jan, you can't imagine how many other Jews had the same idea," smiled Rudolf. Since he had linguistic talent he soon mastered Spanish so well that during the Civil War, in which he participated as a volunteer, he became the chief press censor on behalf of the Republican government. He boasted that he had censored the dispatches of Hemingway and Orwell.

During the first three weeks of May 1 wrote most of articles and reports for the nine pages of the first issue. The remaining three, comprising the front page and the middle spread, I reserved for coverage of the three-week International Labor Conference that began its session at the Palace of Nations in early June. Our press center was on the seventh floor adjoining the press gallery. It became my second home. I spent ten to twelve hours a day there. I arrived at work at seven to have peace and quiet for writing before the bustle and stir of the day's activity began at eight thirty. During the day I rushed from one committee meeting to another to gain an overview of what was going on, and to check on progress made in negotiations. I gave them precedence over the plenary discussions that I could follow in *Conference Records*, where they were published verbatim. I was the only one in our department who read all the speeches and noted down the main thoughts, new ideas and proposals they contained.

I took on all this drudgery as a challenge. I wanted to prove that I was capable of making a good and interesting magazine. I might not be going to stay here, but I am going to leave with flying colors, I repeated this to myself as a mantra, especially when my work did not progress as I wanted, and when I had nostalgia or the blues.

Editorial correspondence and administrative chores I

left to Claude Passet. Otherwise it was a one-man show. I did everything: writing, editing, layout, paste-up, crosschecking facts and names in various language editions. In addition I had to revise and expand the mailing list. I increased the press run of the English edition to twenty thousand copies, the French edition to twelve thousand, and the Spanish edition to eight thousand. Over time their combined press run approximated half a million copies.

I cannot say that the first issue of a rejuvenated *ILO Information* provoked a tsunami of enthusiasm. Its impact was rather like that of a stone thrown into a slow-moving pond: the surface rippled in centrifugal waves that disappeared rapidly. Every bureaucracy is conservative by definition and reacts to new things with caution and a wait and see attitude.

The outside reaction was different. Out of the blue came a call from René Passet, who was a correspondent at the Palace of Nations of the influential Agence France Press. His wife showed him a clean proof of the magazine in French that she brought home. Its editorial caught René's attention and he wanted to use part of it in his report on the June session of the ILO's conference.

"Salut, Jan," said René. "I have seen your salad, may I chew off a bit?" he asked.

"Sure, if you spell *ILO Information* correctly," I said half jokingly, half in earnest, to make him aware that I expected to give credit to the source.

If René is interested, why not other correspondents, it occurred to me. I did not hesitate one second and started out of the office across the park to the Palace of Nations holding two English proofs in my hand. I went to see Hans Neuerburg, a senior correspondent of the Associated Press, and John Calcott, Chief of the Geneva bureau of the United Press International. I had become acquainted with both of them during the ILO conference. They came to see me because they wanted to know what was going on in the Application Committee that was about to put the USSR on the black list because of violations of trade union rights. I told Hans and John that *ILO Information* would be distributed generally in three days but that they were free to choose and use any item from it right away.

"Have a first bite but, please, do me a favor and spell out *ILO Information* correctly," I invited them.

They both did. Hans Neuerburg chose an article entitled 'A Billion Jobs or Generations of Poverty.' It warned that in order to reduce mass unemployment by the year 2000 it would be necessary to create 1,000 million new job opportunities, mainly in the developing countries where some forty percent of working-age people were jobless. The alternative was that future generations would be condemned to poverty and hunger. John Calcott decided to use a report on alcoholism at the workplace. According to an ILO study, more than a half of problem drinkers were gainfully employed and society should contribute to paying their doctors' bills and cirrhosis treatment. Alcoholics were also more accident-prone and had more work absences. The combined estimated cost to US enterprises amounted to some 800 million dollars a year. Both Reuters and UPI disseminated short accounts of the articles that literally circled the world. As a result my magazine appeared on the media radar screen for the first time. Based on this experience, I gradually built up an advance distribution network in which I included the most influential press agencies and leading newspapers around the world.

When I drafted articles for the non-conference pages of the magazine I had to use press material put out by my colleagues over the past two months. It's warmed up salami, I grumbled, this won't do. I cannot wait until a report or study lands on my desk. I must know about it in advance. In short, I have to act as a reporter who seeks out his subjects, with the ILO as my beat.

Immediately after the conference I began to survey and explore one major ILO activity after another. First, I visited the department directors I came to know at the Herricks'. Having easy access to them, I tested their reaction to my pitch.

"I want to make *ILO Information* a showcase of the ILO's work and results," I explained. "I would like very much to give due space to publicize your activities. To do that, however, I need to know what major reports, studies and projects are on your plate in the coming months, who is in charge of them, whom could I interview, and when these activities will be ripe for coverage."

Within three weeks I compiled an overview of the ILO's current and future work. I divided the findings into four categories: social and economic studies; reports to conferences, the Governing Body, and meetings of technical committees; preparation of new international labor standards and recommendations; technical co-operation projects and their results. I listed all these activities in a chronological sequence and I had an editorial plan for the rest of the year. At the same time I gained access to key ILO officials responsible for the different fields of work. I could pop in on them any time to discuss work progress and make sure that I obtained galley proofs of their reports or studies. This enabled me to write them up well ahead of publication.

I wanted to keep the results of my story prospection under wraps but Snow insisted I inform my colleagues. At our departmental meetings, held every Monday, I had to reveal what was on my menu for the given week. Some of the work items Snow assigned to other press officers. I was not pleased at all, but there was nothing I could do about it. Therefore, I decided to keep mum about the best story ideas so that I could do them myself.

On the 30th of October Snow called me into his office. As a new issue of *ILO Information* had appeared the day before I silently hoped it was not about a booboo or that I had unwillingly offended some part of the ILO constituency or stepped on somebody's political corns.

"It's not Christmas yet, I know, but I have an advance gift for you," said Snow and handed me a sheet of paper. "Congratulations, Jan."

It was a new work contract 'without time limit' that guaranteed me employment until the 31st of March 1998. It was some time before I realized that I held in my hand a nomination for tenure.

"I don't get it, Snow," I said. "My probation contract ends on the 31st of December. How is it possible that I receive a permanent contract already? It strikes me as quite unusual."

"It is very exceptional, indeed," confirmed Snow.

The standard procedure was that once a probation contract expired, it was either cancelled, or extended for another year, or changed into a fixed-term one. I had not heard of anyone receiving a permanent contract after ten months of work for the ILO. In my inner mind Jarmilka's warning echoed: Don't go there, you will crap out. I should write to her now: I won't crap out, I am fixed until I am sixty, they cannot throw me out unless I get gaga, and even then it is not sure.

"It's a clever move on our part," added Snow with a sly smile, "because it may cure you of itchy feet."

If he means that I'll stay in the ILO until old age, he

is mistaken, I thought. I give myself three, four years at most and then I'll return home because I want to continue my career as an author, and books I can only write in my mother tongue. I was wrong, but at that moment I had not the slightest idea how very wrong I was.

"Thank you, Snow," I managed to mumble. What else could I say? I was confused by contradictory feelings of gratification, joy, apprehension and doubt. I could not find my bearings.

"And how about a pay raise?" I added to alleviate my emotional distress.

"You will get promotion at the end of the year," said Snow. "For now you will get an office for yourself and in due time a secretary."

This is how I gained my own den with a view of the park and the lake.

"Two things before you go," added Snow. "Number one, tomorrow you will take an oath of loyalty to the ILO at the Director-General's office at ten o'clock. Number two, Casey asks you to come to dinner. No excuses, this is a command performance."

X: THE ANTISPY WHO REFUSED TO COME IN FROM THE COLD

I did not expect, neither did any inner voice warn me, that the first Monday in September 1971 would change the life of our family forever. When I drove to work another sunny day dawned on the still sleepy town of Geneva. The sky was blue, the lake was dozing and its surface sparkled like a diamond. I was happy, content with the world, and full of blissful expectation, a feeling augmented by the prospect of a lunch with Professor John Kenneth Galbraith at the hotel *La Réserve*, where he usually stayed when he came from Boston to Geneva.

The ILO parking lot was deserted. I parked my Mustang near the back entrance, closest to my office. A stack of manuscripts waited on my desk that I had to edit for the next issue of *ILO Information.* The deadline was Friday. The lead article was entitled 'The Challenge of Automation: Blessing or Bane?' The impact of automation and new technologies on employment had become a bone of contention between trade unions and employer organizations in industrialized countries. I attended an international conference in Paris in May where the guest speaker was Wassily Leontiev, a Nobel prizewinner for economics. In his mind, automation is neither good nor bad in itself. It all depends on how it is used, whether for the benefit or to the detriment of working people. Personally, he was an optimist. Referring to the experience of the United States with its car industry, Leontiev pointed out that the appearance of cars put out of work thousands of cabmen and horse breeders, but also brought well-paid jobs to millions of Americans. I asked him if I could turn his speech into an article for our magazine. As he agreed, I sent him a shorter, edited version for approval. To the delight of my journalistic soul, Leontiev signed it for printing without a single change.

For some time, I had been aware that ILO research was often a rehash and did not propose new initiatives to solve topical social and economic issues. This is why I began to enrich the magazine with outside opinions and ideas. To overcome potential resistance from within the ILO to views not its own, I shielded myself by choosing internationally reputed experts and scientists.

As a result, the magazine became more readable and interesting. Professor Galbraith had recently given a lecture at the Institute for International Studies about the problems of migrant workers. It was a timely issue. At that time France lured Tunisian and Algerian workers across the Mediterranean to do the dirty, poorly paid jobs the French natives did not want. Germany did the same with regard to Turks. The migrants were supposed to stay for as long as they were needed as '*Gastarbeiter*,' guest workers, and then obediently return home. Galbraith called it a theory for a perfect world. In the real world, however, the 'guests' bring over their families and settle down permanently. He warned that this could be a source of many social and ethnic problems in the future. I interviewed him for the magazine in another attempt to open its pages to unorthodox opinions. "*Trop d'Americains*" (*Too many Americans*), Carriche said of the articles. He was appeased when I told him that I was planning an interview with René Dubois, a reputed French demographer, on the subject of population aging in Western Europe. According to his projections, this was inevitable and would cause grave difficulties in financing pensions from the beginning of the 21st

century. I added that still another European personality whose views I wanted to feature would be Jan Tinbergen, a Dutch Nobel prizewinner for economics. He fathered the interesting idea that in order to reduce poverty in developing countries it would be necessary to transfer production of certain labor-intensive goods from rich countries to the poor ones within the framework of a new international division of labor.

"And what will happen with the European workers who will lose jobs?" asked Carriche.

"This is exactly one question I want to put to Tinbergen," I said.

The door opened and in came Rudolf Selke bringing his Spanish translations. He had retired recently and to mark the event he married his twenty-five years younger partner. He was a short, flabby man with a great head, both literally and figuratively. When we prepared a family vacation in Ibiza in summer, Rudolf said that we should stop in Madrid on our way and book into the hotel Europe where he had a dear friend Vladimir beside whom he had fought in the Spanish war, and ask him to give us Hemingway's room on the top floor. I did not think much about it. After more than three decades Vladimir could be anywhere, maybe six feet under. But it was like a fairy tale. We found the hotel. Vladimir was behind the reception desk. And we slept in Hemingway's room, and received, as a gift, tickets to a *corrida*.

"Do you have something for me?" asked Rudolf.

Since his retirement I had employed him as an external translator. This way I did not need to kowtow to his successor, de Hoyos, who was of little use to me because his translations lacked the elegance and polish of Rudolf's style.

"A couple of news items for the current issue," I said. "But I shall have a big job for you. I want to submit to the Governing Body a proposal to launch new national editions of *ILO Information*, namely in German, Finnish, Norwegian and Swedish. Mr Larsen who works for the UN in Copenhagen will do the Scandinavian editions. You could do the German here in Geneva."

"When do I start?" asked Rudolf. He never refused any chore.

"The Governing Body will meet in November. I think we could start next January."

"Why don't you also propose a Russian edition?"

"You are asking the same question again," I sighed since he had suggested it before. "The answer is the same: *niet*. Valentin Pavlich put out feelers at the Ministry of Foreign Affairs when he was on home leave in the summer. Moscow is mulling it over, but meanwhile it's no."

Pavlich was a Soviet quota member of our department. He spoke French perfectly but his English was poor. He assisted Dick Woodward in drafting and publishing booklets on the social and economic situation in developing countries. They were not too productive because they had other priorities. Those of Pavlich were assigned by the KGB and those of Woodward by the CIA. Snow showed his sense of humor when he coupled them together in the same office and job.

The telephone rang. I glanced at my watch. It was half past nine. I lifted the receiver and said:

"*Oui?*"

"Honziku…," I heard the voice faintly and tentatively in the receiver.

"Ruzenka, my darling, where are you calling from?"

"From Olbramovice…I am in the Post Office."

"When did you arrive?"

"Yesterday evening."

"I am so glad you called, I was worried…You sound strange. Are you all right?"

"Yes, but…"

"What but…is anything wrong?"

"I have no passport."

"Jesus Christ! Did you lose it? Or was it stolen?"

"I had to give it to the two gentlemen who waited for me at the airport."

"Why? Did you ask them why?"

"Yes…"

"What did they say?"

"That all our passports will have to be changed…and that we get new ones when you arrive. They wanted to know when you will come back. I said that you would come, but that you were still not sure when."

The first shock and panic that overtook me, when she mentioned the two gentlemen and confiscated passport, turned into silent horror. I must not let it show, I must overcome it, I must not go to pieces.

"And how is little Jan and your parents? Are all they doing all right?"

"Jan is an urchin, as you know…My mother and father give you their best regards. I miss you very much. Maybe we made a mistake when I came here without you. What do we do now?"

"I don't know, my love. But I am sure I shall find something…You will see all will be fine, we shall be together again."

"But when…"

"Soon," I promised her and myself. "Meanwhile stay where you are, with your parents, don't move anywhere else…"

"What do you mean…?"

"Just stay home so that I can get in touch with you…I must think it through…Could you call me tomorrow at the same time?"

"Do you love me?"

"You know I adore you…"

Petrified, I held the mute receiver in my clenched hand before putting it slowly back in the cradle. Awareness of the grave danger and of my helplessness left me numb.

"Bad news?" Rudolf's voice seemed to come from far away. Since his mother tongue was Russian, he might have understood the Czech words, and from the tone guessed my consternation

"No, it's nothing." I had to use all my willpower to return to reality. "All is OK."

I gave Rudolf the texts to translate, and we parted quickly.

When I was alone I went to the window and lit a cigarette. I smoked it in deep and long breaths so that nicotine would hit my nervous system quickly.

What can I do? I asked myself. Wrong question, the right one is: What must I do? Damage control! Stay cool. Contain your panic and fear. Don't be afraid. All this was easily said but tough to do.

The telephone rang again. I did not answer. I could not stay in the office; I would not be able to fake 'business as usual.' I ran toward the back entrance and out into the park. Only there did I slow down. I walked on the asphalt path meandering along the lake…just as in the evening of my first day here when I was interviewed for the job five years before…Jesus Christ, is it possible that I have been here such a long time! …How much has happened since then…and what will happen now? What to do? That's the question.

Whenever I have had a problem and found myself in tough straits I have always taken a long walk and let my thoughts flow freely in the hope that a solution will emerge like a subsurface river rising from unknown depths.

What will happen next? A young mother passed me, with one child running around and another in a pushchair. Two pensioners were sitting on a bench laughing loudly. Japanese tourists took pictures of the lake dotted with sailboats. A lone jogger flashed by. I noticed nothing of this. I moved like a sleepwalker.

What are my options? Either I succeed in getting Ruzenka and Jan to return to Geneva and everything will be all right, or I fail and will face two predicaments: stay without them here, or join them at home. The frying pan or the fire. To live without my wife and son appeared to me insupportable, cruel and impossible. If I went back home, they would most likely lock me up, and when they let me out an old family story would repeat itself. I shall have to fell trees like my father, or slave in a mine. My son will have no chance to study because he will be branded like his father. And Ruzenka will be miserable as a result of our misfortune.

What must I do now?

I could not meet Professor Galbraith. I was unable to concentrate on a coherent discussion with him, since I couldn't think about anything else but the fix I am in. I must apologize and tell him that something unforeseen has happened.

Next, I must confide in Snow and ask his advice.

Finally, and perhaps most important, I must get together with Pista to try to find out whether he knows something about what's actually going on in Prague, and who may be behind it.

Then it also occurred to me that, in addition, I should try to meet George if he was in town and available.

Snow pointed out that for a confidential talk at lunch,

291

the ILO cafeteria is not a suitable place. He decided we should go to the restaurant Perle du Lac in the park, a five-minute walk from the office.

When I told him what had happened in a succinct account, prepared and thought out in advance, he asked:

"Tell me, who had this brilliant idea to send Ruzenka and the kid to Prague? Was it you?"

His question was like a whiplash against my remorseful soul. How is it possible that I let my wife and Honzik go? What can I say?

"Ruzenka does not like to live in Geneva," I started my feeble defense. "She misses her family terribly. I tried to stay on good terms with the government so that she could visit her parents, two sisters and a brother. She longs to see them for weeks and months before every visit, and she is always so happy to leave Geneva. When she comes back she puts up with life here more easily. So I wanted to enable her to make these family reunions last as long as possible. I thought that nothing could happen, that she was in no danger over there."

"You did not tell her that you want to jump ship?"

"Ruzenka does not know that I have burned my bridges," I admitted. "I wanted to protect her. Therefore I said nothing. I was afraid that should she know that I did not want to return to Prague, she might give it away involuntarily, if only by being very sad."

"How stupid!"

"I know...now."

"Have you had any signals that you have fallen out of their good graces? Since you are still on speaking terms with Czech diplomats, have you not felt any change in their attitude towards you?"

"No...well, yes, in some way. Now when you ask me, I realize there might have been some hints that something was going on behind my back that I overlooked. One thing that comes to my mind now is a conversation with Mr Stefan Hurin, the First Secretary at the Czechoslovak Mission. You may remember him, he looks after non-governmental organizations in Geneva and attends all sessions of the ILO Governing Body. We had a coffee in the bar of the Palace of Nations during the ILO conference last June, and he mentioned, en passant, that I should return to Prague to negotiate with the Ministry of Foreign Affairs a permit to prolong my stay in Geneva. He said that I was here for five years, and that usually all diplomats and international officials return home after such a period of time."

"But you have a permanent contract."

"Hurin knows it, and I reminded him, of course, but that means nothing to the Czechoslovak side. It's five years, period. Hurin said that my contract was an exception, and that the Ministry would certainly agree to make a deviation from the rule in my case so that I could stay on in the ILO. It was just a formality that I should go to Prague to negotiate. He wanted to know when I would go. I evaded, giving an exact date by saying that I must first publish the after-conference issue of the magazine. We met again on the 1st of August at a reception to mark the Swiss national holiday and he repeated his question. In retrospect I perceive there was a certain insistence in the tone of his question. I said that I was working on the September issue and that I would go once I had finished all the manuscripts and put the magazine to bed."

"And you did not hear the alarm bell ringing in your ears?"

"Sure. I was aware that I should not go to Prague under any circumstances since I would not be allowed to come back."

"But you sent Ruzenka…"

"I thought she might slip in and out unnoticed. We kept it under the lid, not mentioning her departure to anybody. I said to myself that it was the last time, let's risk it."

"And you blew it. What will you do now?"

I told him I was groping in the dark, and that the first thing to do was to see Hurin with whom I had a good and friendly relationship. Maybe I could get some information from him, a lead that would help us to find a solution.

While we were drinking coffee, Snow said that he would talk to the Director of the Legal Department, because it was not clear how my case might develop, and it could cause a conflict between the ILO and the Czechoslovak government. He added that I should put down all the essentials in a minute to the Director-General. The Legal Department would decide to what extent the ILO could get involved and what action it could take on my behalf.

"I must put work on the back burner, " I said, "because I shall have to go to the Czechoslovak mission and talk to Hurin, maybe a couple of times. But your secretary will know where you can reach me at any time. Most probably, I will miss all my deadlines for the September issue."

"That does not matter at all now," said Snow. He took the bill, looked at the total, fished a roll of Swiss money out of his pocket, peeled off ninety francs and dropped them on the table.

"Come to think of it," he said as we were leaving the restaurant, "it occurs to me that you have bluffed for far too long. Now they have called your bluff."

He was right. It is a showdown. The question is whether I manage to escape from the trap.

It was a wonderful sunny afternoon. We walked

silently through the park. At one point Snow stopped and stood still.

"You are facing a dilemma," he said. "When the shit hits the fan, what do you decide?"

"Right now I don't know…but I cannot imagine my life without Ruzenka and little Jan. If the worst comes to the worst…I will just follow my heart."

"I get you," said Snow laying his right hand around my shoulder. He pressed it little and we took a couple of steps in this embrace. "Follow your heart, but use cool judgment as well. You are at the crossroads of your life," he added when he released his hand.

The new building of the Czechoslovak mission in Geneva stood near to the seat of the World Health Organization, a stone's throw from the building site in rue Morillon where the ILO had begun to construct its future nine-storied palace because its old home on the lake could no longer house all the officials. The Czechoslovak diplomats were within walking distance of the Palace of Nations, the GATT, which later became the World Trade Organization, as well as the World Intellectual Property Organization and the International Telecommunication Union.

Originally, the mission was accommodated in a small villa at Conches on the outskirts of town. It was where all Czechoslovak citizens assembled in late August 1968 to express their disapproval of the Soviet invasion of their country. They made a lot of anti-Soviet and anti-collaboration speeches. All of them, except me, since I was sitting in the ambassador's office putting together a protest resolution. It was adopted by acclamation. The participants then signed it one by one, and left.

I knew that the illusion of 'socialism with a human face' would be a failure. Valentin had warned me

295

repeatedly since February that Moscow would never permit our Communist Party to lose its grip on the country, or allow us to leave the Soviet camp. George asked me in April to pass a message home that the American government could not help us in the case of Russian military intervention. "Tell your friends," he added, "to slow down reforms and tone down the rhetoric." I made a turnaround flight to Prague and succeeded in talking about it to Vasek. Having heard me out, he shook his big head and said: "We have also heard such tip-offs, but we must, on the contrary, advance faster and more resolutely. At the beginning, people thought it was just a power struggle in the Party, but then they gradually grasped that it was about real political changes directly concerning their lives, and an avalanche of popular resistance got into motion. We must not disappoint their hopes and miss the chance to sweep away Bolshevik socialism, and go our own way. This will be of capital significance for the future." His words echoed in my ears and tasted as bitter as gall. Within a few weeks no one would give a damn about our aborted hopes, and in a few years from now they will disappear through the trapdoor of time.

In the ambassador's residence I stared at the piece of paper, already a bit creased and dirty, that lay on the table before me. I was fully aware of its futility. It will achieve nothing, and most probably will only result in the persecution of those who signed it during that preposterous August night. I remained alone in the room. All the participants had dispersed like a flock of scared birds. I could leave without putting my name on that incriminating document, and no one would be any wiser. I admit that this thought crossed my mind. But I had already burned other bridges, and one more or less did not matter. I chose the right lower corner of the paper, a place no one can overlook. It formed a triangle into which I wrote transversally Vitek, under it Jan, and I added a cross in the tip of the triangle. My funeral. I am burying my present life.

It was three o'clock when I parked my Mustang in front of the new mission. The offices of the diplomats were on the first floor. I ran up the stairs two at a time. I rushed to energize my body and spirit for my head to head with Hurin. Behind his back, we called him Pista, maybe because he originated from a remote village in the eastern part of Slovakia.

"Comrade Hurin is on the phone, you will have to wait a little," said Marta, a chubby, freckled blond girl who was Pista's secretary.

A copy of the mouthpiece of the Communist Party, *Rude pravo*, lay on the small conference table. I mechanically picked it up and looked at it with unseeing and impercipient eyes. I was focusing on my opening gambit. The best defense is attack, I reminded myself, as if I could possibly forget it.

With this decision imprinted on my mind I entered Hurin's office.

"Hi, Honza," said Pista cavalierly and beckoned me to sit down. A year and a half ago, when he came to Geneva, he greeted everybody with a standard Party greeting "Honor work, comrade." But since he was an intelligent man he soon grasped that it doesn't go down well here. "I am very glad to see you," he continued. "Just this morning I thought of you, as I would need a little favor from you. But let's start with what is bringing you here."

"Two plain-clothes policemen met my wife at the airport in Prague and confiscated her passport. What do you know about it?"

The good-natured smile in Pista's face disappeared. His eyes widened in an unalloyed expression of surprise—either genuine or well-acted. "I repeat my question: what do you know about it?"

"Absolutely nothing…I didn't even know that Ruzenka was flying to Prague. Tell me, how could I have known it?"

"Easy. You just give a call to the local office of Czechoslovak airlines to report to you all arrivals and departures by our citizens…so I ask you once more—what do you know about it and what does it mean?"

"Nothing, cross my heart," said Pista. "Tell me what happened, I want to know everything, every single detail."

"There is nothing much to add. Ruzenka and Honzik arrived in Prague yesterday afternoon to visit her parents in Moravia. We agreed that I would join them as soon as I put to bed the September issue of my magazine," I began my spin story, "so as to negotiate at the Ministry an extension of my stay here as you told me. However, this morning my wife telephoned me that her passport had been confiscated. I want to know: what does it mean?"

"I swear I have not the slightest idea! How do you know they were plain-clothes policemen?"

"Who else could they be?"

"Perhaps officials from the passport department of the Ministry. It may be possible they want to issue her a new passport. Did they show her their ID cards?"

"No idea. You know Ruzenka is young and inexperienced. It did not occur to her to ask for their IDs. I don't buy that they were from the passport department. These bureaucrats would not bother, they would write or call her. Besides, our passports are valid until the end of the year anyway."

"There is something that escapes me," Pista said vaguely.

"Me, too. But the difference between us is that

you…since you say you know nothing about it and I believe you because I consider you as my friend," I laid it on thick, "the difference is that you can telephone or send a fax to find out who is behind this and what's the real purpose. They would not take her passport away without a reason, just out of a bureaucratic spite. Somebody in Prague must have a serious grudge against me. Who? Why?"

"Maybe it's all a misunderstanding…I don't believe someone holds anything against you. Maybe it's just because our comrades want you to come to Prague," Pista babbled. "Forget it, that's nonsense." He immediately tried to cover up his slip of the tongue. "I am sure it is a misunderstanding."

"Between whom?"

"Maybe between the passport department and the department of non-governmental organizations. Search me for an answer."

"Why don't you make a call to Prague to find out?"

"Can't be done."

"Why not. You are the First Secretary and you look after the ILO, it's in your job description."

"You know that I would have to make a safe call from the bunker. To do that I need the permission of the Ambassador."

'Bunker' was the nickname for a well-insulated small room next to the Ambassador's office. It was a place for secret calls and meetings. I knew very well that Pista needed nobody's permission. Once, he confided it to me, to show his importance. It was clear to me that we were both bluffers.

"Stefan," I used his name with great feeling, "you and I, we can be frank with each other. We know each other well, and I appreciate you as an excellent diplomat and a valuable human being. No matter what's behind the scheme against me, let's try to preserve our friendly relationship."

"Honza, I am glad you say that. Let's play with our cards openly. There must be a misunderstanding somewhere that can be elucidated. Buy an air ticket…"

"That's not necessary."

"Why?"

"I have one already. When I bought Ruzenka's and Honzik's tickets, I also bought an open one for me so that I could fly to Prague as soon as I am done here. I don't have the ticket with me but you can check with Czechoslovak Airlines." I made a mental note that I must actually buy a flight to Prague in case Pista followed my advice. "But I still believe that there is no misunderstanding," I continued. "I consider what's happening as a paramount expression of mistrust towards me. I am not ready to let it go."

"Honza, don't take it so much to heart. Bureaucrats are jackasses."

"That's right, but it does not change one iota. In fact, what's involved is more than an expression of mistrust. It is blackmail."

"Come, you exaggerate."

"As a shot in the dark, would it be possible that their purpose is to make me resign?"

"Surely not. You can take it for granted."

I took a folded paper out of my breast pocket, a sham document that I had prepared after the lunch with Snow.

"I submitted my resignation last week. Here is a copy. Read it."

I unfolded the paper and passed it to Pista. It was addressed to Snow Herrick and its head read 'Notice of Resignation.' Underneath was just one short paragraph of two sentences that Pista read very carefully.

"You want to leave at the end of the year…for personal and family reasons…What do you mean exactly?"

"Ruzenka does not like Geneva...I would like Honzik to go to school at home, and I want to return to creative writing. I have already started a book about a lowly international official. It will be a sort of satire, but I need to work on it full time for several months...I could never finish it here."

I let Pista take a breather to swallow the bait.

"You should have consulted me," Pista admonished me. "Such a decision should not be made without careful consideration. Are you sure you want to go back?"

"Dead sure, Stefan. I don't like slaving in the ILO. Besides, as my buddies in Prague tell me, there is more fun over there."

"It's a great pity, but if it's your decision...you will have to explain it in Prague."

"My pleasure. But I am not going there under duress. I am as mad as anyone could be. I have never been more pissed off in my whole life. I feel like..." I stopped in order not to overdo my feigned disgust. "I'll go there on one condition only, namely that I hear from Ruzenka that she got her passport back. I have never been blackmailed, and will not tolerate it. In this case especially I will resist it with all my force and determination."

"These are strong words! You are not being blackmailed!"

"I am not? All right. Let them give Ruzenka back her passport as a proof of mutual trust, and then we can start acting on an equal basis."

"Do you want me to report it to Prague?"

There was an undertone in his question belying a veiled threat. I did not react to it since I did not want to escalate the challenge. Instead, I tuned the temperature down to a more conciliatory mode.

"Stefan, please understand me. Imagine you were in my place. Wouldn't you feel bitterness, humiliation, and inner defiance and revolt? Would you tolerate it meekly? Certainly no! But I want to de-dramatize the situation, since blunders do happen. If it is, as you say, a misunderstanding, then a rectification is easy and simple. Ruzenka gets the passport, I go back to Prague, as was and still is my intention, and the whole thing will be settled and forgotten."

The temperature of our relations when we parted was tepid. We took leave of each other hastily. Pista completely forgot the little service he wanted from me, that he would never obtain anyway. Before I sat myself at the wheel of my Mustang, I pointed my index finger to the window of Pista's office and pronounced the worst Chinese curse I knew: "May you live in interesting times." It had no effect at all on him, but I felt much better.

The branch office of the Danzas Travel Agency in the ILO closed at five. I made it just in time to buy an open air-ticket to Prague. The planes of Czechoslovak airlines were never fully booked, and one could come at the last minute and always find a seat available.

When I returned to my office I dialed George's number. The answer was "Call later."

On my desk I found the English translation of a French article by Marc Carriche about the growing emigration of university-educated young people from developing countries to the advanced industrial states. This phenomenon afflicted Africa especially. It was losing many medical doctors, who went to England and France. The article was entitled 'Costly Brain Drain.' The education of one doctor was estimated to be worth one hundred thousand dollars, paid by African states, an investment from which the immigration countries profited. "It is a development aid upside down," wrote Carriche. "Poor states support the rich ones." Carriche's own style was refined. The English version seemed jerky. I tried to polish it but it went badly because of my lack of concentration. Then the telephone rang.

"Hi, Jan, how did it go?"

Snow was calling me from home. He wanted to know how things went off with Hurin.

"He shuffled and wriggled," I said, "but he surely knows more about it than he is willing to admit, which is understandable. We started a game of liar's poker. We shall see who blinks first."

Snow tittered. Then he told me that his friend Jack Martens, Director of the Legal Department, would personally take care of my case. In his opinion any pressure from the Czechoslovak government was illegal, and he promised that the ILO would do everything in its power and possibilities to help me fight it off.

"Casey sends you her love. Don't stay there too long. Go home, have a good night's rest," he added.

I felt good. When you are in deep trouble it is comforting to know that you have real friends.

Before leaving the office I called George anew, this time using his secret number at which he could be reached at any time. When he finally answered the call, I asked him:

"Could we have a chat?"

"When do you want to meet?"

"The sooner, the better."

"OK…Let's meet tomorrow at seven o'clock at the T-bone steak place."

We had rented an apartment on the fourth floor of a building in rue Daubin, one of the areas of Geneva crammed with small flats. Ours consisted of a living room with a kitchenette, a bedroom, and a small child's bedroom. All this in eighty square meters, but in comparison with the tiny nest we had in Prague it was a palace. We saved money every way we could to buy our furniture piece by piece. Money-wise we were better off because I received two successive promotions and moved from the bottom professional category to the third. I had a substantially higher salary than my starting wage, but the kickback I had to pay to the Czechoslovak mission increased in direct proportion as well. If I jumped ship, as Snow put it, I would save some two thousand Swiss francs a month. But I did not think about that at the moment. After all, money never mattered much for me, most probably because I have always earned enough for my relatively modest way of life.

I sat at the forefront of the dining table in my usual place. I dined on ham, bread and cheese, chasing it down with genuine Czech beer. I bought this, as well as wine, alcohol and cigarettes, from the Czechoslovak mission at a reduced diplomatic price. Usually, Honzik would sit on my right and Ruzenka on the left, which was nearer the kitchenette to bring us our food. I felt overpowering loneliness. I recalled how two years ago my father had been sitting at this table with us. We brought him from Kremze to Geneva by car via Austria and Germany so that he could see part of the Western world. He was seventy years old. He lasted only three days. "I couldn't live here," he said. "This place is not for me." The next day we put him on a plane since he insisted on going home immediately.

If I stay, I shall not see my father and mother again, I told myself. What else shall I miss most? Buddies like Ota, Jirka, Pepik, Tonda, Karel, Vasek…In my mind I called up the faces and names and snapshots of our fleeting experiences. I fondled them as miser caresses gold. What else? Bohemian life that connected me via an umbilical cord to kindred souls that I was already missing sorely, as well as enthusiastic discussions about literature, creative writing and fantastical ideas born during all night extravaganzas. What else? Books I carried in my mind that I should never write. And more? I would not be able to go to the National Theater, Rokoko, Semafor and the little avant-garde theater for which I wrote occasional sketches. Deep in my soul I was aware that all that belonged to the past, that it was impossible to repeat the unrepeatable, and that I could not turn back time.

And what would I gain? A secure existence for me and my family, well-paid employment, the chance to live in a large apartment, to exist in comfort and travel freely. Ruzenka will not have to work. Honzik will be able to study. Yes, Mr Carriche, you are right. Geneva is a golden cage.

Don't be stupid, I told myself, there is no balance to weigh what's imponderable, no scale to measure what's immeasurable. No matter what you decide, it will be a jump into the unknown.

I crushed an empty cigarette box and took a new one out of a carton on the cupboard. I smoked Camels. My first one had been offered me by an American soldier in nineteen forty-five.

I found a worn-out record by Elvis Presley, put it on the gramophone and pushed the button to play:

Love me tender
Love me sweet
Never let me go
You have made my life complete
And I love you so

It was our song. I used to listen to it with Ruzenka in that funny shaped little room that became our paradise. I would have sacrificed all the golden cages in the world if we could return there.

It was already eleven o'clock at night when my daydreaming with Elvis ended. I tried to be as orderly as Ruzenka wanted me to be. I put my trousers and shirt on hangers, folded underwear and socks neatly as in the army. Teeth. Pajamas. Nightcap. I poured myself a good measure of Johnnie Walker and sipped it lying in bed. I felt alcohol mounting from my stomach to my head, and closed my eyes.

I replayed the discussion with Hurin in my mind. I heard him saying: "Do you want me to report it to Prague?" I knew very well that he had recorded every word we said as soon as I left. His report was already in the hands of unknown persons who would decide my fate. Pista certainly added his own conclusion and recommendation. But it's stupid to worry about things that I cannot influence, let alone change. In this situation it was far more important that Ruzenka should not have forgotten what I had told her to do in case it might be necessary for her and Honzik to leave the country in a hurry. "Do you remember the small boarding house Franz Nahrada on the outskirts of Vienna where we once spent a night?" I asked her before her departure. "If you get a cable from me with his name on it, drop everything, rush over the border, and I shall be waiting at that boarding house for you." Was it a premonition?

I had fitful night. I finally fell into a deep slumber, only to awaken brutally almost immediately. It was like sinking into a profound well and then being brought back to the surface in no time. My mind worked at full blast. It was almost dawn when the idea shot into my brain like a red-hot arrow: THE SPY FROM BERNE.

In a jiffy I was awake. I sat up in bed brusquely, for I realized with anguish that I had misjudged the reason for my predicament. Pista may really know nothing. The people who want my skin are not from the State Security Service but from Military Intelligence. In the shock I received yesterday morning I had completely forgotten that in late May a voice on the telephone had informed me: "Best regards from Mirek. He is sending you a bottle of Johnnie Walker and I would like to hand it over as soon as possible."

The first time I was 'woken up' in this way was almost four years ago, sometime in nineteen sixty-seven. After that, total silence. I thought they had written me off.

I assumed a fetal position on the bed with my hands clasping the head. In my mind, like an old black and white film, I remembered how they had broken me down shortly before my departure for Geneva:

The door of my room in the editorial office of the magazine *Vojak* opens and a man enters without knocking. He presents himself as Mirek Kvapil and waves a Military Intelligence ID in front of my eyes. "We must have a discussion about a very serious matter," he says. "Would it be convenient for you to meet the day after tomorrow at two o'clock in the Hotel Krivan in room twenty-two on the second floor? Do you know where it is?" I nodded and smiled. It was the place where I celebrated my marriage with Blanka, and where Vasek smuggled me into the Party. Now, I am being invited there by Military Intelligence. A coincidence, or fate?

I find myself in a shabby unfurnished hotel room with no bed; just a tired wooden table with four chairs. "Meet my colleague Karel," says Mirek. "Sit down Mr

Vitek." He pronounces my name slowly and distinctly with an ironic emphasis on a short i, not as I use it with an accented í. I am immediately attentive and unsettled. I came to the meeting thinking that I would be interrogated in the case of the suicide of a private in a small garrison who shot himself dead while on guard. He could no longer tolerate the bullying by non-commissioned officers that the commander of his unit, an incompetent, lazy captain, was unable to stop. I wrote a feature story about it, 'Death Named Harassment,' which the censor killed. Since such 'extraordinary events,' the politically correct term for tragedies, were always investigated by a special branch of Military Intelligence, I was not all surprised that they wanted to talk to me. I was prepared to protect my sources, but I soon became aware that my whole life was at stake. It began to crumble like a house built on sand under the weight of accusations that Mirek heaped on me as if he were a court prosecutor.

"We know that you changed your name, Comrade Vitek, which, after all is not so important. But the fact that you falsified your personal file is a crime. You are the son of Jan Vitek, a former wholesale cattle merchant, and not of a forest worker as you stated in your CV." Every word was like a sledgehammer blow to my head. "Moreover you concealed your exclusion from the university because of your bourgeois origin and because of your participation in anti-government student demonstrations. What we do not know is how you slipped into the ranks of the Party but that will be up to your editorial office party group to find out so that they can purge you. I assure you that we have witness testimonials and copies of the relevant documents proving your offences. There is no use in trying to deny any of these things."

"As a matter of fact, we are not much concerned

with your, shall we say, embellishments to your political profile, and we might be prepared to overlook them," says Karel. "All that has been said here so far need not even appear in the minutes of our meeting. That, of course, will depend on your attitude."

They are playing a game with me. Mirek pretends to be the bad cop, Karel the good guy. I feel like a rabbit driven into a corner of its cage before being pulled out by the ears for his neck to be broken. I realize that I have a very slim fighting chance, if any.

"What do you want from me?"

"Your help, Comrade Vitek, nothing else but your help."

I know I am trapped. If I refuse, it will be goodbye Geneva. This would not matter, but I shall surely lose my job. Moreover, I shall be blacklisted and forbidden to publish. That is the worst part. It crosses my mind that this is exactly how my father must have felt when his business was closed down and his property confiscated. He did not have a ghost of a chance. I, on the other hand, do have a unique possibility to escape that I must not waste. OK, comrades, you call the tune now, but once I am abroad it will be the other way round. This idea calms me down and strengthens my confidence that I will be able to trump them.

"I don't know what kind of help you expect from me," I say slowly and decidedly, "but there is a certain limit beyond which I will not go. I will never snitch on my fellow citizens."

"We are not the State Secret Service," says Mirek in a huff. "We are Military Intelligence. Geneva is a center of espionage. All major intelligence services are present there. What we want, for a start, is that you do your job and keep your ears and eyes wide open. Later on, we will specify what we are interested in. Now, please choose a cover name."

It occurs to me to choose something that will make it quite clear what I think about this deal.

"Johnnie Walker," I suggest.

"Oh," says Mirek, "are you sure?"

They want me to sign a blank sheet of paper, and I don't ask why since I don't want to prolong my abasement. To spite them I purposefully misspell the first name and write Johny. I do it out of a ludicrous, desperate sense of defiance.

You raped me, but I will not prostitute myself, I swear to my soul. And I later repeat this over and over again. It is branded on my mind and heart forever.

I did what I did because it was the more bearable of two options, both of which were painful, even catastrophic, and in one way or the other both wrong. This is what a grave decision means: whatever you do, you err and suffer.

Mirek visited me twice in Ruzenka's studio when I came to Prague on a short leave. He did not learn anything more about Geneva than what I recounted to my buddies at Pinkas pub the previous night. At that time George had already appeared in my life and our fruitful friendship had started. It gave me an opportunity to retaliate for the rape, and even more important, to settle the score between our family and the Bolshevik regime that pretended to offer socialism.

I got up since I knew I would not fall asleep again. I opened the window in the bedroom. Cool night air streamed in.

They did not write me off after all. After the phone call, the resident officer of Military Intelligence at our Embassy in Berne waited for me in a black Mercedes at the entry to a small village in the neighboring canton of Vaud. When I stopped behind him he put his left hand out of the window and made a sign that I should follow him. We drove through the village at noon. There was not a living soul around. Leaving the lifeless village behind, we branched off on a narrow country road in a valley. There were vineyards on the hillside on the left and a forest on the right. After some four or five kilometers, the Mercedes came to a halt on a small open area that wine-growers used as a parking lot.

The spy from Berne was a thickset, middle-aged man. He wore washed-out jeans and a black leather jacket. Large sunglasses covered his eyes. He sported a baseball cap with the inscription 'Switzerland' and a tiny brown moustache on his upper lip. We talked. He was interested in the same thing as his predecessor: had I managed to identify somebody among my American and German friends who could be won over, bought or blackmailed to co-operate with our intelligence service? He listened to my evasive answer without a question or comment. Then he told me that Mirek wanted to see me in Prague and asked when I would go there. I said that probably I might make it after the ILO conference in June. The conversation was brief. It lasted less than ten minutes.

Now, reviewing the encounter, I realized that there was something fishy about it. The Mercedes had Berne license plates the number of which I memorized but most likely to no avail because it was a rental car, and surely hired under an assumed name. The sunglasses, the baseball hat, the moustache, probably false, the apparent nervousness, the superficiality of our discussion—all this in retrospect appeared extremely suspicious. What was even more disquieting was the choice of such a deserted place for the meeting. There could have been an accomplice of the resident hidden in the forest, observing the encounter and the valley through binoculars, for they might want to know if I am 'clean,' or 'shadowed.' Did they do it out of caution or mistrust? What if there had been a leak on George's side? Or, have we not been discreet enough? Does Military Intelligence have the right to take away Ruzenka's passport? Did they conspire against me with the State Secret Service? Alternatively, did the State Secret Service enroll the Military Intelligence in its hunt? Who started the witch-hunt? Pista? Or was it some local informer? Where and when did I make a mistake? Who was the mastermind in Prague? Questions pounded away at my aching brain, but remained unanswered.

A GAME OF DOUBLE BLUFF

Nancy howard brought me a clean copy of the English version of Carriche's article I edited yesterday. She was one of the rare persons who could decipher my handwriting, an achievement that I really appreciated.

"May I suggest a little improvement?" she asked.

"Go ahead, shoot."

"It is a very good article but it could use a catchier headline than 'A Costly Brain Drain.' How about calling it 'When The Poor Aid The Rich'?"

Nancy was a small, frail bespectacled American in her early fifties whom I delivered from slavery in the English secretarial pool some three years before when I chose her as my secretary on the recommendation of Claude Passet.

Nancy was a pearl: reliable with a genuine eye for detail. Just the person I needed to watch over my bohemian carelessness. She verified all data, numbers, names and references in my manuscripts, and with unconcealed pleasure showed me her treasures—errors and inaccuracies marked in red pencil. In addition, she possessed a natural talent for language and style. When she suggested a change, it was always an improvement,

312

as with that headline.

"You are right as usual," I said. "Your heading is great. Thanks. And since we are changing it in the English edition…"

The telephone ringing cut me short. It was Snow. He wanted to see me immediately.

"We'll use it in all other editions including the French," I added after hanging up the receiver.

"Carriche may not like it," said Nancy.

"Mark is a top-notch journalist. I am sure he will welcome it," I said.

It was shortly after nine when I entered Snow's office. He was evidently impatient to talk to me, for he did not say even "Hi" but plunged right into the matter.

"When I explained your problem to Casey, she had a brilliant idea. She proposes that we call a press conference at the Palace of Nations and announce publicly that the Czechoslovak government confiscated the passport of a spouse of an ILO official, thus preventing her and her child from joining her husband in Geneva. They are hostages of the communist regime…"

"Snow, for Christ sake, you cannot be serious!"

"Just wait to hear the rest. I am going to consult Jack Martensen on how to formulate the announcement to be legally in order, and then we will show it to the Director-General. Casey is his long-time friend; their families lived near each other in New York. So before we go to David Morse, she will touch base with him to make sure that he approves of the announcement. The purpose of the exercise is to stir up international pressure on the government to let your family leave the country."

"I totally disagree. I don't want it."

"Why?"

"A press conference at this moment would be

counterproductive. It would mar all hopes of a conciliatory solution. Hurin reported our conversation yesterday to Prague. Let the situation mellow, or as the French say *laisser pourrir* (*let it rot*)."

"OK, no press conference. But we can leak your case to some friendly journalists."

"That would be even worse."

"As you wish, it's your show," said Snow without conviction. Then his face lit up. "And what if you use the threat of a press conference in your liar's poker game with Hurin to force him to a showdown?"

I had to admit that this was not a bad idea. I could put Pista under pressure and he would have no way of knowing that I was bluffing.

"I shall think about it," I promised.

I was about to leave when Snow stopped me. He remembered that he had an invitation for me from Casey to come to an evening buffet party at seven. No excuses, it is a command performance.

In the corridor I ran into Dick Woodward. He said he had been looking for me in my office and asked me to join him for lunch. If I knew Dick he had something up his sleeve or he wanted to pick my brain. I said I accepted with pleasure and we agreed we would meet at one o'clock in the cafeteria on the first floor.

Never postpone until tomorrow what you can do today, I told myself as I started to dial Pista's number. When Marta switched me through I apologized for the intrusion, adding that I must speak to him on a very serious matter.

"I am calling because I must confess to having made an awful *faux pas*. I hate myself for doing it, but what's done cannot be undone…Yesterday afternoon, after my return to the office, Herrick called me in about a proposal for the Governing Body…We discussed it for about half an hour, and Herrick must have noticed that I was distracted and absent-minded. He asked if there was something wrong that made me look so sad and preoccupied…He has always been nice to me and very friendly…I know I have no excuse but in a moment of weakness I told him everything about Ruzenka and Honzik…I simply confessed to him. Which would be bad enough but there is something even worse." I sighed deeply as if in anguish and then I sputtered in one breath:

"Just a while ago Herrick was here in my office and told me that he had taken up my case with the Legal Department and that on Friday during the routine press briefing in the Palace he would make a public announcement on behalf of the ILO that the Czechoslovak government was holding my wife and son hostages…"

"What!" Pista cried out. "This is preposterous…this…this is a lie!"

"Please, calm down. I told him right away that I did not agree, and that under no circumstances would I want…"

"You lost all judgment spilling the beans!" shouted Pista.

"Totally, I agree. But believe me I have everything under control. Nothing can be done against my will."

"I do hope for your sake that you are not wrong," Pista said icily.

"Please, Stefan, I beg you, let's leave it just between you and me…I leveled with you because I don't want to keep anything from you. I have pacified Herrick, I am sure of that."

"Honzo, you are an asshole," said Pista, and hung up on me.

Putting the receiver back in the cradle I imagined how at this very moment Pista was running to the bunker to call Prague. But certainly not the Ministry of

Foreign Affairs. I would bet my life on it.

At half past ten I told Nancy to protect me from visitors, and said I did not want to be disturbed because I was expecting an important telephone call. Ruzenka was punctual. She was even always on time for our rendezvous—but long minutes passed and I stared at the black telephone as if I were hypnotized. Suddenly it rang.

"Yes, darling?" I said in Czech.

"Come on, Jan, it's me…"

"Sorry, Snow, I can't speak to you now, I must hang up…I am expecting Ruzenka's call any minute now. Ring you up later."

The ashtray on my desk was overflowing with cigarette butts. When I was in trouble I would light one Camel after the other.

Eleven o'clock. Still nothing. Something must have happened. Ruzenka might have been arrested…No, this is nonsense. What will I do if she does not call?

At long last the black box came to life.

"Yes," I said testily.

"It's me, darling," I heard Ruzenka saying. There was a distorting echo in the receiver but for me her voice sounded angelic.

"I have been worried about you. How come that you are calling so late?"

"From here I cannot call directly, I must wait for Prague to relay the call."

"Are you all right, darling?"

"Yes."

"And Honzik?"

"He is right here. Do you want to speak to him?"

"Some other time. I don't want to prolong the call, we could be interrupted…I have had a word with Stefan Hurin. You know who he is, don't you?"

"Yes, I met him at a reception at the mission…"

"Stefan thinks that that they took your passport by error, that there must be some misunderstanding that will soon be elucidated."

"What does it mean, soon?"

"I don't know. Two, three days."

"Do you believe that?"

"Yes," I said without conviction.

I hesitated for a moment. Should I remind her of Franz Nahrada and what we had agreed on? Better not. It is possible, or rather very likely, that our call is monitored in Prague, and it would be unwise to attract attention to our secret signal. I cannot take such a risk. Anyway, it will be better to limit our telephone conversation to the essentials and to the shortest time possible.

"I think that Stefan is right," I continued in a constructive way, in case somebody was listening to us, "because there is no other explanation…When you get your passport back, send me a cable."

"Wouldn't it be better to call? We could hear each other at least."

"There are problems with the phone…like today…Moreover, I'll be in and out of the office in the next few days so it will be difficult to catch me…Simply send a cable."

"Will you come over?"

Jesus Christ, that is a tricky question, if not a trap! What can I say to mystify those who listen in?

"As soon as possible…I will cable you. I love you, Ruzenka, and I miss you terribly. I wish we were all together again."

Hanging up the receiver I noticed it had traces of sweat. I breathed out deeply a couple of times to calm myself. I hope I have not made any blunders, I thought with deep disquietude.

"Do you know that Valentin Pavlich is leaving, that he has resigned?" Dick asked as soon as we sat down at the table.

This was news to me. However, I was not surprised to hear it from Dick who somehow, through some mysterious channels, always knew things first or even before they happened. Gossip, rumors, news and especially confidential information were Dick's business. I told him that I had not seen Valentin since his return from Moscow sometime in the middle of August. He certainly had not given any hint that he intended to resign.

"He has been here only three years. I would like to know if he resigned voluntarily or if he was coerced. What's your educated guess?"

We had roast chicken with French fries and mixed salad, accompanied by a carafe of tap water. I was used to the fact that whenever Dick invited me to lunch or coffee I had to earn it.

"Valentin was fed up with his job. He thought it was degrading to help you put out good-for-nothing booklets," I said. "His first foreign assignment was as Cultural Attaché in Warsaw. Before coming here he was in line for a similar job in Paris but something went awry and he ended up in Geneva. His marriage to Nastia was on the rocks, to put it mildly. I have a fleeting suspicion that he had somebody else in Moscow, which is why he traveled there every so often. I see several reasons why he would want to leave."

"OK, but Valentin ran into trouble with the Swiss police. Some ten days ago they nabbed him for drunk driving. He might even be hauled before a court."

"I know nothing about that. And they can't put him on trial because he has diplomatic immunity. However, I am not surprised that he got caught. He drove home from every reception loaded."

"I have heard the ILO stripped him of his immunity. Maybe the Soviet Embassy wants to hide him away to avoid a scandal."

"Even if they did strip him of immunity, he will just have to pay a fine and lose his driving license for a month or two. I seriously doubt that he would have a problem with the Soviet mission. They do not take such things seriously. Most important, you must not forget that he is a KGB man. Once when we had drunk a lot he confided to me that he had joined the KGB because it was a 'kryska,' a protective shell in which you are above the law."

"He behaves strangely. I'll be grateful to you if you would sound him out and tell me if he is hiding something, and if yes, what."

"OK, if I find a suitable occasion," I promised, to shake Dick off.

I recalled how Dick had 'adopted' me shortly after my arrival at the ILO. At first he invited me to have coffee occasionally. Soon our chats became a daily ritual. There followed invitations to lunch or dinner. Before long we lunched or dined together twice a week. Dick always paid, he never wanted even to share the bill. At the beginning I felt embarrassed but I gradually grasped that Dick was not paying from his own pocket. Towards the end of nineteen sixty-six Dick said to me that he would like to introduce me to a very good friend whom he had told about me and who would be delighted to see me. This is how I met George.

"Do you know that *ILO Panorama* is doomed because the Governing Body crossed it off next year's budget?" asked Dick.

"Yes, Dave Skybar told me."

"What a surprise, don't you think?"

"I am surprised that the magazine lasted that long.

The production of each copy cost five dollars. It was a black hole for money. And moreover, who read it?"

"That leaves your magazine as the only mouthpiece of the Organization. You must feel good about it."

"I certainly have no spiteful feeling, just a certain satisfaction that my conception of a mouthpiece, as you say, is viable. To return to Valentin…if he leaves, I shall miss him."

"The same here," said Dick.

"Don't worry, you will get another KGB guy to baby-sit," I assured him.

Snow and Casey lived at Champel, a fancy quarter of Geneva for the rich. Whenever I called them up a maid replied: "The Herricks' residence." Indeed, their flat was a plush place, like those you could see in Hollywood films. The entrance hall was relatively small but the living room was extra-large, equipped with easy chairs and a couple of low conference tables, and lit by floor lamps and indirect light from halogen bulbs built into the ceiling. It led out to a wide and long balcony separated by sliding glass doors that, on hot summer days, could be pushed back so that guests could breathe the fresh air and admire a splendid view of the town sprawling at their feet.

I came a little bit earlier to talk to Casey in peace and quiet. She invited me to her study cum library. Above her desk on the wall hung an enlarged photograph of Casey's father with President Roosevelt on the lawn before the White House. She came from a rich Jewish family in New York. Snow, whose social origins were much humbler, met Casey at Columbia University NY where he studied after the war on a military grant. Casey's family was well connected and Mike Clark told me once with undisguised envy that it was thanks to her influential connection that Snow could become the Director of Public Information in the ILO. "It's Casey who wears the trousers in their family," he commented.

That evening she wore a long evening gown made of blue velvet. It fitted like a husk to her slim and supple sporting figure. She must have been on the far side of forty but she looked much younger. She wore heavy make-up and her eyebrows were shaved into thin slanting lines under which bulged two dark brown eyes. Vera Sokolova had the same expressive eyes but they were pale blue.

Casey sat down on a chair opposite me and laid her hands on mine.

"Jan, I think of you very much, and I am very worried."

"Don't, Casey, I am like a cat, I always fall on my four feet."

"I can rally all the American correspondents in town. Just tell me when you want to launch a campaign to save your family."

I explained why I was against this for the moment. To amuse her I recounted, somewhat colorfully, my morning conversation with Hurin, and how I tried to put the fear of God into him. I thought she would be entertained but she remained grave.

"Promise me that you will consult me before making any irrevocable decision," she said, pressing my hands.

"OK, Casey," I assured her, despite knowing I would not ask her advice because the decision was mine and mine alone, as well as the responsibility for its consequences.

"Darling, please don't do anything foolish."

With this admonition she rose, kissed me on both cheeks, and we went together into the living room just when the first guests arrived. They all were directors of different ILO departments, all the top D1 or D2 level, accompanied by their wives. Snow described them as 'the usual crowd.'

I preferred a buffet party to a formal dinner when you have to converse with only two or four people sitting near you. At a buffet you could circulate with a glass in your hand, and choose and change your company. Or just park yourself in a corner to observe the human animal.

"Come with me," said Snow. He led me to the balcony where he introduced me to Jack Martenson. He was a lanky, thin-bodied man smoking a big cigar. He said that my case preoccupied him very much, a banal courtesy phrase, and began to lecture me. As an ILO official, bound by its oath of loyalty, I should not listen to, let alone obey, instructions from the Czechoslovak government. He spoke to me with condescension as if I was a first-grader and his pronounced Oxford accent irritated me. He asked me to inform him personally about the further development of my case, especially if the Czechoslovak government should attempt to pressure me to resign. Then he offered me a benevolent handshake as a gesture of dismissal. Jack raised doubts in me, not confidence.

Suddenly I felt as if I had landed here on another planet. I stood in the midst of a whirl of extraterrestrials who were making funny grimaces and producing sounds I did not understand, and never would. Why am I here? What am I doing here? My God, it's hopeless! I do not belong here!

When I spotted Casey, she was momentarily alone. I approached her, put my arm around her shoulder and whispered in her ear:

"I must be going now. Thank you for your invitation. Goodbye, Casey."

I meant it. I was almost sure I was seeing her for the

last time. I shall miss the Herricks. But that's about all. You can take your golden cage and shove it.

I lay in bed fearfully expecting yet another white night. But, mentally drained, I fell into a healthy sleep without dreams and without nightmares.

COFFINS FOR THE LIVING

Since early that morning, nancy and i had worked through manuscripts for the September issue of *ILO Information*. We made the last stylistic touches, mostly suggested by Nancy. She had certainly taken the copy home yesterday, which she did regularly before the printing deadline, and went through it page by page for final polish. Nancy was a spinster married to the ILO.

"What do you know about that graphic designer?" she asked. "What's his name?"

"Fribourghaus," I said. "Not much, but Jean Mohr, who recommended him, thinks he is the best in town."

"When is he coming? At two, did you say?"

I nodded and told her that she need not be present at our meeting, which she appreciated. Nancy like so many Americans had problems learning a foreign language. She spoke broken French although she had already been in Geneva for fifteen years.

Until now, I had done the layout and prepared manuscripts for the printer. I learned the basics as editor of an army magazine, and refined it by studying a graphics manual that Ludek Burianek gave me before I left for Geneva. When I received galley proofs I cut and pasted them into a layout in an amateurish manner. Luckily, the printer, Mr Torriani, was extremely understanding and tolerant. It was evident that such a makeshift arrangement was unsatisfactory and that the magazine could use a professional graphics editor.

The ringing of the telephone was like a dagger in my breast. Every time I heard it, I hoped it was the post office calling to say there was a cable for me. Today is Wednesday, that's too early. Tomorrow will be the optimum day. If I do not receive it by Friday our chances will have diminished. After Sunday they will be nil.

Snow called to come to his office on the double. When I sat down he asked if had received news from Ruzenka..

"You will be the first one who is informed," I assured him. But it was his news he wanted to pass on.

"I have got my cliff in Sicily," said Snow. "My agent just called to say that he has paid for it. It's a bargain, only fifty cents a square meter!"

For Snow, the Second World War ended in Sicily. After landing he was stationed there. His mixed battalion remained on the island as an occupational force. He loved Sicily. He and Casey went there last year in May to prospect for a site where they could build a villa. Of all places they visited, they liked best a cliff overhanging the sea near Sciacca. They photographed views of it from various angles and at different times of the day. The loveliest were the shots taken at sunset when the sun formed a golden bridge over the sea. I asked Snow when he wanted to start construction of his dream hideout.

"Next spring at the latest," he said. "By the way, the Cabinet of the Director General wants you to make some changes in your article about sea transport. It is too sensational, especially the headline 'Floating Coffins on the High Seas.'"

Who raised the objections? I learned that it was a new cabinet member, Keith Stephanson, which did not surprise me, because he was a bureaucrat with whom I had had problems before. The article focused on the fact that some shipping companies hired cut-rate sailors, untrained and unqualified, and mostly originating from Asia, to serve on old, badly maintained vessels flying a flag of convenience to escape international regulations. The result is that these ships become floating coffins. This problem was on the agenda of an ILO Maritime Conference to be held in Genoa in October. I wrote the story as the lead article for the next issue, and what annoyed me most was that the objections came so close to the printer's deadline. Had it not been for my family worries I would have had a shoot-out with Keith. Now, I did not care a hoot. Who knows what will come, and where I shall be in a couple of days.

"OK, I am going to tone down the story," I said.

Rudolf Fribourghaus entered my office at two o'clock sharp. He wore a dark cloak, had a beard and his hair was trussed in a pigtail. I was meeting a Swiss bohemian and, as it turned out, an excellent graphic designer and illustrator who worked for a number of publishing houses. At some length we discussed the nature and purpose of *ILO Information*, its target audience, and ways to give the magazine a new look. Then we went through the copy of the September issue and disposition of articles on its pages. We agreed that Rudolf would bring a model for a new graphic concept in a week's time.

A messenger brought me Keith Stephanson's minute. It was clear that he wanted to soften and obscure all criticism of shipping companies, so as to pre-empt potential flak from the powerful lobby of the Employers Organization. I had a hunch of what was behind it. The post of the Director of the Employers Relations Branch would be vacant as of next year. Keith was a hot candidate to fill it. Therefore, he put all his objections and ideas in the form of an official minute he could use to score points as a defender of employer interests.

I wrote a new headline: 'Problems of Substandard Ships.' Then I mercilessly crossed out almost everything that made the article interesting and readable. It was not first time in my life that I was forced to violate my principles.

Carnivore was one of Geneva's most out-of-the-way restaurants. One had to look for it very hard to find it in a newly built housing development known as 'La Gradelle,' close to the French border. A bus service had begun only recently. At that time 'La Gradelle' represented a futuristic concept for a housing settlement. It was dominated by a sixteen-floor, diamond-shaped high-rise surrounded by five-floor modern apartment buildings, with a park and a children's playground in the middle. It also contained essential shops and services: a grocery store, a cleaner's, a pharmacy, an elementary school, a barber's, two doctors' clinics, a tax advisor, and the restaurant Carnivore.

George was already there, sitting at a table in the corner left of the bar. He was always at the meeting place first, though that day I came almost ten minutes early. He put the menu in brown leather binding aside, got up and offered me a handshake.

"Good to see you, Jan."

His voice sounded affable and warm. He was evidently really glad that we were meeting again. It was mutual. We had known each other for more than four years and had become good friends. George had strikingly blue eyes like the American actor Paul Newman. Initially, he had introduced himself with a surname that I immediately forgot because I knew it was assumed.

"I am glad that you have found time for me," I said. "I need to consult you. It's vital and urgent."

"Let's order first," suggested George.

The specialty of the house was Argentinean T-bone steak with American ('country') potatoes.. We had already tried it here. We didn't need to choose. It was succulent. To accompany the meal George ordered a bottle of Bordeaux, Chateau Margaux. Usually, we discussed 'business' after the meal but I broke the rule this time.

"My wife and son are being held hostage in Prague," I announced dramatically. I wanted to get his full attention right away.

"Really? Are you sure?"

I began to recount the succession of events since last Monday. I spoke for a long time. I gave all the facts, and my interpretation of them. George listened without interrupting. When I finished, he did not reproach me or ask how it was possible that I had been so imprudent as to let Ruzenka and my son leave for Prague. I appreciated it. I had already flagellated myself enough for my thoughtlessness.

"If your family is being held hostage," said George, "the question is, why are you wanted so badly? To make you resign?"

"Hardly. If they wanted me to go back the Ministry of Foreign Affairs would simply send me a letter, or I would be officially informed by Mr Hurin from the Czechoslovak mission with whom I spoke twice during the past forty-eight hours," I said. "I am afraid a far more serious matter is involved. Actually the worst that could ever happen."

"Do you mean that they have discovered our...secret?"

"It's a possibility. But how could they have found out? Has there been a leak from your side? I can't explain. How otherwise they would know about us?"

"A leak from our side is out of the question! Just forget it. Moreover, we usually have a guardian angel when we meet. If there was somebody suspicious around we would have known."

We ate in silence for a while.

"You know, Jan, who comes to my mind? Your friend, the army general, for whom you wanted asylum and a new identity, do you remember?"

"You mean Vaclav Prchlik?"

"You told me he had been arrested. He could have been forced to talk."

"Nonsense. He has been in prison for three years. If he had talked, why would they act only now?"

"OK, have there been other people in the know?"

"Ota Brozek and Jirka Horsky. They were the messengers. Prchlik had asked them to seek me out and learn whether I could help him."

"Couldn't they have blown the whistle?"

"Do you think I am so stupid that I would tell them about you? I only said I would take care of Prchlik."

"But what if they gave that away? It could have been enough to make you suspect."

"I doubt it. Ota is a blabbermouth when he is drunk, but the question still is the same: why only now?"

"Yeah, it's a strange riddle," George sighed.

Once again, as so many times before, I felt the urge to lay my cards on the table and tell him about Mirek and the spy from Berne. And again—maybe for the hundredth time—I rejected the temptation. As a journalist, I had easy access to representatives of governments, employers and trade unions from all the countries attending ILO conferences and meetings. I was invited to diplomatic receptions, I could move freely in the United Nations, and I personally knew many influential personalities—in short, I was valuable material for intelligence work. But what might be even more interesting for George would surely be that I become a double agent. If I confided in him, he would do his utmost to lure or press me into this role. I entertained no illusions that I would have the willpower to resist. I would, consequently, become a pawn in the agencies' game like Alec Leamas in the novel *The Spy Who Came In From The Cold* by Le Carré. But I did not want to be a grain of sand between these two millstones. My only means of defense was silence. Moreover, I felt an overwhelming psychological inhibition: I was terribly, almost morbidly, ashamed that I had broken down and had been violated. If I ever confess to anyone, it will be the Swiss when I ask for asylum.

"You are right, it's a weird riddle that we cannot solve here and now," I said. "Tell me rather, what should I do if Ruzenka and my son are not able to come? Should I stay or return?"

George pensively looked at his glass of wine and remained silent. The headwaiter came, took our plates of half-touched food, gave us an indignant look, and left without a word.

"Should I stay or return?" I repeated the question that I had asked myself a thousand times, and each time answered it differently.

"From a solely professional view it would be more advantageous for us if you returned. Put bluntly, you could be more useful there than here." I understood what he meant: as an emigrant I shall cease to be persona grata at the Czechoslovak and Soviet missions, and I shall be a less interesting for the Company. Clearly, at home I will be a greater asset. Before I finished thinking it through, George added:

"But as your friend I must tell you that if I were in your shoes I would stay in Geneva."

"I can't do that, because it means that I shall never see my family again!"

"Never say never. There is always a way, and if necessary we could help your family to leave the country."

"How could you get them across the border?"

"It might take some time. We would have to wait until you are sort of forgotten. Then Ruzenka and your son could go to Yugoslavia on holiday, and from there it would be possible to spirit them out to Italy or Germany."

"They will not be allowed go to Yugoslavia because it is considered a capitalist country. At best, they could join a group tour to Bulgaria."

"OK, then: we organize an escape from Bulgaria."

"Why would you do all this for us?"

"Number one, we owe you a couple, Jan…"

"You owe me nothing!"

"And number two, we never leave friends out in the cold."

What George was saying made sense, but it sounded too far-fetched and too optimistic, and above all so simple that I could not believe it

"Thanks," I said. "I know that you mean well…that you want to help."

"Right," George confirmed. "And we have great plans for your future, too. I am authorized to offer you a standing contract with the Company," he announced, and paused to enjoy my surprise. "Under the contract you will receive a monthly retainer of five hundred dollars plus bonuses for special assignments payable to a numbered account at a Swiss bank."

It took me a while to fully realize that he was offering me money for my collaboration, making me a paid agent.

"It's a fair offer," said George.

"You are my friend and I take your word for it," I said.

"And we can help you with your career in the ILO," he added.

I had no doubt about it. They could push me upward in the same way Dick was moving up the hierarchy ladder, as if he had propeller on his back.

"I am totally overwhelmed by your…" I stopped searching for a subtle word…"your gesture," I said slowly. "May I ask you a direct question?" When George nodded I continued: "Tell me, what would you expect me to do for that money?"

"Well, more or less the same," George said. Then he indicated vaguely that I would meet with him and with his colleagues more often and would have to carry out special assignments.

Five hundred dollars made two thousand Swiss francs, more than half my net salary after deduction of the 'haircut' I had to pay to the Czechoslovak mission.

An inner voice told me this was an offer one could not refuse. My worries would be over. I would not have to fight hard for my career. But experience had taught me to treat such impulses with suspicion, that I needed to sleep on it.

"All cataclysmal things in life strike like lightning from a clear sky," I said, helping myself out of embarrassment by a cliché. "And this is such a big surprise that I don't know what to say."

"Then say nothing," smiled George. "Mull it over."

"You bet I will," I promised. "But now I must concentrate on Ruzenka and my son."

"I understand, first things first," said George. "But I need your answer as soon as possible, because I am not sure how much longer I'll stay around."

"Are you to leave Geneva?"

"Most likely, yes. So let me know when you make

up your mind. And, of course, we would like to know very much why your family is detained, who is behind it. I need not to stress how important it is for us. I want to know everything you find out, down to the last little detail."

We rose as if to order.

"If you need any help, don't hesitate to call me," said George. "I will do everything I can. And, please, keep me posted on any new developments regarding your family. I wish you the best of luck."

"Thanks, George, but I am afraid that luck alone will not do. It will require a miracle."

We parted. I left the restaurant first. George as usual stayed behind for some time. He had explained me why at our very first encounter, namely that he had seen many compromising photographs of two people leaving a restaurant together who were not supposed to know each other.

It was shortly before ten in the evening and I did not enjoy the idea of going home and being alone. I sat behind the wheel of my car and took a small road leading to the countryside. I followed it through fields and vineyards like a sleepwalker. At little village called Jussy, some twelve kilometers outside the city, I woke up to reality. I turned right towards Vandoeuvres and joined the high road along the lake.

I stopped near the Geneva golf club on a hillside above Cologny. It was my favorite place from which to contemplate perhaps the best view of Geneva. The lake lay below, dark, mysterious. The dipped beams of the quay lights accentuated its horseshoe shape. The town was adorned by neon lights like a Christmas tree. I felt the breeze from the lake on my face. It tasted like water.

I recalled how I stood here with my father when he

visited us. Suddenly, I realized that we would be together every time I returned, and that, in my mind, he would be standing there at my side until the end of time.

MOMENT OF TRUTH

Early next morning i drove my mustang to a small repair shop on the corner of Lamartine Street where jacks-of-all-trades took care of cars of all makes and brands. They worked fast and cheap. The Mustang needed an oil change and a check of all its fluid levels. I wanted to have it in good shape to avoid a repetition of the engine overheating we experienced in Germany last year. On the way back from Czechoslovakia, as we drove through Ulm, we heard a long wailing sound. "Imagine," I said to Ruzenka, "it's more than twenty years since the war and the Germans are still testing their air-raid sirens." Out of the town on a highway the wailing started again, and this time it did not stop. "We are on fire," Ruzenka announced. "I can see smoke coming from under the hood." It turned out that there was no more water in the cooling system. The car had a built-in siren to protect the engine against human stupidity.

Having dropped off my car in the ILO parking lot, I observed Snow trying to squeeze his majestic convertible between two Volkswagen cars. I waited until he had succeeded before joining him. While walking to the back door together, Snow asked me if I wanted to attend the ILO Maritime Conference to be held in Genoa in October with him.

"I don't know," I said. "October is for me a million light years away...I now live an hour at a time."
I sat at my Underwood typewriter. The white page waited for my flow of words that were not coming. My

brain was washed out. I was unable to put together a coherent sentence.

Valentin Pavlich saved me from further pointless effort. Without knocking, as was his habit he charged into my office and said:

"*Jan zdravstvuj dorogoj, pajdom kofe popit.*"

I refused his invitation to have a coffee by saying that I was expecting an important call. But I asked him to sit down and tell me what's cooking.

With a grunt, Valentin pressed his ninety-five kilos into a small armchair at a conference table. His round, pink-cheeked face was lit by a broad, disarming smile. He asked me if I knew what Dave Skybar did to Claude Passet last Sunday. I had it from her direct, but said to Valentin to go ahead and tell me. This way I would be able to switch off and not have to prick my ears all the time to understand his rapid Russian. I told him many times that he speaks like a machine gun, '*kak pulomjot,*' but it was no good.

I heard his voice but did not pay attention as, with many colorful words, he recounted how Dave Skybar, after a Saturday night binge, called up Claude Passet and said: "I hope I am not disturbing you…" Claude cut him short: "Dave, do you know what time is it? Five in the morning." "Oh, I am sorry," Dave droned on," but you see I am sick, so please tell Herrick I won't be in the office today, and that…" Claude interrupted him again: "Dave, you do not need to come in today, it's Sunday!" I laughed to be polite. I knew that Valentin did not come here just to tell me this story. It was his usual conversational gambit: first a joke and then '*nemnozko druhuj razgovor,*' some serious talk. So I kept mum and waited.

"I am leaving the ILO," he announced at last. "I have submitted my resignation."

I feigned surprise, and asked when and why he had

resigned.

"Last Friday," he said. "The post of First Secretary in Paris will be free next January and they want me to go there."

I immediately grasped that it was disinformation. The first part was true; the other was a white lie. I knew very well that when a Soviet diplomat ends his assignment abroad he must spend at least three years in Moscow to get used to the life at home again and to purge all foreign influences from his mind. Valentin was being recalled, but certainly not because of drunkenness. '*Eto nicevo,*' that's nothing. But what was the reason? I felt sorry for him not only because I would most probably meet with the same fate, but also because Valentin was a decent human being. Once, when we discussed the Soviet occupation of my country, he declared: "*Eto byla bolschaja ashibka*" (*It was a grave mistake*).

The telephone rang. I grabbed the receiver with a lightning speed. As heard the message I jumped up.

"*Oui, merci beaucoup,*" I thanked the caller for the great news that flooded me with happiness.

"I must be going, I have urgent business to take care of," I mumbled to a perplexed Valentin, and dashed out of the office. I sprinted along the corridor, turned right, then right again. The Post Office was also located on the ground floor but on the opposite side of the building. I entered the room breathless. There was a female colleague at the counter paying her bills. It seemed to me that she was taking too much time. Get on with it, I urged her silently, to hell with you, get lost…

At long last the clerk handed me a rectangular piece of paper with three printed words: 'I got passport.' I looked at them as if I could not understand their meaning, let alone believe them. Yet it stood there black in white: 'I got passport.' No signature.

I did not hesitate a second. I took a blank form from a case on the counter. I wrote Ruzenka's address and underneath I added: 'Franz Nahrada now.' No signature.

Again I had to wait an eternity for my turn, calculating in my mind the time it might take for the telegram to be delivered. It's almost eleven…two hours? Maybe. And what if they block it? Or if it gets lost? It cost me two francs fifty centimes for the dispatch. If all turns out as planned, it will be the best investment in my life.

On the way back to my office I thought through what I must do immediately. I must inform Snow, leave a message for George, close up shop, go home, change my suit, grab some things for the road such as cigarettes, chocolate, passport, and money. Did I forget anything?

"Snow, Ruzenka has got her passport," I reported breathlessly. "I am driving to Vienna to meet her. Please, tell Casey…"

"That's great news!" Snow was jubilant.

Rather, it was just encouraging news, I thought. It's not altogether sure that she will be able to cross the border. They might have returned her passport but at the same time they could have given an order to stop her from leaving the country.

A RACE AGAINST TIME

I started out of Rue Daubin at two o'clock sharp. Before me lay one thousand three hundred kilometers of roads and highways. If I spurred my Mustang it drove at two hundred kilometers an hour easily. That, of course, was possible only on the German Autobahn, and even then not everywhere. I should be happy to average ninety kilometers an hour, provided I do not lose much time in traversing Zurich with its dug-up streets, and then in squeezing through the congested roads of Munich. I could be in Vienna at Franz Nahrada's boarding house around three or four in the morning. We slept there last year on our way to Olbramovice where Ruzenka's parents live, and where she and Honzik are staying now.

"You can take a train to Vienna to the Franz Josef Bahnhof, the main railway station, or a bus that has its terminal nearby," I had advised Ruzenka when we discussed the eventuality of meeting in Vienna in case something unforeseen happened that would prevent me from joining her at Olbramovice. "What do you mean by unforeseen, are you afraid of something?" she asked. "No, I am not afraid of anything," I tried to calm her. "This is just a standby arrangement, emergencies happen, what do I know?...Take it easy, just remember boarding house Franz Nahrada. Any taxi driver will know where it is."

On the highway between Berne and Zurich the eight-cylinder engine under the hood purred silently at a traveling speed of one hundred and sixty kilometers an hour. For a while I forgot where and why I was speeding, and fully tasted the pleasure of driving a powerful car. I had found it some two years before in a garage show-window on rue Servette. Its color was golden green. It looked like the sports car I have always craved. It was love at first sight. I stood in front of the show-window bewitched. The running horse was its radiator ornament like the legendary Mustang Steve McQueen drove in a dramatic car chase through the streets of San Francisco in *Bullitt*. Still dreaming, I entered the shop. I woke up to reality when I learned that it cost twelve thousand five hundred francs. I felt like a small, penniless boy who finds himself an ice-cream parlor. "We are selling it at such a bargain price because it was used by our director, but it has only six thousand kilometers on the meter. It is a four-liter with two hundred eighty horsepower, that means it can easily do over two hundred kilometers an hour," said the salesman. He added that he would be prepared to accept my car as a trade-in. What do I have? "A Simca fifteen hundred, six years old with over eighty thousand kilometers." The salesman looked at me with compassion. He consulted a worn-out booklet with the prices of used cars. With a sigh he told me that at a maximum, making a gesture, he could give me one thousand francs. I could try to sell it myself to somebody and possibly get a better price but that would take a long time, and, meanwhile, the Mustang would be gone. But if I were really interested he would reserve it for me for a day or two. I ran home to find out how much my economical Ruzenka had laid aside from my salary. It was thirteen thousands francs. The following morning I went to empty our account at the bank…and I have never regretted the money I paid for the Mustang. It became a source of joy and manly pride. Whenever I sat behind the wheel it was as if its enormous power passed into my body. In my Mustang I was the master of the driver's universe.

And what if I have to return? I cannot take my Mustang home, the people there would be green with envy, and if they lock me up, it will be confiscated and some Communist Party hack will drive it. No way! If I had to return to Prague I would rather give it to somebody here for free. With this resolution, all my worries suddenly returned.

I picked up a tape cassette on which I had recorded the golden hits of Elvis Presley and put it into the player. Instantly, the music and lyrics of one of his greatest hits, *Heartbreak Hotel*, filled the car. One always can use company on a long trip. I could not have had better accompaniment. With the King the kilometers raced by. Elvis is closely linked in my mind with the 38th parallel, Panmunjom and inspections in the North and South in the Land of Morning Calm. I heard his voice night and day from the American Forces Network in Korea. Memories themselves fade as do the photographs I took in Korea and China, left unsorted in shoeboxes at home. I have never found time to put them in an album, and I never shall. But the songs stayed as fresh as ever.

Somehow in my mind there rose blurred images of the day when the Americans had expelled us from Pusan…We are boarding a military plane for paratroopers…My alternate, Vanek, and radio-operator Bican and I are seated with American soldiers along both sides of the plane. We carry parachutes. A black sergeant with a Brooklyn accent announces that at the first alarm signal we should stand up, at the second get in line, and at the third begin to jump one after the other…and he makes a joke adding: "And to those who do not know how to hit land safely, I say thank you for flying with us…" Reporters and TV crews are waiting for us on the tarmac of the airport in Seoul…Cameras focus on me and voices want to know: what is my reaction to the termination of our inspection activities?…I repeat over and over "No comment, no comment"…We all have our fifteen minutes of glory, said Varhol.

It was already half-past six when I was driving down a slope toward the Lake of Constance on the Swiss–German border. This was somewhat later than anticipated in the schedule I made in Geneva. Zurich delayed me considerably and I had not managed to make it up. I shall have to spur my Mustang on the highway between Ulm and Munich. The Swiss customs officer, seeing a Geneva license plate, just waved his hand and I crossed the borderline. However, I stopped in front of his German colleague because I was sure he would say *"Ausweis, bitte."* (*Papers, please*). He did not disappoint me. When he looked at my Czechoslovak diplomatic passport he asked me to pull over to the side and wait there, and disappeared into the building. He will be telephoning somewhere, copy the passport and check that it is not falsified. This was a standard procedure at every border and I was used to waiting.

Constance. This is where in 1415 they burned to death our Jan Hus, the Czech priest and philosopher who was the first Catholic reformer. It made me think about how many people have sacrificed their lives on the altar of truth, or what they believed was truth, and how few of them influenced the course of history…A great Czech author, Karel Capek, writes in one of his short stories that as mankind moves forward like a herd, from time from time somebody branches off in the hope of finding a new course, but he gets lost, disappears, and what he leaves behind him is only a trampled grass-blade; and that later on somebody else sees it, breaks off two and disappears leaving another trampled grass-blade; and so it goes on until one day the crushed grass-blades form a pathway, and ultimately a broad road which leads the whole of mankind in a new direction. I don't wish too much for myself. I would just like to leave a trampled grass-blade when I am gone.

"Danke vielmals." The German customs officer interrupted the train of my thoughts. He thanked me and wished me a nice trip.

A mist descended on the port. I was lucky to get on the ferry at the last moment. When the boat began to move I went up a narrow staircase leading to the deck where there was a restaurant. I ordered a Frankfurter with bread and mustard, a beer and cup of strong coffee. After the bananas and chocolate I ate in the car, it tasted like a king's feast. With an enormous appetite I lit up a Camel, the first since I had started. When I want to drive at top speed I concentrate on the road and steering so intently that I cannot be disturbed by anything else. Besides, nicotine is replaced by adrenaline. And Ruzenka does not like, or rather hates, my smoking in the flat or the car. "You smoked again," she says with rueful voice when I come back from the office. She is so sad about it that if I ever give up smoking it will be because of her, to make her happy.

From the restaurant I went out on deck. As the ship cruised lazily across the lake an earlier memory from far away came into mind. The Germans call Lake Constance 'Bodensee,' and during the war they made a movie of that name staring Zarah Leander who swam in the lake completely nude. This was something so extraordinary at the time that we, as pubescent boys, could not miss it at any cost even though the film was for adults only. My chum Gusta Kriz and I decided to sneak into the auditorium after the projection started and hide among the standing spectators who could not get a seat. But the cinema's ever-vigilant usher Havel spotted us and dived into the crowd after us. He missed Gusta but found me and drew me out by my hair. Now, as I was regarding the shore that approached, I imagined Zarah Leander running to the beach, taking off her clothes and jumping into the water naked…What strange things come into your mind at times of crisis.

The main road from the lake to Ulm was narrow and serpentine. Overtaking was often forbidden. It was impossible to drive fast. I told myself to be patient, hoping that when I got on the highway from Ulm to

Munich and farther on to Vienna I would be able to improve my average speed.

The first time I drove from Geneva to Olbramovice was also in an emergency, but a happy one. And I had also started out after receiving a cable from Ruzenka that I impatiently awaited. And it was also brief: You have a son. The maternity ward was on the first floor of a hospital at a district town, Moravian Krumlov. A nurse took me to a glass wall and asked me to wait a little before she found the mother. Suddenly, as if switching on a television set, Ruzenka appeared in hospital garb, holding in her arm swaddling clothes, out of which peered a little bald head and a red face with a small chin and a prominent nose. I could not deny the newborn child, who evidently inherited a typical Vitek hooter. Ruzenka radiated pride and happiness. I was standing there mute, dumbfounded, grateful, amorous, daft with joy, and perplexed because I did not know what to say. Through the glass wall I read Ruzenka's lips. She mouthed: "Honzik." I answered in the same way: "Thank you." Which was all I found to say.

With surprise I realized it was four years ago. The years had passed like seconds. The first two were martyr's years, filled with daily struggles in a new, strange environment. I worked in a foreign language, and I strove to show that I was as good as an American or Frenchman. Often, I felt that my colleagues imagined that at home we washed in the toilet bowl, and we were barbarians and savages. They did not say it explicitly, of course. They let me know their superiority in an elegant and sophisticated manner that was all the more wounding. To perform favorably was not good enough, I had to excel, and do the work of two people in order to become noticed and indispensable. At that time I wanted to leave the ILO; but as a success, not a failure.

The occupation of our country in August 1968 and the purges that followed dampened my desire to return home. All my friends suffered. Ota Brozek, Josef Tichy, Vaclav Jelinek and Rudla Franz were dismissed. They now lived as construction workers and spent their nights in a trailer. Vaclav Prchlik was arrested and imprisoned...The question was no longer how to leave the ILO, but rather whether to stay, or not to stay. Inwardly, I was afraid of exile because I know myself: I am a sentimental Slav, and I am sure to miss my country. Once, two decades ago, I wrote a short novel entitled *Walking in Circles* about a man who searched for fortune in foreign countries where he became very rich but unhappy, and in the end returned to the place where he was born. The motto of the story was a poem in which Mother Homeland says to her son: "If you leave me I shall not perish, but if you leave me you shall perish." It must have been a masterpiece of melodrama, full of clichés, and later on I congratulated myself that it had been completely forgotten, as well as the obscure magazine in which it had been serialized. But it was no wonder that it had lately returned to my memory.

The Mustang's dashboard glimmered its grave green light. The needle of the tachometer hung at two hundred kilometers per hour but the engine still had some extra power as I was not pushing the gas pedal to the floor. No other car overtook me. I drove in the fast left lane leaving Mercedes, BMWs and Audis behind. For my manly ego it was as if I had sniffed coke. All worries, fears and hopes disappeared. The world was the Mustang, the highway and me.

I slowed down in Munich and the obligatory fifty-kilometer speed limit felt like a senile crawl from one red traffic light to another. At half past nine the traffic was still dense but, luckily, not congested. I had the fleeting idea of phoning up Tony Pospichal from some pub or call box. He had settled down here in exile. In that fatal year 1968 Tony was a press attaché at the Czechoslovak embassy in Belgrade where the then Minister of Foreign Affairs, Jiri Hajek, found refuge and from where he organized an international campaign against Soviet occupation. As a press spokesman Tony got into the limelight and the new Prague regime put him on its list of enemies of the State. The authorities sent two secret agents to Belgrade to watch him and to ensure that he returned home. However, Tony succeeded in escaping under dramatic circumstances, and the German government granted him and his family asylum. I could imagine what he would tell me if I asked his advice whether I should stay in Geneva or not. I will stop by on the way back, perhaps, I promised myself, if everything goes well.

Having passed through Munich, I stepped on the gas and the needle pointed to two hundred again. I had a new companion, one of my most favorite crooners, Frank Sinatra. Now he was singing for me one of his greatest hits, *My Way*.

I lived a life which is full
I traveled each and every highway
And much more than that
I did it my way…

I was humming along. I have no musical ear and I could not sing even the simplest tune without false notes. Therefore, melody is secondary for me. I like songs that have good lyrics that touch my heart and soul; lyrics inherently connected with profound, emotional experiences making them unforgettable. I found them in the songs of Presley, Sinatra, Piaf, Brassens, Aznavour, Okudhava, Vysocky, among

344

others.

Yes, there were times
I'm sure you knew
When I bit off more than I could chew
I ate it up and spit it out
I took the blows and did it my way...

I grew up and lived in a divided world. During the war Kremze was on the new frontier with Nazi Germany established following the Munich agreement in 1938. After liberation in 1945 I crossed the demarcation line between the American and Russian occupation zone every day on my way to the lyceum in Budejovice. In the late 1950s I worked three years on the 38th parallel dividing the two Koreas, North and South. I had the possibility of getting to know each side of the divided country. Now in the ILO I could observe and study the two antagonistic blocks separated by the Iron Curtain. After all this experience I arrived at the conclusion that those who want us to believe that the world is black-and-white are liars. No country, no block of countries, is a personification of good or evil, but each is rather an amalgam of good or bad people and things. Man is *basically* good but, unfortunately, easily manipulated and dominated. It all depends on the ways and means used, artfully and consistently, by both secular and clerical leaders to brainwash people, and, most importantly, to what purpose. Deceived and confused masses are an easy prey to irrational hatred and frenzy that leads to massacres within and between nations. It's a mad, mad world, but to be indifferent to it is out of the question. One has to take a stand, to be engaged, to raise one's voice against, and to say no, if necessary.

Regrets I have a few
But then again, too few to mention
I did what I had to do
And saw it through
Without exemption

Once Professor Galbraith told me that the do-or-die competition between the two antagonistic blocs had at least one advantage: both systems have to disguise their ugly face. "I know what the Soviet regime wants to obscure," I said, "but I have no idea what the capitalist system tries to hide." "Greed, the law of the jungle and social Darwinism," he replied. "We experienced it in our country in the Thirties." I should have asked him if a relapse was possible if capitalism became the victor. That, however, has occurred to me too late.

For what is man, what has he got?
If not himself, then he has naught
To say the things he truly feels
And not the words of one who kneels
The record shows I took the blows
And did it my way…

During the trip so far just one Porsche 911 had overtaken me, and only because I was lost in dreams, listening to Frank's *September Song*.

The highway changed to a two-lane road climbing a little hillside on the top of which were the customs and border police. The German guard just waved me on. The Austrian one looked at my passport and suggested I park my car beside the customs office. He disappeared in the building to photocopy and verify my passport.

"*Fahren Sie nach Hause?*"

I nodded that I was on my way home. Why should I

346

tell him? That I would love to drive home, but it's impossible. Well, who knows, maybe I will snap and end up at Olbramovice.

I drove slowly down the other side of the hillside into Austria. I was so exhausted that I succumbed to momentary drowsiness. After five kilometers I spotted a lay-by surrounded by high bushes. I turned off and parked my car there. I switched out the lights, pushed the seat back almost horizontally, and closed my eyes. Almost immediately I was lost to the whole world.

Somebody knocked on the window. A flashlight lit my face, waking me up from a deathlike sleep. I pulled down the window and shaded my eyes. I saw a policeman.

"Sind Sie in Ordnung? Brauchen Sie etwas?"(*Are you OK? Do you need anything?*)

"Nein, danke. I war nur müde." (*No thanks. I was just tired.*)

"Ausweis, bitte."(*Papers, please.*)

When the policeman saw my diplomatic passport, he changed his austere official tone for an almost friendly one and apologized for having to wake me up to know who I was and what I was doing there. He added that sleeping in a car on a deserted lay-by could be dangerous. He wished me *"Gute Reise"* (*Have a nice trip*), saluted and disappeared into the dark.

I don't know how long I slept but I certainly felt better. I was ready to drive on. The clock on the dashboard showed that it was thirty minutes past midnight. So far, I had managed to make a decent average speed but I still had some three hours of driving in front of me.

The highway was totally empty in both directions. I switched on my high-beam headlamps and gunned the Mustang. I drove on the line. Its intermittent white strip

347

was shooting visual projectiles into my eyes.

Disquieting questions besieged me again. Did Ruzenka receive the telegram? Could she leave right away? How? I did not know what connection she had from Brno, whether she could take a train or a bus. Which would leave sooner and arrive earlier? Will they let her go, or stop on the border?

I put in another tape, Bing Crosby for a change, to chase the clouds away. I began humming along with Bing: *I'll be loving you always*, and then my favorite: *True love, true love*.

I tried to figure out what to do when I arrived at the boarding house. If Ruzenka and Honzik are not there yet, I'll book the large corner room where we slept last time. I'll jump into bed without even taking off my clothes. If they are already there and asleep, I'll slip in silently like a thief and wait until Honzik opens his eyelids and cries out joyfully "Father is here!" waking up Ruzenka.

Visualizing this scene I realized how much I loved my boy and how little I showed it to him. I was so much preoccupied with myself, my ephemeral worries, and with fighting battles for survival, real or imaginary, that I found no time to go with him to a park to build sandcastles, swing him on the see-saw or buy him a carousel ride. All this will change now, I decided, once we are together again we shall become a real family, and I want to be a real father, present and attentive. My father told me once that he had missed my childhood, and I don't want to do the same.

I found the Vienna orbital transit road easily. Once I was driving on it I could not get lost. The town was slowly coming to life. Cars began to accumulate at traffic lights, there were some early risers rushing to work along the pavements.

A silky fog descended on the bridge over the

Danube River. Having passed it I took a main road and after several hundred meters I branched left into a narrow, dimly lit street. I did not see a sign but I was sure I was in the right place. I drove very slowly staring into the dark night and searching for a white sign with block letters saying FRANZ NAHRADA, and underneath in small letters '*Fremde Zimmer*,' *Rooms To Rent*. I saw nothing. I put the car in reverse gear and began to back up. My eyes scoured the darkness. I discovered the contours of small, one-floor villas…Suddenly I came on a yawning hole. This is where the boarding house had been! I turned the car sidewise to aim the headlamps on the vacant lot. Besides a heap of earth there was nothing.

I got out of the car to make sure that I wasn't mistaken. The boardinghouse had really disappeared. I don't know how long I stood there like some marble statue. I thought I was ready for every eventuality and had foreseen all contingences. Except for this surprise. The devil is in the details. It was always one detail that foiled so many infallible plans.

What could have happened?

No, this is the wrong question. The right one is what now?

I cannot do anything else but stick to the original scenario. I parked the car at the street curb where we were to meet at the boarding house that no longer existed.

What now? It was five in the morning and the only reasonable option was to crawl onto the back seat, nestle up and try to catch some sleep. I should at least take some rest, even if I don't fall asleep. A big day was before me.

The back seat was short and hard. I had to pull up my legs and prop my head against the door. Lying there I ruminated that what I needed was a fallback position in case, due to a combination of unforeseeable circumstances, everything went awry. I should develop a plan for the worst-case scenario: that I have to return home to Czechoslovakia. I needed an ace up my sleeve. What if I tried to redeem myself? What could I offer? Not much...unless I find something to offer, some sort of bait they might swallow. I might offer them what they have always wanted from me: somebody who could be recruited as a spy. It cannot be just anybody...it must be a credible recruit. How about Dick Woodward? You wanted an American, comrades, here he is! Wow, why not? Diamond would cut diamond!

This idea exhilarated me. But I soon realized its defect: I would have to reveal to George and Dick my secret, tell them that I had been broken, and explain why I had not confessed earlier. If I told them the truth, that I was unfathomably ashamed of myself and mortified by having been so violated, they will say that they believe me because I will be giving them on a silver platter a unique opportunity to use me to infiltrate Czech military intelligence. How would you like to become their puppet?

To agonize about it was useless. There was no alternative, and I would have to become entangled in a spy game. To hell with it, I decided, let the antagonists fight it out, I shall stay in the background as a shadow and break my chains at the very first opportunity. To set myself free must become my ultimate goal. Free as the wind. Free, but with a mission: I must not allow my mind to be put in hock, and I must not accept the leaden yoke of a subject relation. Never again, ever! I must keep my coat-of-arms immaculate and unblemished for the rest of my days. This resolution brought me relief and consolation. I began to think about how I could present the decoy to Mirek...For instance, I could say that Dick is a left-wing intellectual and a former peacenik who had campaigned against the war in Vietnam. But I need not worry much about it because the Company will surely take care of fabricating a convincing story that I should use.

Then gloom took hold of me again, and inner peace turned to a dread that I had lost all judgment.

IN THE MIXER

Cold woke me. my muscles were bone stiff. I crawled out of the car with great difficulty. Standing up I tried to take a couple of steps but I staggered like a drunken sailor.

A glance at my watch told me that I had slept for three hours. The street meanwhile came to life and there was bustle and stir of a working day. From the passers-by I chose an elderly man who looked like a born Viennese and not one of thousands of immigrants who populated the outskirts of the town. Having greeted him, I asked what had become of the boardinghouse Franz Nahrada that used to stand here.

The man spoke a rapid German with a local accent. It was difficult to understand everything but I got the gist of it. The boardinghouse "*war im Brand vernichtet,*" (*was burned down*). Was it arson? The man shrugged his shoulders. "*Man weisst nicht genau...*" (*Nobody knows exactly...*)

Well, at least this mystery was solved, but it did not help me much. I was in a terrible jam— '*dans le pétrin*' (*in the mixer*), as the French say. I knew from past experiences that I must not gnaw away at my feelings because this led to a paralyzing self-pity and anguish. I must act, perhaps not in the right way, but act I must. To sit here twiddling my thumbs was senseless.

I fished out a pen and a visiting card from my

pocket. On the back of the card I wrote a short message for Ruzenka, trying my best to do it legibly: 'Darling, I am going to the railway station to look for you. Please, wait here, I'll be back. I love you.'

I put the visiting card behind the windshield wiper and started walking to the main road. I found a petrol station I had driven past last night. At the cashier's counter sat a young, perhaps teen-age, girl who for lack of business was polishing her nails. When I explained that my car had broken down and that I needed a taxi, she took mercy on me and personally called a cab.

She smiled and said the taxi would be there in ten minutes. Then she turned her attention to her nails again.

I directed the driver first to the bus terminal. The schedule hung on a wall in the waiting room, which was completely deserted. I learned that there was only one bus a day between Brno and Vienna, arriving at half past four in the afternoon. The main railway station was nearby, so I walked there. According to the timetable the next express train from Prague that made a stop at Brno was to arrive at ten forty-five on platform two. The last express train in which Ruzenka and Honzik could come was due at seven that evening.

My rumbling stomach suggested that I should have breakfast, since I had to wait more than an hour. The restaurant was crowded but I found a small empty table not far from the bar. I ordered coffee, toast, butter, jam, ham-and-eggs and grapefruit sauce. It was my first hearty meal since noon yesterday.

I asked for another cup of coffee, lit a cigarette and began to plan my next step. Wait for the express train. If Ruzenka is not in it, return to the Mustang, to see if by chance she is there. That probability was minuscule but I must check it out. Stay in the car until one o'clock. Then lunch at the railroad station, which was to be my principal observation point. If Ruzenka and Honzik do not come on the afternoon bus I would wait until the evening express from Brno arrives. If they are not on it, it is clear that Ruzenka cannot leave the country.

I have two possibilities.

One: return to Geneva and let Snow call a press conference at the Palace of Nations during which I declare that my wife and son are being held hostage in Czechoslovakia, and thus launch an international campaign for their release.

Two: kidnap my son. I have a valid passport, and there are only some fifty kilometers to the border and another sixty to Olbramovice. I could drive there tonight and try to convince Ruzenka to consign Honzik to me to take him to safety in Switzerland. He is inscribed in my passport, so we shall be able to get out of the country by using another, less frequented checkpoint tomorrow morning. There is no reason for the Czechoslovak security police to issue an order to arrest me at the border. For them I am still in Geneva. I must persuade Ruzenka that our separation will not be long and that an escape via Bulgaria will be easier for her and for the people who will organize it. But it is very likely, if not certain, that Ruzenka will not agree to the separation. What then would be my options?

When the crunch comes, I told myself, you have two options: either return to Geneva, or go home. If I join my family in Czechoslovakia there are two possibilities: either they leave me in peace, or they lock me up. If they let me be, that's fine. If they lock me up, there are two ways it could go: either they put me in prison for a short stretch or for a long time. If for a short period, OK...I realized that I was trying to look at my predicament in the same way as the tragicomic hero of Franz Werfel's 1944 play filmed as *Me and the*

Colonel, the Prague-born author's character, Jacobowsky, a small-time Jewish businessman, who flees to France to escape the Nazis. When the German army approaches Paris he consoles himself with the thought that no matter what happens he would always have two possibilities. Either the Germans occupy Paris, or they attack Britain. If they don't come, fine, but if they occupy Paris, he has two possibilities: either he ends up in a good concentration camp, or a bad one. If it is a good camp, fine. But if it is a bad one, he still has two possibilities...If I am imprisoned for a long time I'll also have two possibilities: either they send me to Bory, or to Jachymov. If I end up in Bory, fine, but if I had to mine uranium ore at Jachymov, I have two possibilities: either I survive, or I kick the bucket...

A waiter passed by holding a tray with a bottle of beer and a tumbler of the hard stuff, a chaser, and suddenly I recalled the days of my bohemian life in Prague. What would I not give to be back and free in the smoky, roaring Pinkas pub of the olden days! I would even sacrifice the Mustang with no regrets. What would I not give not to have left my country! For an instant I was tempted to raise my hand for the waiter and order a glass of beer and a tumbler of vodka, my cure-all for trouble and blue mood.

I called the waiter and paid the bill.

At the exit for arriving passengers a dozen men and women gathered. They did not form a group, but stood apart as if to show that they do not want to fraternize. What will I do and say when I see them? I'll lift Honzik up and tell him that Grandma's food has fattened him and that he must have gained a couple of kilos, or something similarly banal. I will embrace Ruzenka and whisper in her ear that she is the love of my life and we must never separate again. But I am not going to tell her about exile, definitely not here at the railway station. And what if she wants to know why she had to leave in such a hurry? I'll beg her to have patience: I will explain everything once we are home.

Suddenly I had the feeling that I recognized somebody in the waiting crowd, a chubby figure with an expanding paunch and round head on a thick neck. There was no doubt. Grisa Laub.

"Grisa," I called. The corpulent young man jerked as if stuck by a pin.

"Honza!" he cried joyfully. "What are you doing here?

"I would expect a more intelligent question from you, Grisa. Who are you waiting for?"

"My sister-in-law. And you?"

"My wife and son."

"I thought you had found refuge in Switzerland. How come you are here?"

"We have a rendezvous here in Vienna," I replied evasively. "Tell me what are you doing? I heard you were in Hamburg and have started writing in German."

"I have finished my first book," said Grisa. "I am not writing epigrams any more, but short stories."

Grisa Laub was one of the young, talented authors we published in the magazine *Vojak*. I learned from Ota Brozek, when he visited me in Geneva, that after the Soviet occupation Grisa immediately packed his bags and left the country to stay with relatives in Hamburg. Grisa was a born writer and an ambitious young man. He would have made it anywhere.

He asked what I was doing in Geneva.

"The most important thing is that you have a steady job," he said when I answered his question in a few words. "It's a time of exile…There is the rule of darkness at home."

"How long do you think it will last?"

"One generation. Maybe longer," said Grisa. He

shook hands. "Take care," he added. "See you in better times, I hope."

A stream of passengers began to flow through the exit door. Grisa ran to a woman carrying a big valise in each hand.

I stood on tiptoe and craned but did not see what I wanted. Then I paced nervously back and forth as the human stream thinned. Two or three belated people passed by. I remained there alone. I tried to console myself with the hope that there would be another chance in the afternoon and a last one in the evening. But it did not help much.

It was a beautiful sunny day. The air inside the taxi that was taking me across a half of the town back to the Mustang was oppressive. I pulled down the window, but shut it again because of the insupportable smell of diesel engines. We crawled at snail's pace. The taxi driver observed that we were caught in a midday traffic jam. I did not mind. I was in no hurry.

I stretched out my feet and leaned my head back. I closed my eyes and tried, as so many times before, to find a solution to my dilemma: if Ruzenka does not confide Honzik to me, will I leave them or stay with them? In my mind I projected the film of the last four days again and re-read the scenario of the next few hours. Had I made a mistake somewhere? Did I underestimate Pista? How could I have known that the boardinghouse would burn down? What else did I miss?

In the afternoon I will drive to the railway station in my car and park it there. If Ruzenka and Honzik are not on the evening express train, I will immediately depart for Olbramovice. I cannot survive another night of misgivings and anxiety.

We left the bridge over the Danube behind.

"*Die erste Strasse nach links*," I said. (*First turning on the left.*)

"*Ist gut*" (*OK*), said the driver and turned left.

We had not driven a couple of hundred meters when I sighted a miraculous apparition.

"Stop!" I cried out. "*Halten Sie, bitte. Ich steige aus.*" (*Please stop. I'm getting out.*)

I got out, paid the fare and impatiently waved the driver away. For a while I stared with watering, incredulous eyes. My head was spinning. The blood pulsated in my temples, my heart was about to burst, and my stomach was clamped in an iron fist.

About two hundred meters away Ruzenka was leaning on the hood of the Mustang. Her hand caressed my son's blond head resting on her lap. She was a picture of the Madonna of tenderness personified. The scene entered my soul. It made me love her even more.

Then Honzik looked in my direction.

"Mom!—Dad!" he cried out and began to run towards me while I was running toward him. We met halfway. I lifted him up on my shoulders. When we approached Ruzenka, I saw she was weeping.

I put Honzik down and embraced my wife.

"Don't cry any more," I said soothingly. "Nothing will ever separate us again."

"We were waiting for you here yesterday, where were you?" she said. "I was afraid that we would never meet, when I could not find the boardinghouse and you were not here."

"Where did you sleep?"

"We walked to the main road and found a little hotel…It's not far, I left my luggage there. I could not sleep. I was afraid that you did not come because something had happened to you. It was an awful night. I was delirious with delight when I saw the Mustang this morning."

"Dad, when are we going home?" asked Honzik.

"We'll collect the luggage," I said. "And then we'll return straight to Geneva."

"But I want to go home!"

"Home, where?"

"Home at my grandma's."

"Do you hear?" whispered Ruzenka with a silent reproach.

"I promise you, Honzik, that you will go there…We will all be going to Grandma…soon. As soon as possible." I lied to both of them and to myself as well. Anguish gripped my breast and my heart almost stopped. "But now we must go to Geneva," I added. "Home is also Geneva."

Ruzenka was putting our son to bed. Through the closed door of his room in our apartment I heard her singing: "Orangutan was jungle king, all little she-apes admired his swing…" Honzik loved this song. He did not want to go to sleep without it. Usually, they both dozed off. Tonight, after thirteen hours in the Mustang whose spring suspension left much to be desired, it will not take them long. I was also as tired as a marathon runner reaching the finishing line, but there was one important matter that I had to settle. Since I had come to an irrevocable resolution based on innermost conviction, why postpone it?

I slipped out of the apartment and left the house. The first thing I did on reaching the street was light up a Camel because I was not allowed to smoke in the car. I walked slowly to the call box on the corner, mulling over again what I must say, and how best to explain and substantiate it. A blizzard of words and phrases filled my head but they were not exactly what I wanted. Something important escaped me. Well, I shall simply spit it out, I decided.

When I started to dial George's number, I unwillingly recalled that one of his first lessons was: never call me from your flat. He did not answer for a long time, but that was to be expected because they had to look for him.

"Hello, Jan, where are you? In Geneva?" I heard him say at long last.

"Yes, we are all here, the whole family."

"How did it go?"

"Apart from a minor hitch, fine."

"Great, you'll tell me all about it later."

"Can I take up something with you now?" I bit down on the bitter subject. "Do you have time?"

"Not much, but shoot."

"It's about your offer," I said slowly. I was still searching for suitable words to explain that I was not interested in money and career; what I want and seek in life is something that has no blemish, something intangible—what's called sometimes a question of higher principle...a higher moral standard...I do not know what is the exact English word for this notion...Therefore, whatever I might say would sound hollow, conceited...

"I do appreciate your generous offer but I cannot accept it," I blurted out finally.

"Why? Are you sure?"

"I don't know how to explain it but I am sure." It's very likely I shall regret it later, but now I was absolutely certain that I was doing the right thing. To soften my refusal I added: "I highly esteem our relationship and I want to keep it as it is. Let's stay friends, George, just good old friends."

We were both silent for a while.

"If I understand you correctly," said George, "you want to preserve your integrity."

George found the word I had vainly been searching

for. Yes, integrity is of the essence. It is all that matters. Not to be beholden to anyone or to anything, but on the contrary to be free and independent. This is the ultimate luxury that has to be paid for dearly. However, even if the price is exorbitant, it is never as enormous as the one you pay if you are in the clutches of somebody, or some system, or an ideology. Great God, this is the sum of my lifetime's experience! Preserving and protecting your personal inviolability has never been easy. Yet it has never been so hard as in our disjointed, Orwellian epoch in which evil is good, decadence is prosperity, greed is virtue, the lie is truth, and the law of the jungle is economic freedom.

"You are dead right, George," I said. "And I am glad that you understand…"

"I regret your decision, but I respect it," said George. "See you one of these days."

"Yes, one of these days." I hung up.

Although we promised that we would meet again, the words somehow seemed like a goodbye. Maybe it was. But what does it matter at a time of great partings and separations? Today I turned my back on a great chunk of my life and said farewell to a lot of people who were dear to me. I did not care a damn.

Silently I opened the door of my son's room, dimly lit by a bulb on the bedside table. Ruzenka lay on her back on his bed. It was too short for an adult, so that her legs were on the floor. Honzik's curly blond head rested on her breast. Ruzenka held him in her arms, pressing him close as if she wanted to protect him against something. Never before had I so painfully realized how infinitely I loved them as in this fleeting moment. And shall love them as long as my heart beats. Nothing else matters, all the rest is unimportant. The only ultimate value is our threefold being. I must not endanger it in any way. I must guard it, with all my force and means, all my life. Suppressed tears burned my eyes, and unfathomable anguish was strangling my throat.

I stood there as if turned to stone and for the first time in my grown-up age I began to pray, sincerely and ardently.

My Lord, whoever you may be, let nothing separate us again and let us love each other forever. Make it come about that Ruzenka loves me, notwithstanding all the stupid things and troubles I may, even involuntary, be responsible for. Protect her from all evil because she is a vital source of love and togetherness. Forgive me my errors for which we are now paying. Give us strength and courage not to collapse under the burden of exile, uncertain existence and vain nostalgia for the home country.

In the life of every man there are defining moments that change, forge and brand him. I lived them in those five days and nights in early September, filled with fear and daring, desperation and hope, cowardice and bravery, rapture and premeditation, hatred and love, and God knows what else is incommunicable and non-shareable. They mark my soul even today.

THE CAGE DOOR CLOSES

Ten days after our return to geneva Ruzenka and I sat in the ILO coffee bar facing Pista. When I had phoned him with our decision to ask for political asylum in Switzerland, he insisted on a personal encounter on the grounds that he must tell us something very important. We agreed to meet on a Friday at ten in the morning when Honzik would be in a day-care school so that Ruzenka could also come.

"I advise you to think it over very thoroughly," said

Pista. "You will destroy yourself and your family. I can guarantee you that nothing bad will happen to you back home, that you will be able to continue your career. Did we return the passport to you wife? We did, so you know that…"

"I know that it was a trap," I cut him short. "As soon as Ruzenka left home two secret police agents turned up in a black car. Someone among those who want my skin belatedly grasped that the telegram I had sent Ruzenka was an agreed signal. Consequently, plan A, namely to lure me into the trap, had failed. Therefore, plan B was immediately launched—to hold my wife and son hostage. Ruzenka's mother sent us a letter describing the gist of the discussion with the two agents as follows: We must talk to your daughter…She is not here…Do you know where she has her passport?…In her handbag…Where is she now?…Her father took her to a bus stop…Where is she going?…To Vienna…How long has she been gone?…Two hours, maybe less…When the two gentlemen heard that, they jumped into the car and drove away without saying goodbye. Had Ruzenka hesitated with the departure, and had her father not taken her and Honzik on a motorcycle to the bus stop at Pohorelice, a mere half-an-hour from the border, what do you think would have happened? They would have confiscated her passport, and then put a dagger to my throat."

"You exaggerate and overdramatize, "said Pista with a wry smile. "You did nothing wrong, so nothing can happen to you."

"I know people who for nothing spent ten years locked up," I said. "I don't know who is after me, but I definitely don't want to find out by returning home."

"Is that your last word?" asked Pista.

"We are not going back, we are staying here," I said taking Ruzenka's hand in mine. "This is our common decision."

"We can put pressure on the ILO to dismiss you," Pista threatened.

"I don't know what will become of me, or whether I will be dismissed from the ILO. But this does not change our decision one iota."

"Honza, you know that I always wanted the best for you," said Pista in a soothing tone. "I am the last person to do you wrong. I just don't want you to do anything stupid…I suggest that you sleep on it. Tomorrow is another day and you will see everything in a different light. Think it through and carefully consider all consequences. If you tell me tomorrow that you have changed your mind, I will forget this conversation, as if it never happened. Done?"

He offered me a handshake. I did not accept it.

Pista did not lose any time. In his capacity of First Secretary at the Czechoslovak mission he demanded and obtained a meeting with Wilfred Jenks, Director-General of the ILO. He managed to enroll the support of the Soviet Ambassador, who accompanied him. In the name of the two governments they demanded my immediate dismissal.

Jenks was an Englishman, an international lawyer, and above all an honest and principled man.

"We have a contract with Mr Jan Vitek, not with the Czechoslovak government," he said. "There is nothing to discuss. The case is closed."

And so the trap door shut. I was caught in a cage. Even made of pure gold, it would, nevertheless, be a cage. At the same time, and incongruously, I felt completely free for the first time in my life.

XI. SHOWTIME, ROSEBUD!

"Maybe, your wife might make a good fortune teller," said Dr Sitavanc puffing out a cloud of cigarette smoke, "but, please, don't let her dabble in my craft."

"The trouble is that she is usually right," I said. "Can you imagine what life's like having such a spouse?"

"I don't, and I don't even want to. However, diagnosis, my friend, is a science, not female intuition, especially in a case of a potential cancer." This always sun-tanned man in a white coat took another cigarette from his pack and lit up from a still burning butt. "To show you how wrong she is, I shall send you to Dr Stuckelberg who is the best colonoscopy specialist in town."

Dr Sitavanc was our family practitioner. I liked him. He was a fellow countryman, smoked like a chimney, and to amuse his patients would regale them with jokes. That day, before we parted, he told me the story of a chairman of an agricultural cooperative in the South of Bohemia who assembled all its members to deliver them the following speech: "You ungrateful bastards, you have complained about me to the Directorate, saying I am a lousy organizer and you don't want to work under me anymore. Well, all right, I will show you how much you will miss me when I am no longer here." He took a jackknife out of his pocket and stabbed himself in the chest. To be sure he would die, he staggered to a nearby pond and jumped into the water. It was winter and very cold. When they fished him out and put him on a stretcher he started to shout desperately: "Cover me up with a blanket, you fuck-brained idiots. Don't you know I could catch pneumonia."

Dr Stuckelberg's consulting room was located at Avanchet Park, a brand new urban settlement of apartment buildings painted in motley colors. One of them had a medical center for all sort of specialists. For patients it was very convenient because they did not have to run around town from one doctor's office to another. Dr Stuckelberg asked me if I wanted to follow the examination on a screen, in which case he would just give me a local anesthetic, or did I want a full dose to be completely unconscious. I opted for the latter.

When I woke up, Dr Stuckelberg revealed to me with compassion that he had found a tumor as big as a fist in my large intestine, but that I should not worry too much. In men of my age—I was fifty-two—it was nothing unusual, and the tumor might be benign. However, to be sure he had taken a sample of the tissue and sent it to a laboratory. We had to wait a couple of days for the biopsy results. I called Dr Sitavanc. He was also very optimistic. A previous test of my stools had shown no internal bleeding. Thus most probably the tumor was not malignant. He encouraged me take a rest at a sea resort if I felt tired, and hoped I would enjoy myself there.

Indeed I did feel lousy lately. I was exhausted, no juice left, burned out. This was why Ruzenka, who should have studied medicine instead of pharmacology because she had a natural gift for clinical diagnosis, concluded that I might have cancer and pressed me to seek professional advice.

I took a week of leave and left for Juan-les-Pins on the Côte d'Azur. A friend and tennis partner, Clive Drummond, owned a flat there that he rented out to us whenever we wanted. In the early Seventies, Clive had been the Public Relations Director at Geneva-based Investors Overseas Service, run by Bernard Cornfeld. Mr Cornfeld promised clients and employees twenty or even thirty percent return on their investments. For some time he actually paid out such dividends in company shares. Some people had become rich, mainly his small group of cronies, but on paper only. In fact, Geneva authorities became convinced it was a con game, a variation of Ponzi scheme, where new clients financed payments to former ones, until one day the whole edifice collapsed. When that happened in 1970, Clive was broke, except for the flat he had bought. It was located in an enclave of luxury buildings on a hillock with a beautiful view of the Mediterranean Sea. Fenced off and guarded, it included a swimming pool, a bar, tennis courts and palm trees. It was an oasis of calm and peace even in the summer high season, when Juan-les-Pins was overcrowded. We spent our vacations there for several consecutive years.

I took a train to get there because it was more comfortable than in a car. Côte d'Azur in mid-May is especially charming. All around is green. The flowerbeds in the parks are in full bloom, and tourists do not yet infest the promenade along the shore. In the spring sun Juan-les-Pins was sleepy and seemed to purr like a kitten.

On the third day of my stay, shortly before noon, Ruzenka and Honzik suddenly appeared in the flat.

"We have come to bring you back," Ruzenka said. "Sitavanc called up to say that the tumor is malignant. You must return immediately."

"Have you had lunch?" I asked in an effort to avoid reacting to the bad news. I refused to acknowledge it. It's nonsense, I cannot have a cancer, I feel fine, don't tell me otherwise, I am a healthy man. "We could eat at Pepe le Moco. They serve fine sea food there."

"Do you get what I'm saying? Did you hear what I told you?"

I nodded.

"You must have an operation. Sitavanc said he would find you the best surgeon, but we must hurry."

"That's very nice of him," I said. "But you surely do not want to drive back to Geneva today. Since we are all here, let's enjoy the day. We'll worry about the other thing tomorrow."

I stubbornly refused to discuss the result of the biopsy and what it meant for me. We had lunch in a small Italian restaurant. We hung around the beach for an hour or two and then we went shopping, since I insisted that Ruzenka buy a new swimming suit. We also visited all the bookshops because Jan was enthralled by science fiction and wanted to enrich his collection. We remembered one summer when Ruzenka's mother had been in Juan-les-Pins with us, how she had waded in shallow water with her skirt tucked up and a straw hat on her head, looking majestic and happy.

That night I lay in bed a long time with my eyes wide open. I told myself: what will be will be, don't ruminate on it now. All of sudden, a picture of a girl's face surfaced in my mind—a lovely, freckled face with blue eyes and a slightly turned-up nose, framed in straw-color hair. I saw Blazenka again sitting in my attic room in our house at Kremze, listening to a Bing Crosby record I got from American soldiers. It's the end of vacations, of bathing in the pond, of campfire nights. We embrace tenderly, and I hear her whisper: I want you to be the first…it's my gift to both of us…We make love for the first time, we are seventeen, it is 1945, a unique, unforgettable year. A wide, sunlit road opens before us leading to a horizon with a rainbow-colored archway through which we shall enter a world where dreams become reality. I did not know at first why I thought of all of this so clearly and precisely though more than thirty years had passed. But then, in the last moments of consciousness before falling asleep, it occurred to me that I was beginning to make an audit of my life: what I received, gave, owed. I was analyzing and reviewing my whole existence.

Going home we followed the Route Napoléon, the road he took back to Paris in 1815 returning from Elba. It was narrow, sinuous, climbing up from the sea to the hills of Grasse and further on to Digne-les-Bains. Every turn presented a new fascinating view. On all slopes lavender was in full blossom. The sun shone brightly. The sky was blue. It was a beautiful spring day.

The following day we went to the Geneva City hospital. At first, I did not want Ruzenka to come along, but after that I was glad she did. It was blissful to have her palm in mine, for from this gentle touch sprang forth a warm stream of love and courage flooding my soul. That was exactly what I desperately needed.

Professor Dr Roehner invited us to sit down. He was a tall man of approximately my age, with an ascetic face and penetrating eyes that made you feel he was able to see through you. His voice was gentle and calming. He said that my tumor had been discovered relatively soon, hopefully in time before it could metastasize, but that, of course, would only be known with certainty once he opened me up. I was looking at Roehner's hands holding the findings of the biopsy. For a man of his great stature his fingers were slim and long, like those of a concert pianist, cultivated, manicured. Unwillingly, I imagined that instead of a paper the fingers of his right hand held a scalpel while his left hand rested on my abdomen. My life will be in those hands. Meanwhile Roehner continued the explanation of the surgery. It will have to be penetrative. Most probably it will not be possible to save the rectum, given the unfavorable location of the tumor.

"Does it mean that you will have to make an artificial anus?" asked Ruzenka.

"Yes, Madame. But it also means a much better chance that there will be no relapse. I could conserve the rectum—we'll see what can I do during the surgery—but I consider it risky, which is why I would not recommend it."

He asked me what I thought. I had no opinion. I left everything to God, or rather to the hands with the fingers of a virtuoso pianist. Ruzenka wanted to know a lot of other things, but I did not even follow the discussion. I made up my mind that the less I knew about what I must undergo, the less material I would have to ruminate over, for there was no use in worrying about the unavoidable. For me the most important question was: when?

"Monday, the fifth of June," said Roehner after consulting his dairy.

"As long as two weeks!" I said with exasperation.

"I cannot do it sooner," said Roehner. "Don't worry. There is no risk in a slight delay."

After the meeting with the surgeon I ceased my inner resistance. I understood, at last, fully, that I had cancer. At the same time I was overwhelmed by a tide of indignation and revolt. Why me? What have I done to merit such punishment? Is it because of my misdemeanors? What have I sinned against? I began to scrutinize myself against the Ten Commandments. Did you steal? Never. Well, perhaps some ideas and thoughts, but only from dead authors…Did you take the name of the Lord in vain?…Not very often, so far as I remember…Did you covet your neighbor's wife?…Yes, once or twice…Did you commit

369

adultery…Yes, guilty as charged…but would that justify such punishment? What the heck, to hold such communion with oneself is stupid. After all, there's no God anyway, and even if there were, He would definitely be extremely unjust and uncharitable. Why me of all people? Why was I dealt such a ghastly card?

The following nights were endless. I slept in fits, interspaced by a recurring nightmare…Kyril Tidmarsh, the ILO's Director of Information, appeared sitting in his directorial chair shrouded in a gown. Terry Davidson, a colleague, had a stack of paper before him and was posing as a prosecutor. What's the Director-General Francis Blanchard doing here? Why is he floating in the air on angelic wings? I hear Terry saying: "Vitek must be fired. Without him the magazine will be better and successful. The problem is his lack of culture. We know where he came from…" I shout: "When I took *ILO Information* over, it was not worth the paper it was printed on. I gave it new contents and a new look. It now appears in seventeen languages, even in Chinese, and it has a press run of half a million copies." Terry laughs: "Bullshit." Who is supporting him? Of course, it is Bob Mott, who also wants me out. They are both after my job, sly buzzards. If they do away with me, they will peck out each other eyes, because only one of them can get the promotion. My God, how long has their campaign been going on? Two years! "The magazine has no impact at all," says Mott. "This is a white lie. We get thousands of cuttings with reprints from newspapers all around the world." I lose my breath, I suffocate, I drown. Blanchard raises his hand and is saying something, but I never hear what because here I always wake up. Davidson left the ILO long time before, and Mott returned to Chicago because his contract was not extended. Out of all this there remained just this nightmare that keeps persecuting me. I replay it every night. It reminds me of all the other futile battles I have won or lost in my life. They were many, and I know, there will be more, if I live.

Ruzenka sleeps on her back, right hand cranked over her mouth with an elbow sticking out as if on guard. I palm her forehead. She sighs uhmmm, turns on her right hip, sighs again, and turns on her tummy. I lift the duvet and caress her back, once, thrice. Uhmmmmm, she lets out a long sigh and with an unexpected facility she pulls her nightgown up. I fondle her neck and shoulders. "*Plus bas,*" she whispers. Obediently, I stroke her along the spine. "*Plus doucement,*" she commands. When in a trance, she always speaks French with me. My palm glides in gyratory caresses down to her left hip, then to her right hip. Uhmmmm. I kiss her shoulder, savoring the dazing aroma of her skin. I recall with unfathomable gratitude all the happy, unforgettable moments we have lived out together that bind us to each other forever. Uhmmm. I wish from the bottom of my heart that every touch and caress would tell her: I adore you, my only dearly beloved, and my *femme fatale.*

I cannot imagine that this morning ritual might end and never be again.

Work became my refuge, for it took my mind from the accursed six-letter word. At seven in the morning, I was already sitting at my desk and drafting articles for *ILO Information* or rewriting contributions by others because I found them not good enough. At nine, when all the officials arrived, the telephone began to ring and people were knocking on my door, meetings started. All this bustle and stir became a merry go round, leaving no time for creative work. I had to provide some fifty pages of manuscript for each issue of the magazine. But with special, targeted materials for national and regional editions it was almost double the number.

Every article and every news item had to run a gauntlet. To begin with, the content had to be approved by the department concerned. Often, it led to a sort of ping-pong game with members of various departments. Their factual remarks and suggestions were welcome. However, some of them suffered from an editor's complex and made stylistic changes. Since it required a lot of time to talk them out of this, I simply disregarded such comments. The next stage was political clearance. It had three rounds. Every story had to be seen and approved by the Workers Relations Director, Mr Mukharjee, an Indian, whom I knew very well and who made no problems. His counterpart, Mr Hammar, a Swede, Director of the Employers Relations Branch, was a stickler. When he spotted something in the text, even a slight hint or implication, of something that might rub the wrong way certain industries or, most particularly, multinational companies, he started cutting and changing the copy mercilessly. Since we belonged to the same tennis club, I began to play matches with him so that we could get to know each other better and become friendly. Once we were on a first-name basis, I could call him up and tell him: "Hans, be reasonable," which helped at times. The final round of negotiations was with the Chief of the Cabinet of the Director-General. He had to vet every article and news item keeping in mind the various sensibilities of member states to avoid any negative reaction on their part. I often looked back longingly to the army magazine, *Ceskoslovensky vojak*, where we had just one censor, and a drunkard at that.

On Wednesday I had a business lunch with Jean-

Jacques Maillard, who represented the influential International Employers Organization in the ILO. He was a corpulent Frenchman, some forty years old, whom I got to know during the regular meetings of the ILO Governing Body. Now he was sitting with me, sipping an aperitif on my invitation, because I had a problem to solve.

I wrote an article in the April issue of *ILO Information* about asbestos, whose production and use constitutes health risks for workers and in some cases also for ordinary citizens. When microscopic asbestos dust penetrates the lungs it remains there and becomes a time bomb that may explode in twenty or thirty years in the form of cancer. While asbestos in car brakes helps to save lives, in building materials it is a hidden health hazard for whole generations. At that time, in the spring of 1980, ILO for the first time ever sounded an alarm bell that hundreds of thousands people were carrying deadly asbestos in their lungs. The article was picked up by international press agencies and the warning swept the world. Monitoring services sent us press cuttings with full or partial reprints of the story from some six thousand newspapers in Europe and America alone.

Mr Maillard wrote a protest letter on behalf of his organization to our Director-General in which he contested the results of the ILO research, branding them as 'dubious.' But the main thrust of his attack was against my article, which he described as 'biased' and 'sensationalist.' I wrote a three-page reply in which I suggested to Mr Maillard that we discuss the issue face to face. This is why we found ourselves in a chic and expensive restaurant, the Lion d'Or, tasting tournedos with Lyon sauce and drinking an excellent Chateau Mouton Cadet. We talked about the forthcoming ILO conference in June where the guest of honor would be

373

Willy Brandt, the German Chancellor, who would present a plan to reduce poverty and unemployment in the world.

I left the thorny issue of asbestos for cognac and coffee. I explained to Mr Maillard tactfully, that to my great regret I could not publish his letter, because that would open a Pandora's box, but that I could offer him another possibility to make his views widely known.

"I'd be pleased and honored to publish an article by you on a general theme of the concern of employers with working conditions and workers' health, dealing also with unsolved, often controversial problems such as asbestos. From this platform you can air your personal views as well as those of your organization. If you agree, your contribution will be published in the pre-conference issue in June."

I knew that Mr Maillard had a hidden agenda because he aspired to be elected to Chair of the Employers Group in the ILO Governing Body. He was a top candidate and the elections would take place after the June Conference. So I hoped he might appreciate some discreet personal publicity in the magazine and its timing.

Mr Maillard mulled over my offer for a while, turning a half-empty glass of cognac in his chubby hand.

"How long should the article be?" he asked.

"Seven hundred words," I said with great relief. In fact, I have long considered the idea of introducing a new section in the magazine for external authors entitled 'By invitation.' Why not to start it with a libation to Mr Maillard now, and kill two birds with one stone?

When I paid the bill I groaned inwardly, but I consoled myself with the thought that it was a necessary investment that might bring long-term benefits, if I lived.

I spent another white night. I thought about death. I read somewhere that in birth and in death, man is alone. I dismissed it then as a cliché, but now I was discovering it is true: I am alone in the throes of my agony, and no one can help me. We all have to die…Yet another cliché until your turn comes to pass away. Nothing happens—until it happens to you.

And what if a miracle comes about as in Zermatt?

In my mind I see Little Matterhorn and his big brother whose top is in the clouds. The camera of memory focuses on a mountain saddle between the two giants covered with a glacier, Theodulgletscher, and eternal snow.

It is the end of March; a strong icy wind is blowing. I ask the ticket clerk: How is the weather up on the glacier? Is it skiable? He shakes his head and says: *Ich glaube ja, aber Vorsicht* (*I think so, but be careful*). There are four Italians in the cabin with me, clad in the latest ski outfits, talking and gesturing all at the same time. When we get out, their voices gain in high-pitched intensity. *Pericoloso* (*dangerous*) is the only word that I understand. As I put on my skis I wonder about the visibility. It may be ten meters, probably less, and a thought crosses my mind that I should give up. The Italians head back to the station, silent, as if defeated. Deliberately, to show off, I start with a jump right into a cloud that descends on my head. I breathe vapors that irritate my throat and make me cough as if suffocating. Now visibility is down to three or five meters at most. Maybe I can make it…You must do it, if you give up, I tell myself, then you are really, truly old! I start to ski slowly ahead. The track has been freshly made. My skis rattle on the frozen prints of a piste tractor. Suddenly the visibility is at zero. I am blinded, a prisoner of the white darkness. I stop. Should I go back? It's too late. I must continue—but how? I know that the ski run turns to the right. I have already done it many times before. Then it goes downward. But beyond that I have no recall. Be cool, I caution myself, you must go ahead, you must listen to the rattle of your skis. As long as you can hear that, you are on the right track. And when it stops? Then you finish in a ravine where nobody will find you. I move forward very slowly, as if that would be a solution. Am I at the turn? Do I have to ski down? I am covered by a cold sweat. I move my skis to the left...nothing. I move on them to the right...they clatter. I am paralyzed by fear. I cannot move. I don't know how long I just stood there. A minute? An hour? I try to get hold of myself. Simultaneously, I feel a burning, painful feeling going down my spine like the tip of a long red-hot needle. It penetrates my brain and sets off a sparkling firework of memories. Each sparkle is a remembrance, a place, a fraction of time, a smile, a name, a face...precious elements of my being. They reflect my life. It was good and generous to me. I lived in a way I could and knew. It was wonderful while it lasted. And suddenly I see John Wayne prodding soldiers to get out of a trench and I hear him shout: "Get out, you bastards, do you want to live forever?" Thanks, John, for reminding me of this. I heave up on my poles with all my force and loose off. The skis rattle as I dash through the cloud at full speed. I feel great, serene, reconciled with my destiny.

It was the day when I was born again. Since this miracle happened in Zermatt, why could it not happen also in Geneva?

I got up. It was four o'clock in the morning. I went to the kitchen, opened the icebox, took out a bottle of milk and poured some in a cup. I took a sip. Then I went to the balcony, propped myself against the balustrade and looked at the building across the street. It was a hospice for old people. Several windows were lit up. I tried to imagine the people behind those yellow boxes, and what troubles and sorrows kept them awake.

A thought shot through my head: you should write your last will and testament. It lodged in my brain and I could not drive it away. Last will...After all, why not? Every reasonable person in my situation would do it. The document should have the right form, it should have a date and place and a statement that I am of sound mind...and what else? Maybe a signature certified by a notary, but that would be a useless expenditure considering what little I own...a flat owned by the bank, a used car, a couple of thousand francs in the kitty, altogether not much. After all, according to Swiss law Ruzenka will inherit all my property. So why bother? I should rather just state my last wishes regarding disposal of my body...For instance, that the hospital can harvest any useful part of my body...not the liver which is surely burned up by alcohol or the lungs decimated by tobacco smoke...nonetheless, maybe, they still will find something usable, let them have it. And what about the rest? Incinerate it, and spill the ashes in the lake that I loved so much. In its bosom I will rest for eternity. And no obituary notice, please, no burial service, dust to dust.

I heard, from somewhere in the downtown, the faint wailing of an ambulance that filled me with sorrow. Not for myself but for the poor fellow in a coma who might pass away before I do. I silently recited the 17th-century poet John Donne's lines: "Any man's death diminishes me, for I am involved in mankind. Therefore send not to know for whom the bell tolls, it tolls for thee."

I chaired an editorial meeting on Friday to discuss the

contents of the June issue.

"The outcome of this year's ILO Conference will be rather meager, except for the adoption of a draft of new labor standards," I said. "Therefore, we will put on the front page just a box headed *Conference Report Card* with a succinct summary of this meeting. The other stuff will go inside on the middle spread. I shall not be around to write a special report, so you can use the closing round-up issued by the Press Service."

The editors present sat silently and passively. Most likely they thought: Say what you like, when you are not here, we shall do it our way. They all knew that on Monday morning I should be on the '*billiard*,' the operating table. I felt six pairs of eyes casting sideways glances towards me. There was a strange atmosphere in the office, like a Last Supper.

I elaborated the main stories in the issue—maybe for the last time.

The lead on the front page will be 'Baby-boomers Meet Catch-22,' an article about the influx of the generation born in the Seventies onto the job market, stating that some sixteen percent will simply swell the ranks of the unemployed in the western market economies. The editorial 'Too Old at Forty' warned of the trend in Western Europe to copy the American attitude toward older workers, who, under various pretexts, are dismissed and then encounter enormous difficulties in finding work. Both stories will be pre-distributed before publication to the international wire services. Fromont will offer the copy to Agence France Press and the Agence Télégraphique Suisse, Trachtenberg to the Spanish agency EFE, Knight to Reuters, Associated Press and United Press International, Pouchov to the Russian Novosti, Gleyzes to the Deutsche Presse Agentur. Usually, I handled this operation myself.

I entrusted the co-ordination of translations and production control of the international editions to Claude Choin, and the dispatch of materials for the regional and national editions to my assistant Esther 'Skippy' Boylan. This, too, I used to do myself.

I was breaking up bread—my work—and giving it to others. I felt the poignancy of the Christ story, though I did not consider myself in the least bit holy.

Then came the toughest part: saying goodbye. I decided to be short and snappy. And to those who might think that this was my swan song as Editor-in Chief, I would make quite clear that they are wrong.

"Now you will have some respite," I said, "but when I come back we shall work on a new layout and presentation of the magazine. Meanwhile, you can give it some thought." And I dismissed them with "Thank you for coming."

My colleagues dispersed with unusual speed, as if I had thrown a grenade into the room. Only Claude Choin, my deputy, and Esther Boylan stayed behind.

"*Jan, bonne chance*," said Claude.

"Good luck," said Esther.

If I ever needed luck, it was now.

I stayed in the office until late evening. When I was sure that all my colleagues had left, I opened the drawer of my desk and pulled out a glass-framed letter. It was written, some ten days before, by former ILO Director-General David A. Morse, who left an indelible, prominent mark on the Organization in twenty-two years at its helm. Reading it I felt a greater professional and personal satisfaction than I would have if I were awarded a Pulitzer Prize.

There was a calendar on the wall opposite my desk. I took it off and hung Morse's letter in its place. I took a step back and and read its text one more time.

Dear Jan Vitek:

An awful lot of material comes across my desk and I
find it very difficult to keep up with it. However,
there is an exception to my rule when I look at your
latest issue of ILO Information. I thumbed through
it and then found myself reading the entire issue
because of the subject matter. It is very well
presented, the articles well written, and the subject
matter relevant to today's preoccupations.

Congratulations!

Sincerely yours,

David A. Morse

A sly thought crossed my mind. If I don't come
back and somebody else sits here in my stead he will
have Morse's letter in front of his eyes—my legacy and
challenge.

It is my last night at home before the operation. I wish I
could sleep, but it does not come. I try a trusted
stratagem, to evoke something beautiful and
exhilarating, such as my first encounter with Ruzenka.
It has worked many times, but not now. Instead a
picture of little Jan emerged into my consciousness, and
with him a besetting question: What father was I to
him? A frank answer is: Occasional and moody...After
I said no to George...It occurs to me that I could have
refused his offer more gracefully by a Chinese saying:
'Even if the whole world were for sale, I want to be
unsellable; even if all people are drunk, I want to stay
sober'...Thank God I did not say it, because I would

380

look like a bighead...After my rejection of his offer, it might have been a coincidence, but Davidson and Mott started to attack me, and I was vulnerable and alone. I came to know what being solitary means. You carry a heavy burden but there is no one you can tell about it, no one who can help you. I did not even confide my troubles to Ruzenka, for I did not want her to worry. I would get up at six o'clock in the morning to be in the office before seven, and I would return home late in the evening with a briefcase full of reports and files to study. Those were my years of struggle for survival. I know it's no excuse. I just want to explain to you, my son, how I lived and why I neglected you...But still, we went on a vacation every year, to the sea in summer, to the mountains in winter...Once on a Spanish beach I pulled you out of a big wave that almost drowned you...In Sicily we fished starfishes...In Montana I taught you how to ski and I can hear myself shouting after you: "Bend your knees, ski in parallel..." I did not help you at all with your problems at school...You are left-handed and dyslexic, writing neatly was so difficult for you...Once your French teacher asked your mother to come to see him and advised her to take you out of the gymnasium and send you to a vocational school...and it so happened, by sheer luck, that your class master, a mathematician, passed by and stopped to say to your mother: "I am glad to meet you, Madame Vitek, I want to assure that there is no doubt that your son has great scientific potential..." and since then your French teacher let you be...You want to be a film director...Gracious God, why, of all things, must you have inherited my artistic aspirations!...I never uttered a word to reveal that I was stage struck at your age...So I told you what my acting idol Mr Vasta told me then: "Finish your studies first..." I promise that after you take a degree in economics or computer science I'll send you to a film school in Los Angeles...Never mind the cost, I'll pay...But I secretly hope you will change your mind, because I cannot see you in the Hollywood jungle, you are too soft and timid, you don't have sharp fangs and a Teflon stomach...Once you are at the University, I can arrange for you to study at the research institute of Professor Leontief in New York. He has promised me to accept you. He is a great and generous man. Working for a Nobel Prize winner will be enriching and may open new vistas for you, because there are encounters that mark a man forever...There are so many things I wanted to tell you and have not for lack of time...So many things. But the most important is that I love you...I am so grateful to Ruzenka that she gave birth to you...Often I ask myself what would have become of me had I not met her...I would not be in Geneva, I would live like a bohemian in Prague...I would end up like most of my friends, sign Charter 77, be blacklisted, lose my job and vegetate in a van like Ota, or languish in prison like Vasek...I owe her so much, my whole new life......I can still see the street padded with fallen leaves that glitter like drops of blood, the ancient house on Charles Square with its peeling façade rendering and arched entrance...She comes out in a light pink coat and the lightning strikes me again with devastating force. In its burning flash I see a girl who is the personification of my youthful ideal of true love. She is laughing, she is coming my way...

Here the stream of subconscious images faded out. I fell asleep at long last.

In the hospital, on the fifth floor, Sunday, late afternoon.

"*Un peu d'effort, Monsieur Vitek, vous approcher le record de l'hôpital,*" said the nurse. (*A little more of an effort, Mr Vitek, you are approaching the hospital record.*)

"*C'est combien?*" (*How much is that?*)

"*Vingt à cinq litres.*" (*Twenty-five liters.*)

My torturer in a white coat had poured water into my throat liter by liter for the past two hours. She explained to me that my intestines must be washed out to become spick and span before the operation. It's just a hard part of life, I consoled myself. The worst is yet to come. I did not break the hospital record of twenty-five liters; I missed it by one pint.

I arrived at the hospital directly from our tennis club, where with Ruzenka I played a double against Clive Drummond and John Simons from two to three o'clock. On Saturday night we went to the cinema. I wanted to chase away dark thoughts and enjoy some Hollywood kitsch. I chose a picture with a promising title, *All That Jazz*, a musical that should be good: the Geneva reviewers raved about it. The subject of the film turned out to be the life-story of Broadway choreographer Joe Gideon with Roy Schneider in the lead role. Joe led a bohemian lifestyle. During the day, he was high on benzedrine, valium and nicotine. He followed LSD with alcohol in the evening. When he woke up, he pulled himself in shape with a cold shower, caffeine, a handful of pep pills, and atropine in his bloodshot eyes. Then he said: "It's show time, folks." He burned the candle at both ends, day after day, night after night, purposefully and mercilessly, until he collapsed on the set and was transported to the hospital. This was where most of the film took place, in the operating theater. The camera focused on the shining dissectors and scalpels, nurses wiping sweat from surgeons' foreheads, the floor covered with bloodstained bandages. In his delirious hallucination he saw a mysterious, enticing Lady in White, wearing a cloak, with a face covered by a muslin veil. Sometimes he used to get glimpse of her before in real life, or so it seemed to him, and she had attempted to tell him something he did not grasp. Now when she was so near all the time, he craved her, he tried to embrace her, but she kept escaping his outstretched arms. When, finally, he succeeded in holding and kissing her—she was revealed as Death. The music played a sentimental melody and the beautiful Lady sang: "*I tried to warn you somehow, but you had your way, so you must pay, too late to be sorry now.*" I learned later that it was a projection of the director/choreographer Bob Fosse's own life. As a preparation for my Monday operation and a spur to heart-searching, I could not have made a better choice.

When Professor Boehner came to see me I was lying in my hospital bed, enfeebled and dim. In his soothing, calm voice he was telling me something about tomorrow's operation, that I should not be afraid, that everything would be all right, and so forth. Then a nurse brought me a glass of water and a little blue pill.

I lay looking at the ceiling, white as a projection screen. I closed my eyes and continued with the game I had played with myself every evening over the past two weeks. I would name a place and let it wash up memories out of the ocean of time.

Chum: I knock out knots from the barn door with a hammer, making a sieve of it. The landlord, Sahan, shouts: You damn rascal…I wade a brook on the way to my grandmother, who always has some sweets for me…*Pasicka*: It's harvest time, I am bringing my mother a jug with milk…I have a fever. I'm bathed in sweat. Mom gives me Zatka lemonade. I shall never drink anything tastier in my whole life…*Kremze*: An ice hockey field. I attack on the right wing. The puck seems glued to my stick. I shoot, and hear the crowd shouting Goal!...I stand on the corner looking toward the open windows of a building on the other side of the village square in the wistful hope that I will see my secret love, Lida...*Krumlov*: I am on the stage in the spotlight reciting a poem by Aragon...I climb a ladder to the first floor, Blanka opens the window and puts a finger to her lips...*Panmunjom*: I drive a jeep in the Demilitarized Zone along a narrow, neglected road, lose control, and end up in a rice paddy where mines have been laid...*Prague*: An October evening on Charles Square. I see a frail young girl in a pinkish coat coming toward me...

Tired as I am, I am unable to recall other places. I switch my association game to the names of girls I loved. *Vlasta*: We are in a sleeping bag, naked, I caress her short curly hair and call her my little rabbit like Jordan in Hemingway's novel *For Whom The Bell Tolls*. Drops of rain drum on the cloth of our tent. The Vltava river is humming nearby...*Radka*: Hotel National in Moscow. She slips into my room after midnight. We make love silently on a narrow, squeaky bed while two other occupants of the room, Party hacks, sleep—or rather pretend to, because in the morning they threaten to send me home if we repeat last night. The Russian poet Yevtuschenko takes mercy on us and offers us a couch in his study, where we spend the remaining days of the World Youth Festival...

Here my memory fails me again. I have a total blackout. Anyway, it's no time for games. It's time to think of death. I silently repeat death, death, death...and several times more to get used to this word, to reconcile myself to its implications, and to chase the scariness of it away. We are born, we live and we die. This is our destiny. There is nothing more to it. I wish I could believe that there is an afterlife. That we have a soul that will live forever, or that we are reincarnated. It's bullshit. And it is this knowledge that is our nightmare: the nothingness after death. People say of somebody, "He had a beautiful death." The first time I heard it was at the funeral of my uncle. I was eleven years old, and I was terribly shocked. No, rather I was outraged. How can anybody say that death can be beautiful! Now I conceived what it means: you die peacefully, painlessly in your sleep. It's deliverance. A blessing that will not be granted to me, because dying of cancer can be long, weeks, months or even years. I don't want to languish in hospital beds losing my hair after chemotherapy and having my intestines burned by irradiation. I am not afraid of death. I fear dying. And when my time comes, I fervently hope that I shall have the courage, determination, clear mind and strength to shorten the agony. This is my living will: Don't waste your fancy, expensive life-supporting gadgets on me! Just put me in an artificial coma, and let me fade away.

A strange feeling took hold of me, one that a soldier apparently has in the trenches before a bayonet charge: in a few seconds I relived my whole life. Childhood and boyhood seemed like a beautiful mountain meadow in full bloom, youth like sparkling wine, adulthood like a bunch of lovely girls, middle age like a broad, quiet river in summer sunshine.

In one of my short stories I wrote that man, when he is in a desperate situation or mortal danger, thinks of the people who had done much for him and for whom he had great respect because they had changed his life. So I think of Prchlik, who gave me the chance to be a player instead of a mere onlooker; I think of Herrick, who helped me to start a new meaningful existence. I recall other names and faces...Cihlar, who in spite of all troubles he had with me, let me pass the baccalaureate, Brozek, who taught me how to write, Chyle, who guided my first steps in diplomacy, Leontief and Galbraith, who helped me to uncover new insights into the world's social and economic order, Jenks, who protected me, Blanchard, who helped me in my struggle for professional survival...I want to tell you all what a pleasure it was to know you and how lucky I was that I had the privilege to be a part of your life for some time. I do not know how or for what reason and even if at all I merited your friendship, but I admired and loved all of you from the bottom my heart.

And what if you survive? What if you got another chance, would you do things differently? Would you change the way you lived? Yes, but the problem is that my life has been so wonderful and purposeful...Still, you might not have dribbled your energies out into newspapers. Instead I could have written something that would last, books that would make people happy. But why? In the coffin we are all the same, overweight or underweight, the difference is only for the porters.

Do you have regrets? Yes, I cannot forgive myself that I left my parents alone. But did I have a choice? Yes, you could have returned home. And what good would have come of this? How could I have helped them if I were in prison? So, in fact, you don't regret anything. *Non, rien, je ne regrette rien, ni le mal qu'on m'a fait, tout est égale...* (*No, nothing, I regret nothing, not the evil that's been done to me, it's all equal*). Do you want this song be played at your funeral? No I have a better one: *My Way...I had my ups and downs...the record shows I took the blows...but I did it my way.*

I could paraphrase Goethe and say that I am a man who always says no: *Ich bin der Geist der stets veneint.* I left a paper trail behind me that proves it, for everything I ever wrote was embattled, I always wanted to disturb, rouse, give people food for thought, state things the way they were, look forward, be a part of the vanguard. I brought on myself a heap of trouble and problems. Why must I always bang my forehead against the wall like a ram? The reason is very simple: I cannot do otherwise. It comes out of the depth of my soul. It's stronger than I.

Before falling asleep, I reflected that I had burned the candle at both sides, raced through life breaking all speed limits and behaved in a devil-may-care way— and now comes the time of reckoning, I shall have to pay, it is too late to be sorry and to expiate. I am fifty-two years old, I have had a good life, and should the curtain fall, I shall leave the stage levelheaded and reconciled. I lived life hard and fast, burning red lights and disregarding stops, but I lived well and at full blast.

I don't know what sort of blue pill it was, but its effect did not wear off in the morning. I was half-groggy when they pushed me on a movable hospital bed through the corridor to the lift, then somewhere down and through another corridor to the operation room where they put me on the *billiard*. A circle of people in green smocks surrounded me, the blindingly strong light of ceiling mirrors bore into my eyes. I had a feeling of *déjà vu*, despite being in a hospital for the first time. Then it dawned on me that I saw all this in a cinema the day before yesterday. The only thing missing was the Lady in the White.

Somebody asked me to count aloud…

Réveillez-vous, Monsieur Vitek, c'est fini! A hand slapped my face. *Réveillez-vous!*

It was a female hand, but it did not belong to the Lady in White. The nurse was trying to wake me up.

"*C'est fini, Monsieur Vitek!*" (*It's over, Mr Vitek!*)

So I shall not meet the mysterious, enticing Lady yet. All the better. That's fine by me. I was weakened and still half drugged. All I wanted was to sleep and dream, dream and sleep. Later, when I was fully awake, I lay on the bed in my room, a needle stuck into my left arm and connected by a tube to a bottle with some life-giving liquid that hung above my head.

Professor Roehner came to see me. He sat down on the edge of the bed and in his professionally soothing voice told me about the surgery. It had lasted three hours and was very successful, because he managed not only to remove the tumor but also some potentially affected tissue. Unfortunately, the rectum had to be removed, so he used the large intestine to create an artificial anus on the left side of my abdomen, below my beltline. It had to be done in this manner to avoid a relapse and increase my chances of survival.

"You must understand that you had surgery that saved your life," he repeated several times. "It is a small price for staying alive…"

Oh, my God, dear doctor I know best why I have to pay…for all my sins, which I heaped up and up over many years…I had my way…wagonloads of coffin nails, hectoliters of wine, beer, vodka, rum and cognac…so I must pay, too late to be sorry now.

"You will see that you can lead a normal life with this little handicap," the soothing voice came to me muffled as if from far, far away. "I shall send you a nurse who will show you how to handle and control the artificial anus. Thousands of other people have learned it. You will also master the procedures, but you must accept your handicap and come to terms with it. I am sure you can do it because the surgery, I stress again, saved your life. You do want to live, don't you?"

I did not answer since I felt so lousy that I was not at all sure if I wanted to live or not. Then I asked Roehner how long I would have to stay in the hospital.

"Tomorrow you will be able to get up," he said. "In

389

five, or seven days at most you can go home."

As soon as the surgeon left, Ruzenka and Honzik came to visit. She sat down on the edge of my bed, as Roehner had, caressed me and asked if I was in pain. Her delicate, still maiden face untouched by any make up, radiated love and concern.

"You know what they did to me," I said.

"My mother had the same surgery several years ago," Ruzenka said. "When I spoke to her on the telephone yesterday, she said that the first thing you must learn is how to do irrigations, because that will allow you to be at ease and in comfort for forty-eight hours. It may not work well in the beginning, but later on, it will all be fine."

She asked me to sit up, smoothed the pillow and the duvet, poured fresh water in a glass, and washed grapes somebody had sent me. At the same time she told me the household news and enumerated the friends who had called up to find out how the surgery went and to give their best regards. Meanwhile, a nurse came bringing yet another bouquet of flowers, followed by a technician who installed a TV set in my room, courtesy of my colleagues in the ILO.

Little Jan was sitting on a chair near the window, quietly, without a word.

"How is school?" I asked him.

"*Ça va*," he said with a shrug.

I have always had difficulty in engaging in conversation with my son, mainly because of my awkwardness, as now. To ask a fourteen-year-old boy how was he doing in school is a non-starter. I sensed that he was not at ease, for he did not know what to say, and that he would rather be out of the room.

All of sudden, both of them, the most precious and closest human beings in my life seemed strange, as if I saw them for the first time. What are they doing here? Why do I waste time with them? So many important things are swarming in my head, a whole hurricane of them. I must think through what happened to me, and what will become of me. In that, no one else can help me, I must do it myself. I said that I was tired and needed to sleep.

"We'll come tomorrow," said Ruzenka. "All will be better tomorrow."

Her parting words stayed ringing in my ears. I sorely wanted to believe them.

A little rosebud appeared on the smooth stomach skin slightly below the waistline, the creation of professor Roehner. I saw it for the first time when a nurse changed my bandages. Its picture burned the stigma of a physical handicap into my mind. I lay at night in my bed, eyes shut but wakeful, examining the rosebud that had become my destiny.

Initial resistance slowly gave way to acceptance and submission. I made my peace with my lot, for there was no alternative. At the same time an unbreakable resolution was born in the deepest region of my soul. It emerged like an underground river and took hold of me.

I will learn how to live with my rosebud. I will master it so well that no one, except for Ruzenka and our family doctor, nobody else, not even Honzik, if possible, will ever notice our interdependence. I shall play tennis, I shall ski and swim, I shall go to work and to parties as before.

What if this is not feasible? Or if I don't make it?

No, these are wrong questions. Forget them. You can do it. In the lifelong struggle that awaits you, you shall overcome. There is no other way.

I played tennis four weeks later. My usual partner, John Simons, inquired where I had been since I was absent for such a long time.

"On vacation in Ibiza," I said.

"How was it?"

"Great. I am on form, full of beans."

Four months after the surgery, at the end of October, I set out on a business trip around the world. The first stop was in Cairo, from there to Islamabad, New Delhi, Bangkok, Hong Kong, Tokyo, Los Angeles, San Francisco, Washington, New York, London and back to Geneva.

The purpose of the trip was twofold (I wrote in my justification for the ILO): namely, inspection of national and regional editions of *ILO Information*, and establishment of co-operation with the media in the countries visited.

But the real reason was to prove to everybody, especially myself, that the show goes on, that nothing is changed, that I remain on stage in an active role.

Doing my level best to be a full man I carry my cross through life silently, secretly and humbly. I have come to realize that Nietzsche is right: What does not kill me makes me stronger.

ILO Director-General Francis Blanchard (left) and Jan
Vítek in the aula of ILO headquarters in Geneva.
(Photo Wolfgang Steche)

EPILOGUE

When i retired from the ILO it seemed natural to go back to journalism. I thought I would be a journalist until my dying day. One chapter of my life was finished and another is beginning, I told myself. Now I shall write in my mother tongue. It will be easier, and a kind of liberation. My fellow Czechoslovaks were also freshly liberated—from the shackles of communism. I had an important message for them, I thought, based on what I learned in the ILO, and on experiences from my travels around the world, especially from what I saw in the United States. I wanted to warn them: don't be suckered by the siren call of unbridled capitalism and neoliberal ideology since they represent a clear and present social danger.

So I took up a fight that lasted twelve years. I published in various Czech newspapers and magazines hundreds of articles, commentaries, essays, feuilletons, satires, and even science-fiction stories. I used all sorts of ammunition in defense of the concerns and rights of working people at a time of profound economic upheaval and an uncertain future.

It was a losing battle. As market fundamentalism and neoliberal dogma vanquished other voices in our country, the situation in the Czech media began to change. Editors with whom I collaborated disappeared, and so did their interest in social and economic issues related to societal development. I lost. But I was not alone. All other dissenting journalists and writers were ostracized. The common denominator in our defeat was bad timing: we expressed our criticism of the world super-capitalistic disorder all too soon. Nowadays, though, the writing on the wall is flagrantly obvious

395

and unequivocal.

I have no regrets. I know I stood my ground on the right side of the barricade, and that the search for paths and ways towards social solidarity and equitable distribution of wealth, in which I took part, will continue because these ideals constitute perennial and unfulfilled goals for humankind.

My modest contribution was not made out of some messianic ardor. If I have to be frank I must admit that I did it for myself—I wanted to give my life a sense of purpose. For human life has no other meaning than the one we give to it ourselves.

I was born under a lucky star. But the greatest and most precious gift I received was to have met many good people who liked me and helped me to sail through all my problems. I may have been a pebble in the torrent of life, but they all aided me to come through its rapids battered but unscathed. I think of each and every one of them with gratitude and love.